Amitav Ghosh's

The Shadow Lines

Amitav Ghosh's
The Shadow Lines

edited by
Novy Kapadia

Asia
book
Club

Published by
asia book club
New Delhi 110 058

Composed by Vivek Mathur, Delhi 110 006 Ph. 3981867
Printed at Chaman Offset Press, New Delhi 110 002

Contents

Part I
The Shadow Lines
Textual Analysis and Evaluation

by
Novy Kapadia

Part II
Critical Perspectives

Contributors

Shyam S. Agarwalla	Ram Manohar Lohia College Ranchi
Urbashi Barat	Rani Durgavati University Jabalpur
Seema Bhaduri	Nasik Maharashtra
Shakuntala Bharvani	University of Bombay Bombay
N. Eakambaram	University of Madras Madras
Pallavi Gupta	A.R.S.D. College University of Delhi
Louis James	London U.K.
Novy Kapadia	S.G.T.B. Khalsa College University of Delhi
Rama Kundu	University of Burdwan Burdwan
Sharmila Guha Majumdar	Kalyani University West Bengal
O.P. Mathur	B.H.U. Varanasi
Alpana Neogy	R.L.A. College University of Delhi
D.K. Pabby	R.L.A. College University of Delhi
Murari Prasad	D.S. College Katihar
K. Damodar Rao	Kakatiya University Warangal
Rahul Sapra	S.G.T.B. Khalsa College University of Delhi
Nandita Sinha	Mata Sundari College University of Delhi
S.P. Swain	Municipal College Rourkela
G.R. Taneja	R.L.A. College University of Delhi
Brinda Veerappa K.	Mangalore University Mangalore

Introduction

NOVY KAPADIA

Author's Background

Amitav Ghosh was born several years after 'Midnight's Children' made their tryst with destiny on 15 August 1947. He was born in Calcutta in 1956 but grew up in East Pakistan (now Bangladesh), Sri Lanka, Iran and India. As a youngster, he was greatly influenced by the stories of Partition, Independence and the Second World War. These stories and anecdotes of such epochal events related by his parents, family members and neighbours made an indelible impression on his mind.

Recalling childhood memories about his mother, in an article in the *New Yorker*, Amitav Ghosh said: "My mother grew up in Calcutta, and her memories were of Mahatma Gandhi, non-violence, civil disobedience, and the terrors that accompanied Partition, in 1947." (104) Recalling his childhood, Ghosh admits that his mother's stories were very appealing, as they had a straightforward, compelling plot line and, in Mahatma Gandhi, an incomparably vital and endearing protagonist." (Ghosh 104) Yet, unlike the fiction of an earlier Indian English novelist, Chaman Nahal, Mahatma Gandhi does not figure prominently in the four published novels of Amitav Ghosh.

History is Amitav Ghosh's prime obsession and his fiction is imbued with both political and historical consciousness. However, when evaluating a segment of history, like India's Independence movement, there is little mention of Mahatma Gandhi in Ghosh's fictional framework, So, despite the charismatic appeal of Mahatma Gandhi and the impact of stories he heard from his mother, the legendary 'father of the nation' and his tactics of 'satyagraha' and non-violent struggle do not feature prominently in his writings. The major influences on him were the stories of his father, which dealt with the Second World War (1939-1945) and the Indian soldiers of the British Indian Army who fought against the Germans and the Japanese. About his father, Ghosh said:

> My father came of age in a small provincial town in the state of Bihar. He turned twenty-one in 1942, one of the most tumultuous years in Indian history. That was the year the Indian National Congress, the country's largest political party launched a nationwide movement calling on the British to quit India: it was when Mahatma Gandhi denounced the Raj as a "poison that corrupts all it touches." And in that historic year of anti-imperialist discontent my father left home to become an officer in the British colonial army in India. (104)

From his father, Ghosh learnt that many Indian officers and soldiers had ambivalent feelings about serving in the British Colonial Army. Many of them realised that without their active collaboration, the British would struggle to rule over such a vast subcontinent. History shows that there were many failed mutinies, the most well documented being the great Sepoy uprising in 1857, which nearly pushed the British out of north India. During his formative years, Ghosh learnt through conversation and silences about the subterfuges and silences of his father's generations. It is this aspect of historical reality, which has fascinated Amitav Ghosh. He has used these memories to construct the concept of freedom and its numerous connotations in the modern world, which is the dominant theme of his most well-known novel, *The Shadow Lines.* In a way the quest in this novel is quite universal as it examines and investigates the meaning of freedom for human beings in the modern world. It is a complex novel, interweaving memory, history and contemporary life. Thus it can be seen that the narratives of his parents and the socio-political changes in India in the turbulent decade of the 1940s had a deep impact on Ghosh and form an integral part of his fictional landscape.

Amitav Ghosh graduated from St. Stephen's College, University of Delhi. For a short period during the Emergency, he worked with *The Indian Express* newspaper. There is a reference to his stint as a journalist, in *The Shadow Lines*, when the narrator as a research student reads newspaper reports in the Teen Murti House library about the causes of the 1964 communal riots in Calcutta. Later he joined the Delhi School of Economics as a lecturer in the department of Anthropology. After some years he received a scholarship to do a D.Phil. in social anthropology at Oxford University. In 1980, he went to Egypt to do field work in the Fellaheen village of Lataifa. The work he did there resulted in *In an Antique Land*. Ghosh has done fieldwork in Cambodia, lived in Delhi and written for a number of publications. Starting in Fall 1999, Amitav joined the visiting faculty at Queens College in the City College of New York as Distinguished Professor in the Dept. of Comparative Literature. He currently lives in Brooklyn, New York with his wife Deborah Baker.

His novel *The Calcutta Chromosome* won the Arthur C. Clarke Award for 1997 and is soon to be filmed by Gabriele Salvatores, the Oscar-winning director of Mediterraneo. He was a finalist in the reporting category for the National Magazine Awards, the most important magazine prizes in the U.S. in 1999 for a story he wrote the previous year for *The New Yorker*. He is the winner of the 1999 Pushcart Prize, a leading literary award, for an essay that was published in the *Kenyon Review*.

Ghosh has admitted that campus life and his constant travels have contributed to his ability to move his characters in and out of their native settings with confidence and ease. As G.R. Taneja remarks in his essay "*The Shadow Lines*: A Note": "His experience as a social anthropologist at the Universities of Delhi and Oxford shows in his handling of the characters and the context in which they exist. He reveals a sense of history and a firm grasp of socio-cultural and historical material that underlies his narrative."

The Works of Amitav Ghosh

Till now, Amitav Ghosh has written four novels, a travelogue and a booklet exposing the nuclear arms race in both India and Pakistan. He published his first novel, *The Circle of Reason* (1986), when he was teaching at the Delhi School of Economics, at the University of Delhi. This novel was translated into many European languages. Its French edition, received the *Prix Medici estranger* a prestigious literary award in France.

His next book was *The Shadow Lines* (1988) considered by many critics as his best work of fiction till date. It is an acclaimed masterpiece and evokes postcolonial situations, cultural dislocations and anxieties in the period between 1962 and 1979. In this novel, the interpretation of fractured nationalities is both vivid and intriguing. For this outstanding novel, he was awarded the coveted Sahitya Akademi award in 1989.

Amitav Ghosh's third book *In an antique Land* (1992) shows that he is not a mere fiction writer but a serious researcher, social anthropologist and a keen traveller as well. This novel bears testimony to Ghosh's interaction with at least four languages and cultures spread over three continents and across several countries.

In his next novel, entitled *The Calcutta Chromosome* (1996), Amitav Ghosh amalgamates literature, science, philosophy, history, psychology and sociology. It is a unique experiment in the post-modernist form and the result is a complex, and imaginative story of quest and discovery that weaves past, present and future into an intricate texture.

Besides these four books of fiction, Ghosh has written a gripping and meticulously researched travelogue *Dancing in Cambodia, At Large in Burma* (1998). It is a travel book that reveals the writer's perceptions about the socio-political situations in both Cambodia and Burma, two countries, which practised the politics of extreme isolation in the recent past. This recent publication shows Ghosh as an excellent socio-historical chronicler.

Journeys are a very important part of Ghosh's fictional

landscape. In his first novel, *The Circle of Reason,* Nachiketa Bose known simply as 'Alu' or potato because of the shape of his knobby and bumpy head moves from Lalpukur in East Bengal to Malabar, then onto to the African port of Al Ghazira and finally to El Qued on the north-eastern edge of the African Sahara. In the next novel, *The Shadow Lines* the narrator journeys from Calcutta to Bangladesh and onto England, while Abraham Ben Yiju in *In an Antique Land* moves from his small Israeli community in the Middle East to Mangalore on India's West Coast to become a prosperous trader. In his postmodernist text, *The Calcutta Chromosome,* the story moves from the god-forsaken village of Renupur in north India, which abounds in ghosts and ghostly trains through a little Egyptian hamlet on the western edge of the Nile Delta with its "brilliantly sunlit vision of sand and mud-brick and creaking water-wheels" (177) to New York in the 21st century. These journeys are not mere quests, they also provide Ghosh with the means to explore the ramifications of history and the impact of violence on human behaviour.

Another significance of the journeys in Ghosh's novels is that they are meant to do away with history and restrictions. Traversing borders becomes almost an obsession with Ghosh. For instance, the young narrator in *The Shadow Lines*, who has not been outside of Calcutta till he is an adult, crosses borders easily with the help of imagination. His cousin, Tridib, who is both his hero and teacher, constantly relates experiences. In fact, three-quarters of this novel's fictional life is Tridib's story as seen through the narrator's eyes. Borders are thus meant to be crossed. Ghosh shows that men and countries set up borders to exclude people and create differences based on nationalities, race, culture and religion. In his novels, Ghosh makes it clear that the borders set up by men are mental constructs, that the lines on the maps are mere shadow lines.

The Circle of Reason by Amitav Ghosh is specifically a contemporary work. The basic technique used in this novel is the well told-story, a tradition as old as Homer's epics. Around the bare outlines of the plot which moves over continents, are clustered an infinite number of stories ranging back and forth in time. Each story, whether it moves backwards or forwards in time, continues and subtly explains any ambiguities in the previous story. So in this novel, story telling is Amitav Ghosh's main narrative technique. However, the author does not use the conventional, linear chronological narrative. Instead, the novel starts in the past with Balaram's excitement at exploring the shape of the skull of his nephew, Nachiketa Bose, popularly known as Alu. It then moves further back in time, exploring Balaram's relationships with his group of friends, all in their mid-thirties. The next phase is a return to Balaram's relationship with Alu. The novel then moves forward to the present with Inspector Das interviewing Gopal, a friend of Balaram and then narrates the early years of Balaram's life, including his years at Presidency College. Each story is a distinct episode and yet unfolds in linear time, creating an overall final experience. Connections are made subtly, episodes being linked by a certain vision of life and understanding process. The final experience is an extraordinary achievement in which past and present co-exist, whilst constantly asserting their difference. Like Salman Rushdie, even Amitav Ghosh displays a mature historical sense. *The Circle of Reason* presents history as a collective memory, a link between past and present. The past, a reference point for understanding what is happening, is equally dependent on the present, to determine the perspective. Ultimately, *The Circle of Reason* can be viewed as an epic of restlessness. Ghosh's concept of history colours all his writing. *The Circle of Reason* presents history as a collective memory, which gathers, in a symbiotic fashion, all that existed in the past into all that happens in the present. His narrative method combined with his treatment of history weaves delicate connections between different phenomena, so that no event becomes absolutely autonomous. There is no attempt on the part of the author to squeeze history into a preconceived shape.

In *In an Antique Land,* Ghosh blends fiction, fact and history so skilfully that the combination appears seamless. Abraham Ben Yiju, his family, his slave Bomma and his friend

Khalaf ibn Ishaq travel a medieval itinerary that links the Levant and the Eastern Mediterranean with Mangalore on India's West Coast in 1148 AD. Their journeys and trade dealings account is discovered in the twentieth century. Ghosh writes on two parallel planes of time: one recounting his visit to Lataifa and Nashawy, small Egyptian villages, in 1990 and 1988, the other reconstructing the life of Bomma, the Indian slave. The two narratives initially seem arbitrarily connected, but they gradually illumine and complement each other. So in *In an Antique Land*, Ghosh reconstructs the tapestry of life in twelfth century India and the Levant against the backdrop of Egyptian life in the 1980s. The quality of slavery, the price of raisins and the shortage of good writing paper in the twelfth century are juxtaposed against the gains and losses of the villagers of Lataifa in the Iran-Iraq war. In this novel, the author himself is the protagonist. The people of Lataifa cannot comprehend a religion (al Hindu) which burns its dead and worships cows. The most unique part of this innovative novel is the manner in which the author has woven details of personal life with historical processes to arrive at new ways of looking at things. Disparate narratives seem to echo into each other, playing on and amplifying the same themes.

In his next novel, *The Calcutta Chromosome*, Amitav Ghosh again uses the experimental mode and combines various themes and techniques. This novel has two major strands of story line. At one level it is the narration of the life story of Antar, an Egyptian computer clerk working on his super-intelligent machine Ava in the early twenty-first century to locate the whereabouts of Indian-born American scientist, L. Murugan. This research scientist had mysteriously disappeared in Calcutta in August 1995. The second narrative goes backwards in time and revolves around Ronald Ross's discovery of the malarial parasite in 1902. The novel is divided into sections "August 20, Mosquito Day" and "The Day After." It reads like science fiction with multiple characters and swift turns in the plot. However, it is not just a science thriller but the work of a serious social anthropologist. In the novel, Ghosh cleverly uses arguments that undermine the rational view of science and the universe. The book has been described as "a medical thriller, a Victorian ghost story and a scientific quest." It is an experimental work in the post-modernist phase in its use of explosion of information, technology and virtual reality. Subhash Chandra, in his learned article "*The Calcutta Chromosome*: A Postmodernist Text," has shown how Ghosh has developed a questioning attitude towards certain obvious historical fixities and the dissolution of temporal boundaries in this novel. By combining literature, science, philosophy and fantasy in this novel, Ghosh approaches human affairs from unconventional points of view.

Travelogue is a queer genre of writing. One perhaps can never be too categorical about them. There is this unique sensitivity required to make a good travel writer, a sensitivity which recognizes well not only the passage of time but that of distances as well. The only way to catch up with the transient is to be able to flow with it. Travel writing is always nostalgic for it is through those captured images of various places that the writers make a meaningful expression. Although quality travel writing is something which can be called a neglected genre by Indian writers but travelogues find a decent amount of audience in India.

Travelling comes as naturally to Amitav Ghosh as to his writings. Thematically speaking, displacement has been a central process in his fictional writings, departures and arrivals have a permanent symbolic relevance in his narrative structure. *Dancing in Cambodia, At Large in Burma* is a travel account by the celebrated author of *The Circle of Reason* and *The Calcutta Chromosome*. The Far East has been an area of interest for Ghosh, also because of some personal reference points. Weaving personal lives with public events is something at which Ghosh could be said to have become a master. In this travelogue also we get some glimpses, although fleeting, of this trait.

The historical perspective again is something which Ghosh seldom misses. *Dancing in Cambodia* begins with a deft evocation of the first ever visit to Europe by a troupe of Cambodian dancers in 1906. Their performances in Paris and Marseilles were ecstatically received. In 1993 the author visited Cambodia, a land torn apart by tyrannical 'Pol Pot years' from 1975 to 1978 and the incessant turmoil thereafter. Amongst other things, he met members of Pol Pot's family and went to the village where he was born. The author gives insights into Pol Pot's background, the impact of his brutal regime and the importance of dance in Cambodia even when the country was reduced to near destitution. The tenacity with which Cambodian people held on to one of the principal elements of their culture is itself deeply moving and provides an illuminating account of cultural courage.

Ghosh visited Burma twice in 1995-96 and the last piece in this volume, "At Large in Burma" brings alive the recent history of the country, from the death of the great leader Aung San in 1947 to his daughter Suu Kyi's ongoing struggle for the restoration of democracy in Burma. The book contains the author's interviews of Suu Kyi. Amitav Ghosh also travelled to the jungle camps of the Karenni insurgents and gives a rare picture of their life. Burma is one of those countries like Bhutan, about which not much is spoken or written in India, despite their immediate proximity. As Prabhat Choudhary says, "Amitav Ghosh's approach is always interpretive. He presents the obvious realities relentlessly till the subterranean starts surfacing. Another strength of his writing is his deep understanding of socio-political patterns. In this volume Ghosh gives the entire socio-political and also the economical backdrop of the countries he visited the space of language. All this with a predominantly humane core makes this travel collection instantly readable."

His latest work is a booklet, *Countdown* (1999), in which he exposes the nuclear lobby in both India and Pakistan. The book also challenges and questions the views of George Fernandez, Defence Minister of India in the cabinet of Prime Minister Atal Bihari Vajpayee. It may be recalled that some years ago, Fernandez had opposed India becoming a nuclear power but later valiantly defended the nuclear blasts in Pokharan. Amitav Ghosh sums up his argument for the nuclear weapons very succinctly.

He states that the motivation for India's nuclear programme was enhancement of status, and not imagined threat to our northern frontiers. According to Ghosh, the primary intention behind the programme is to push India into an imagined circle of powerful nations so that she could be counted as a 'great power.' After much research, Ghosh feels that the motivation behind Pakistan's nuclear programme is also similar. In this booklet, Ghosh warns of the danger of nuclear accidents and war and the subsequent economic breakdown, if over-ambitious politicians hold sway. Amitav Ghosh cites the opinions of scientists like Raja Ramanna and scholars like Kanti Bajpai on the impact of a nuclear holocaust in terms of destruction of cities and human lives in Mumbai, Karachi, Delhi and Lahore. He says: "Has the gap between the realities of the subcontinent and the aspirations of the middle classes ever been wider? Talking to nuclear enthusiasts, I had the sense that what they were really saying was: 'The country has tried everything else to get ahead. Nothing worked. This is our last card and this is the time to play it.' I am convinced that support for India's nuclear program is occasioned by a fear of the future. The bomb has become the weapon with which the rulers of the subcontinent wish to avert whatever is ahead. The pursuit of nuclear weapons in the subcontinent is the moral equivalent of civil war: the targets the rulers have in mind are, in the end, their own people."

Ghosh reveals that it will engulf the whole of the subcontinent and spread noxious gases to even distant Bhutan, Tibet and Myanmar (formerly Burma). The booklet is written largely in the first person and is based on his travels to Pokharan, Delhi, Kashmir, Leh, Ladakh, Siachen Glacier, Lahore (this was his first visit to Pakistan). It is highly readable with lucid arguments and interpretations. He concludes with the statement: "A celebration was organized near the blast crater. There was talk of sending sand from the test site around the country so that the whole nation could partake of the glow. Nawaz Sharif, the Prime Minister of Pakistan, wanted better relations with India. For fourteen years, India and Pakistan have engaged in a high-altitude war, exchanging artillery fire over a piece of land nobody wants. "We are fatalistic nations who believe that whatever happens—a famine, a drought, an accident—it's the will of God."

Narrative Techniques in the Novel

The narrative structure of *The Shadow Lines* is fragmentary. There are sixteen sections in the first part of the novel, known as "Going Away" from pages 3-112 and fifteen chapters in the second part entitled "Coming Home" from pages 115 to 232. Both titles become ironic because the impression that emerges from Ghosh's handling of distances is that a person can neither 'go away' nor 'come home.' Also both the sections do not create an organic whole with a beginning, a middle and an end. The author uses a non-linear, multi-layered narrative technique. Instead of mimetic realism, the narrator uses defamiliarising perspectives including mystery, bafflement and indeterminacy. So narration becomes a search for elusive meanings at both the personal and national level and an act of memory. (For details read Rama Kundu's article in this book.) There is no linear central narrative. Other narratives often interrupt the central narrative.

Commenting on this multiple use of narratives by Ghosh, critic Nivedita Bagchi observes, "The story or the chief narrative line evolves sporadically and is constantly interrupted and diverted by other narratives. The only fixed centre is that of the chief narrative voice through whom the other narratives are filtered." (188) Ghosh employs the technique of the narrator to tell the story of the novel. The narrator shuttles between London and Calcutta to collect material for his Ph.D. thesis. The novel also contains multiple stories of his grandmother and her sister, of his uncles, Tridib and Robi, of his cousin Ila who marries an Englishman, and of May Price a family friend in London. Many stories that belong to the oral sphere in the extended family memory get their validation by being written about in the novel. This is a distinct feature of postcolonial writing. The narrator has inherited the central story from Tridib, who in turn inherited it from Snipe. So the narrator appears as a mirrored image of Tridib and tries to reflect time past and time present, places and people.

The narrator also traverses across a time span from 1981 to the 1960s onto the 1940s and even earlier. Amitav Ghosh seems particular about years, months and even certain dates. However these important dates which are like signs seem to follow one another in an arbitrary manner. For instance 1959 is followed by 1940 (17), March 1963 in Calcutta and 25 September 1940 in London converge and melt into a December night of 1980 in the cellar of the Price house (182). A sequence of 1979 in Delhi slides back to October 1962, the days of the Indo-Chinese war. Another significant date is 2 January 1964, the time of the Calcutta-Khulna riots which leads us back to 27 December 1963, when the Hazrat Bal had disappeared from Kashmir. Ghosh constantly uses the zigzag movement, going backwards and forwards to present a complex pattern of time. Various points of the past and present continuously intersect and overlap in the unpredictable manner of an interior monologue. By this technique the author shows the difficulty of blending the enigmatic past and the confusing present. (For a detailed discussion read Rama Kundu's article).

The narrator's mind is especially drawn to one crucial event, the troubled days of the 1960s when his uncle and childhood hero, Tridib, was killed in a Hindu-Muslim riot in Dhaka. At the time that this catastrophe took place, the narrator, a twelve-year-old boy, had been told that Tridib had died in an accident. It is only years later in 1981 that he learns the truth from Robi, another uncle who had been an eyewitness to the event. Another version of Tridib's death is provided by May Price, an English family friend, also an eyewitness to the gruesome killing. The oblique manner of the revelation of Tridib's death is very effective. It is more effective than a direct presentation as it represents the timeless moment in the tortured consciousness of the family. The narrator—whose name is not given—is the bearer of this troubled memory.

There is an extraordinary density in the narrative texture of *The Shadow Lines*. The overall story emerges in layers and each layer is a fusion of private lives and public events all linked into a thematic unity. Ghosh uses first person narrative from a dual viewpoint, that of the child and the adult "I." This gives a sense of inhabiting both past and present simultaneously. Nandita Sinha, in her perceptive essay "Perspectives in Time: The Narrator as Child in *The Shadow Lines*," says that "the narrator as child comes into close contact with the protagonists of the story and this serves to weave together its multiple facets." The narrator thus interacts with his grandmother who recalls her East Bengal background and memories of her childhood days in Dhaka in a sprawling house with its idiosyncratic occupants. The narrative takes us to what Nandita Sinha terms as "the odyssey of her [grandmother's] search for an old uncle left behind in what was by then East Pakistan and its tragic consequences." Through Tridib, whom the child narrator hero-worships, an authentic vista of Calcutta life is presented, the streetside 'addas,' between Gariahat and Golepark, the strollers around the Lake, the squalid tenements and a tender portrait of a childhood in a middle class Bengali family. Calcutta is also depicted by the Gariahat fish-market from where Ila's mother bought the best 'Ilish' fish and mention of Howrah, Sealdah, Rajabazar, Free School street and Grand Hotel.

The image of the journey is central to the novel. Tridib goes away from India to England, with his family and the child narrator "relives the experience vicariously through Tridib's imaginatively vivid descriptions, so that when he himself grows up and goes to London, it is an effortless transition, a 'coming rather than a going.'" The vivacious Tridib expands the knowledge and frontiers of the boyhood world of the narrator. Tridib makes the young narrator value the importance of imagination. The narrator realizes that imagination reveals a world as concrete and real and more exciting than the world experienced through the senses. His journeys into the past with Tridib provide him with a vivid recollection of wartorn London. It enables him to understand the heroism and stoical attitude of the citizens of London when they withstood the aerial blitz by the German Air Force in the Second World

War. Tridib, as an eight-year-old boy had stayed with his parents, Datta-Chaudhuri and Mayadebi, with Mrs. Price, a family friend in London for a whole year in 1939. It was the year the Second World War started. Tridib had told the narrator about their life at 44 Lymington Road and other places and the terror of the German air raids. Mrs. Price's brother, Mr. Alan Tresawsen and his three friends were killed in one such air raid. They were young intellectuals whose life had been snuffed out all of a sudden. Tridib's narration had been so vivid that even after forty years, the narrator on a visit to London went to explore these places. His rationale for a trip down memory lane was: "I wanted to know England not as I saw her, but in her finest hour. Every place chooses its own and to me it did not seem an accident that England had chosen hers in war." (57)

In the second part of the novel, the grandmother Tha'mmas journey to Dhaka becomes a symbolic search for a point of fixity. The prospect of a return to a home where she has inexplicably become a foreigner baffles her. Initially the child narrator misinterprets her confusion as anxiety at the prospect of travelling in a plane. Later in life he realizes the actual source of her mental conflict. It was her inability to understand how her place of birth has become alien to her and is at odds with her nationality. The encounter with the old uncle who fails to recognise her adds to her confusion. In her bid to resurrect the past that memory has indelibly imprinted in her mind, she fails to take into account the altered realities of the present. She does not realize that the Muslims Khalil and Saifuddin who befriended the old man are his family in the truest sense of the word and she who crossed the borders to the safety of Calcutta is now an alien. The narrator deftly uses minor details to show the grandmother's allegiances to the past, such as changing into a red-border sari at the moment of departure. However, clinging to the memories of the past limits the vision of the grandmother.

Similar references and techniques can be found in the 1999 Booker Prizewinner, the South African J.M. Coetzee. A pre-occupation with apartheid in South Africa and its traumatic transition to a multi-racial, multi-ethnic society forms the backdrop of all his novels as well as non-fiction. In his prize-winning book *Disgrace* (1999), one of the main characters Lucy triumphs because of her ability to forget. Unlike the grandmother in Ghosh's novel, for Lucy memory of the past is a curse. Lucy who is engaged in an experiment with an alternative lifestyle undergoes a traumatic experience. During her stay there, she is brutally raped by a group of black youth. She tries to forget this memory. Lucy realises that the only way in which the present can be made better is by immense generosity and neutralising evil by an excess of compliance. Coetzee's novel thus searches the colonies of the mind of its characters. He suggests that the focus of values must necessarily be beyond history. Lucy thus does not become a slave to memory. In contrast the grandmother in *The Shadow Lines* is unable to break away from the memories and values of the past. She is trapped in a web of memories. Her pre-occupation with the past leads to the catastrophe of the death of Tridib and her elder relative. Thus at the end of the novel, she remains isolated in the Mercedes, while the mob butchers the old man in his rickshaw as well as Tridib who sacrifices his life in trying to save him.

The query that arises is, why did Tridib sacrifice his life? Was it a symbolic gesture or a foolhardy act? The heart of *The Shadow Lines* is the death of Tridib. The manner in which the narrator as a child and later as an adult comes to know of this death is very revealing. His parents are reluctant to speak of Tridib's death and label it as an accident. The child narrator accepts these versions, as death for him was just a word, whose meaning he knew from reading comics and watching films. The narrator's adult experience is different. He hears two versions of the violence that led to Tridib's death. For his uncle Robi, the memory is a nightmare from which there is no deliverance. Robi who has now qualified for the Indian Administrative Service (IAS) has developed a cynical view about sacrifice and freedom after years of experience as an administrator. He feels that human nature has remained unchanged and that the concept of freedom is just a catchword to condone killing and that political freedom is also an illusion. For May, who is guiltridden at the thought that in some ways she was responsible for Tridib's death, it is a mystery, a sacrifice and martyrdom that defies understanding. May considers it as an idealist's heroic stand against the tide of madness and bloodshed. By such different interpretations of Tridib's death, the author cleverly shows separate insights about a single event. The narrator thus goes backward and forward in time before understanding this traumatic experience.

Arundhati Roy uses a similar narrative technique in *The God of Small Things* (1997) with reference to a very painful sequence. Her narrator also goes backward and forward in time, drifting away and veering around the most crucial event, the death of Velutha. Arundhati's narrator also fails to summon the courage to describe the death. It is finally conveyed in detail towards the end of the novel. The narrator in Amitav Ghosh's novel also struggles to find words, struggles with memories and silences before writing about Tridib's death. He says, "I can only describe at second hand the manner of Tridib's death: I *do not have the words*, and I do not have the strength to listen." (228)

The novel can therefore be described as the narrator's journey backwards in time in quest of a fuller meaning in life. It is an attempt to impose a pattern on experience. This novel also does not narrate events sequentially, nor is the experience of the hero-narrator limited to the events of his own life, for beneath the surface of everyday happenings he lives a 'truer' life in his memory and imagination. Commenting on the author's narrative technique, G.R. Taneja says, "*The Shadow Lines* takes us into the mnemonic fund of a young narrator who as a wide-eyed adolescent hero-worshipped Tridib, an uncle, who fed him on his memories of his one visit to London during the war, and his grandmother who shared with him her nostalgic memories of East Bengal where she was born and spent her childhood." The young nameless wonderstruck narrator also hears accounts of the foreign travels of his cousin Ila. The father of Ila, who is the young narrator's uncle, is India's consul general in Sofia. Due to frequent diplomatic postings

Ila has been to Cairo, London, Paris, Florence and several other cities. So memory is one of the narrative techniques used by Amitiav Ghosh in this novel. Explaining how he uses their memories, the narrator says that they "form a part of my secret map of the world, a map of which I only know the key and the coordinates, but which was not for that reason any more imaginary than the code of a safe to a banker." So as G.R. Taneja explains, "from the three whose memories form his own consciousness, he learns to see in different ways." Tridib teaches the narrator to see with precision and to see with imagination. It is through the stories narrated by Tridib that the narrator, a young boy, validates his experiences. "Tridib had given me worlds to travel in and he had given me eyes to see them with." From Ila, he learns the superficial responses to life. The grandmother establishes to him the "oneness of the memory for according to her neither space nor time can divide it." Amitav Ghosh's *The Shadow Lines* is basically a memory novel with a dexterous blending of private lives and public events into a mosaic of history. The narrator's story unfurls itself through fragmentary streams of consciousness where the private turmoil of the individual is reflected in the public chaos and crises.

The narrative can also be seen as an impressionistic rendering of a perceptive middle class youth's world of these changing times. Critic Seema Bhaduri says that Ghosh uses the stream of consciousness tradition, "through sketchy, disjointed outlines of memory, associations and fancies as they pool into the narrator's mind and consciousness by way of reminiscence, fusing gradually into a coherent pattern of stories mutually interrelated yet disparate, the profile of a multi-lateral world." Through the random diversions of the narrator's memory, the socio-cultural ambience of Calcutta and partly of London are conveyed. So it is a novel of memories, with the narrator recalling his past associations in order to shape his visions under the influence of Tridib. The personally experienced reality of Tridib colours the imagination of the storyteller. It is through Tridib, the grandmother and Ila that the narrator views reality and lends meaning to his meaningless infantile fancy.

Though Tridib is the uncle of the narrator, he is functionally a friend and guide. He is doing research in anthropology. "In fact he was working on a Ph.D. in Archaeology—something to do with sites associated with the Sena dynasty." (7) It is Tridib who makes the narrator understand that reality lies not in the obvious but in what it evoked and understood by memory and imagination, in different times. The title of the novel, *The Shadow Lines*, thus becomes an ambivalent symbol. It suggests the dichotomy of one's mind, the shadow lines that pervade the minds of the people. As the grandmother's son says: "This is the modern world. The border isn't on the frontier; it's right inside the airport. You'll see. You'll cross it when you have to fill in all those disembarkation cards and things." (151-52)

Suvir Kaul's scholarly essay, "Separation Anxiety: Growing Up Inter/National in *The Shadow Lines*," says that the narrative technique in this novel is based on the narrator's search for connections. This is yet another view on the narrative technique of Ghosh. Describing this technique, Suvir Kaul says that the narrator's quest is "for the recovery of lost information or repressed experiences, for the details of great trauma or joy that have receded into the archives of public or private memory." (268-69) So it can be seen that in the novel, memory is a restless, energetic and troublesome power. The shaping power of memory in the novel is "enormously productive and enabling but also traumatic and disabling; it liberates and stunts, both the individual imagination and social possibilities; it confirms identities and enforces divides." (Kaul 269) Explaining the nuances of this technique, Suvir Kaul says: "As the repository and archivist of family stories, stories told by his grandmother Tha'mma, by Tridib, by Ila, and finally by Robi and May, the unnamed narrator of *The Shadow Lines* is constantly engaged in the imaginative renewal of time. This remembering is often tinted with the sepia-tones of nostalgia, often darkened by the dull shades of grief, but in each case it is fundamentally a search for meaning, for explanations and reasons, for the elusive, formal and casual logic that will allow the narrator's autobiography (and equally the national *bi-*

ography that is interwoven with it in the novel) to cohere, to make sense." (269)

The pressure of the question, "do you remember" generates the form of the novel, "its partial answers, digressions, its looping, non-linear, wide-ranging narrative technique. (Suvir Kaul 269) So it is basically a memory novel which skilfully weaves together personal lives and public events in three countries, India, England and Bangladesh. Coil within coil of memories unfurls in the narrator's story. Even as he is rooted in Calcutta, his imaginative universe knows few boundaries. He is transported by Tridib's and Ila's stories to places and times, which come alive for him with a powerful immediacy.

His curiosity aroused, the young narrator in his imagination touches the Great Pyramid and visualises the "world's first pointed arch in the mosque of Ibn Tulum" (20) in Cairo. Tridib's stories create new vistas for him, a young sixteen-year-old schoolboy in Calcutta, who had never been more than a few hundred miles away from his native city. He tries to rationalise such experiencc to his attractive cousin Ila.

> Tridib has given me worlds to travel in and he had given me eyes to see them with: she who had been travelling around the world since she was a child could never understand what those hours in Tridib's room meant to me. (20)

Thus for the narrator, as Usha Hemmadi explains in her essay "Amitav Ghosh: A Most Distinctive Voice," "cultural differences can be collectively contained to create not a fragmented self but one that belongs to many places." (297) In contrast for Ila, cultural differences create only a small unsure self, incapable of meaningful action. For Ila who had travelled with her diplomat father to many cities of the world, the recollections of Tridib aroused no curiosity or awe. "It had for her a dull familiarity no less dull than the Lake had for me and my friends." (20) All that Ila remembers of exotic places like Cairo is the inconvenient location of the "Ladies" on the other side of the departure lounge. Using such an unusual narrative technique, Amitav Ghosh raises certain fundamental questions on imagination and reality.

The importance and role of imagination in human life and art has fascinated thinkers for centuries. The Greek philosopher Plato gave no importance to imagination. In his book *The Republic* (387 B.C.) he considered all art to be mimesis or representation, interpreted to mean a rather literal imitation. In contrast the Elizabethan poet-cum-critic, Sir Philip Sidney suggested that imagination was the distinguishing factor for any creative writer or individual. The world of imagination, according to Sidney, is better than the world of nature.

> Nature never set forth the earth in so rich tapestry, as divers poets have done: her world is brazen, the poets only deliver a golden. (21)

In this age-old debate, Amitav Ghosh upholds the value and importance of imagination. In fact the author seems to suggest that there is a 'shadow line' between reality and imagination. So by his narrative technique, the author implies that reality is multi-faceted. It cannot be limited to mere chronology or physical contours. The places imagined by the narrator, after listening to Tridib and pouring over Bartholomew's Atlas were as much a vivid experience, as the cities Ila visited. Ila's reality is mundane and her memories are confined to souvenirs and personal items like a school Yearbook. According to Amitav Ghosh, the imagination can create a more vivid and sustained reality. So, using the technique of uncoiling memories, the author develops on the role of the imagination that is an important factor in the political themes of this novel also.

Thus, as Usha Hemmadi in her essay points out, "Ghosh establishes that there is no dividing line between imagination and reality, for imagination is experience in reality. Memory is all-important, and there are no lines dividing an event from what is remembered." The death of Tridib is an excellent example of the manner in which Ghosh blends theme and technique. Tridib's death actually occurs in East Pakistan in 1964, but the details are spread out for the narrator years later in

London. At this juncture, there is still no separation of what is narrated and what is heard. Tridib had rushed into the frenzied mob, to save the old uncle from the agitators and had been killed in this attempt. His death is seen and narrated by different people at different times. Thus, in Ghosh's novel, events and characters are seen through time-spaced narratives.

The imagination as an ideal retreat, is another narrative technique that Ghosh has used. For instance, the grandmother of the narrator returned in 1964 to Dhaka, her homeland, before Partition. Dhaka has changed, but in the grandmother's mind the place of her childhood remains as real as ever. So though the Dhaka of her youth has changed, the memory of her ancestral home becomes an ideal worth living for amidst the travails of daily life. Imagination thus helps in sustaining memory which provides solace, comfort and a sense of belonging. For the narrator, visiting Dhaka provides a different type of excitement. He is stimulated by thoughts of places he had just heard of. There is clarity in his vision because his grandmother is skilled in the art of recollection.

> I could see Kanu-babu's sweet shop at the end of their lane with absolute clarity. For me Kanu-babu's sweet shop at the end of the lane was as real as the one down our lane, and yet I could not tell whether the lane itself was paved or unpaved. (194)

Thus by skilfully manipulating the narrator's developing social consciousness and his interactions with multicultural representatives in a fictional construct, Ghosh makes this novel the subtle medium of sophisticated comment on current realities. Describing Amitav Ghosh's story telling technique, P.K. Dutta, in his learned essay "Studies in Homogeneity: A Reading of Two Recent Indo-Anglian Novels," says that the impact is "of one passage rather than of montage." (67) Dutta elaborates that the idea of a passage allows Ghosh to constitute his novelistic experience as "oppositions founded on co-existing paradoxes rather than on antagonism. In *The Shadow Lines*, "the world of war-torn London is overlaid by memories of Calcutta and Dhaka. In this way, Ghosh is able to remove realism as the procedure of organising social experience." (67) Instead, according to Dutta, he relocates it to provide the method of describing society for the purposes of narrative meditation. By using such a narrative technique, Dutta feels that Amitav Ghosh extends his thematic concerns to explore human relationships. Characters are not seen as autonomous entities but instead Ghosh examines the logic of human relationships.

By letting his stories interplay with time, Ghosh achieves an unusual synthesis of time. In *The Shadow Lines* the movement is from the present to the past to the present again and this enables the novel to achieve a symbiotic narrative texture. A significant difficulty in *The Shadow Lines* is the identification of the narrator as the authorial voice. Rajeswari Sunder Rajan, in her essay "The Division of Experience in *The Shadow Lines*," says, "We are strongly pressurised by the narrative tone and stance at once judicious, reflective, intelligent and sensitive—to accept the narrator's account and his interpretation of men, women and events as the definitive versions of reality. This is a novel that comes to us entirely filtered through a single consciousness . . however resonant it may be of an entire civilizational ethos." (296-97) Rajeswari Sunder Rajan feels that there is no suggestion of irony or resistant points of view or any other forms of checks to the overall reach of this central vision. She feels there is a powerful control of meaning by the central voice.

So, in *The Shadow Lines*, it is ultimately the male narrator's growing imagination, empathy and intellectuality which leads to exploration and understanding of complex themes. Explaining this technique, Suvir Kaul says, "As his horizons expand and become international in scope, his questions, memories and experiences provide the structure of the narrative. But even as his consciousness mediates and frames other voices, stories and experiences, we become aware that some of these voices counterpoint his narrative, and even interrogate his telling of the story." (285-86)

So there are many stories in this novel which tend to overlap at points and even become contentious at times. With this method, "*The Shadow Lines* becomes not simply a male bildungsroman, an authorised autobiography, with its obvious agendas and priorities, but also a dialogic, more open-ended telling of the difficult interdependencies and inequalities that compose any biography of a nation." (Suvir Kaul 286)

An Overview of the Novel

The Shadow Lines tells the story of three generations of the narrator's family spread over Dhaka, Calcutta and London. It lines up characters from different nationalities, religions and cultures in a close-knit fictive world. The novel is written against the backdrop of the civil strife in post-partition East Bengal and riot-hit Calcutta. The events revolve around Mayadebi's family, their friendship and sojourn with their English friends the Prices and Tha'mma, the narrator's grandmother's links with her ancestral city, Dhaka. The riots in 1964 claimed the lives of Jethamoshoi (father's elder brother) Khalil and Tridib. Jethamoshoi's actual name is Shri Goshtobihari Bose and he worked as a lawyer in the Dhaka High Court. These deaths raise questions and pose a challenge to the concept of intercultural understanding and friendship in contemporary society divided by arbitrary demarcations of national boundaries.

Section I: Going Away

Beginning in colonial times, the story is woven around two families, the Datta-Chaudhuris of Bengal and the Prices of London. The relationship between these two families spans three generations and involves several passages to and from India on both sides. As A.N. Kaul explains in his essay, "A Reading of *The Shadow Lines*": "Towards the end the story also crosses the newly created frontier between India and East Pakistan (now Bangladesh), engaging or acknowledging along the way the proximate presence of other foreign countries and continents through the Indian diplomatic and the UN postings of the Datta-Chaudhuris." (300) The narrative begins in the year 1939. This is an important year in the history of mankind and particularly in the West as it was the year, in which the Second World War commenced. The novel ends essentially in 1964 with the eruption of a cycle of violence in both India and Pakistan. Explaining the importance of these dates, A.N. Kaul says, "In 1939 Tridib, the narrator's father's cousin, then aged 8, is taken to England, and in 1964 he is murdered by a street mob near his mother's original family home in Dhaka. His boyhood experiences in war-time London and his violent death twenty-five years later in Dhaka constitute the end points of the novel's essential narrative." (301-2)

The novel has a large group of characters that are interconnected to each other either as friends or by family relationships. The narrator's family consists of his grandmother, Mayadebi's elder sister and his parents. Mayadebi and her diplomat husband have three sons, Jatin an economist with the UN, Tridib and Robi, who later joins the Indian Administrative Service (IAS). Jatin's daughter Ila is always travelling to various countries with her parents. In contrast the narrator's family is settled in Calcutta where his grandmother was a schoolmistress. The only member of Mayadebi's family who spent a long time in Calcutta was Tridib who lived in his ancestral house in Bollygunje that is in the vicinity of the narrator's house. Tridib is doing research for a doctorate in medieval archaeology.

Now Tridib saw May Price as a little baby when he went to England with his parents in 1939. They stayed with Mrs. Price in London. Tridib's parents went to England because his father was in need of an operation that could not be done in India. The friendship between the families began when Mrs. Price's father Lionel Tresawsen and Tridib's grandfather Chandrashekhara Datta-Chaudhuri met during the British Raj in Calcutta at seances. By the time Tridib again meets May in 1962 in India, their friendship has blossomed into love. The May-Tridib relationship is central to the thematic concerns of this novel. The narrator's uncle Robi accompanied Tridib, May, Tha'mma and Mayadebi to bring the grandmother's old uncle Jethamoshoi from Dhaka to Calcutta. They all witnessed the killing of Tridib, which is not described directly but later conveyed to the narrator as part of the haunting memories of both Robi and May Price. The narrator's meetings with May Price form crucial junctures in the chronology of the novel. "I met May Price for the first time two years after that incident, when she came to Calcutta on a visit. The next time I met her was seventeen years later, when I went to London myself." (19) The stretch of history during these seventeen years between 1962 and 1979 is the effective background of the novel. Using this background, the author evokes postcolonial situations, cultural dislocations and anxieties and interprets the issues of fractured consciousness in close and telling encounters. Another relationship in this novel is the narrator's 'crush' or admiration for the liberated charms of his attractive cousin Ila. This theme is the sub-text of the first section of the novel. The infatuation for Ila is part of the growing up process of the narrator. As an adolescent, the narrator is fascinated by Ila's exotic appeal. Her foreignness, western ways and easy informality attract him. In contrast, her liberated gestures and overtly off-beat demeanour arouse Tha'mma's contemptuous dislike for her. However Ila later marries Nick Price, the younger brother of May Price. Ila's preference for Nick Price is indicated towards the end of the first section of the novel. Her later disappointments in marriage are conveyed in the second section and it exposes her wobbly adjustments in the Western culture. Her dislocation stems from her penchant for illusions devoid of any real understanding of the cultural interface. The adult narrator sees through Ila's hidden anxieties and discomfiture. Her last words in the novel are aimed at consoling the narrator and her cousin that everything is all right between her and Nick. Commenting on Ila's role in the novel, Suvir Kaul notes that she is central to the narrator's coming of age and functions "as a narrative scapegoat, a fixture who acts as a lightning rod for a great many sexual and cultural anxieties." (273-74) So the Nick-Ila pairing is a counterpoint to the Tridib-May kinship in the thematic framework of the novel. In his mature phase, the narrator realises that Ila's seductive foreignness is a cover for her snooty ways and cultural contradictions.

In the first section of the novel, called "Going Away," the storyteller in the first chapter establishes the important influence of Tridib and the latter's eccentric behaviour. Tridib is described as "a familiar figure within the floating, talkative population of students and would-be footballers and bank clerks and small time politicos and all the rest who gravitated towards the conversation-loving stretch of road between Gariahat and Gole Park." (8) He is described as a very knowledgeable person with "vast reservoirs of abstruse information." (8) Much to the delight of the narrator who hero worships him, Tridib could hold forth on all kinds of subjects—"Mesopotamian stellae, East European jazz, the habits of arboreal apes, the plays of Garcia Lorca, there seemed to be no end to the things he could talk about." (9) The impressionable young narrator hears the story of Tridib's journey to England in instalments. So in the first section of the novel, the narrator concentrates on London on the eve of and during the Second World War. The narrator has only a vicarious experience of these events. His knowledge of the war was not gained from books but from the experience of his uncle Tridib who taught him to use imagination and conjure up vivid pictures, which gradually merge into a perception of history. In the subsequent sections the author uses the same method to exercise his historical imagination. The narrator is in England on a year's research grant, "to collect material from the India Office Library, where all the old colonial records were kept, for a Ph.D. thesis on the textile trade between India and England in the nineteenth century." (13)

In the novel, the memory of the narrator shuttles back and forth in time. Memories of Tridib's account of his first visit to London influence the narrator's chronicling of events. Tridib and his family stayed at 44 Lymington Road with the Prices on the eve of the war. In 1939 Tridib's father, jocularly known as Shaheb because of his immaculate suits and anglicised behaviour, took some photographs of Alan Treswasen, Mrs. Price's brother and his friends Now, every object and instance, however trivial, has for Ghosh its relevance to the greater reality of its times. The simple photograph encapsulates the entire history of England of the times. In the photograph, there was the freshly dug pit to serve as an emergency trench. There was also a picture of Mrs. Price's brother, Alan Tresawsen, a freelance journalist writing for socialist papers. Others in the photograph were Dan a Trotskyite (followers of Soviet Communist leader Leon Trotsky who rebelled against Joseph Stalin in the 1920s and was expelled from the USSR), Mike an Irish nationalist, Francesca Halevy and an academic Snipe, the husband of Mrs. Price. Now Dan, the son of an eminent Cambridge physicist, had studied at the prestigious London School of Economics, fought in the Spanish Civil War and written for left wing newspapers like the *Daily Worker.* The twenty-eight-year-old Mike's concept of nationalism is also militant like that of Tha'mma. When he meets Tridib's father he nonchalantly asks him, "Killed any Englishman yet?" (63) Mrs. Price who describes her as "altogether too elegant, too brilliant, too worldly" (65) does not like Francesca who shares a house in Brick Lane with the three young men.

A couple of pages later in the novel, there is a vivid description of the house where on that fateful night of September 1940, Dan and Alan Treswasen died in the intensive German bombardment. Ian F.W. Beckett writing in his article "Total War" puts the civilian loss of life in Britain from the Luftwaffe's bombing campaign at 51,509. To put it into context, Hamburg suffered about the same number of deaths in a week in July and August 1943, whilst various estimates of a single night's bombing of Dresden range from 35,000 to 135,000. Total loss of German life from Allied bombing is put at a staggering 593,000. The total loss of civilian life in Europe during the Second World War is put at 30 million with the Russians suffering 20 million of that figure.

Again the deaths of Dan and Alan are reported by using the memory technique. The narrator is in England on a scholarship and Ila has taken him to Brick Lane to buy new clothes at a cheap price. When they reach Brick Lane, the narrator on seeing the signboard of the Taj Travel Agency recalls that Alan, Dan and his mates lived there at the outbreak of the Second World War. Imaginatively recalling Tridib's descriptions, the narrator describes the manner in which Dan and Alan died during the German aerial blitz. After the deaths of Alan and Dan, the companions split up. Francesca was "sent to an internment camp for enemy aliens in the Isle of Wright." (103) Mike survived but signed up for the Navy and died in action. This death is recalled through a newspaper report: "In 1943 Mrs. Price read his name in the casualty list in *The Times* and learnt later that his ship a minesweeper, had been torpedoed by a U-boat, not far from Lowestoft harbour." (103)

After seeing this house, Ila and the narrator quarrel about the importance of radical politics. Ila considers the deaths of Alan, Mike and Dan who raised their voices against war-mongering as sad because they were casualties of a ruthless nationalism. She also thought that Alan and his friends, who were witness to the war and the fight against fascism, must have been happy as she was in her political activism. She says, "that's why there is a kind of heroism even in their pointless deaths." (104) The narrator calls Ila and her group as "her pathetic little welfare-pink friends" who "knew nothing at all about courage or politics." (104) The quarrel about courage and political activism continues between Ila and the narrator. Finally the narrator does admit that some form of commitment reflects involvement and political activism which he and his middle-class friends would never have dared to do. He says:

> For I had been with Ila once, when she had come out of her hairdresser's shop, her hair all new and curled, and marched straight off to Brixton with her little crew of friends, to confront a gang of jack-booted racists armed with bicycle chains. As for me, I knew I could not have dared. (105)

Incidents such as these provide an insight into the personal and human aspects of political violence and the impact of historical events on the lives of characters in this novel.

The historical events that form the backdrop for this novel

are the freedom movement in Bengal, the Second World War, the partition of India and the feelings of communal hatred that erupted in East Pakistan (now Bangladesh) following the Hazratbal incident in Srinagar in 1964. The novel is not a recapitulation of these historical events in the subcontinent. In fact, as has been mentioned earlier, to call Ghosh's novel as mere political allegory would be facile. Instead what Ghosh shows is the impact of politics on the lives of ordinary people and on human relationships. Historical events have provided Ghosh with raw material against which he studies the historical truths like the meaning of nationalism and political freedom in the modern world. There is a nexus between the historical moments and the world of fiction. The past is reconstructed through references to houses, photographs, maps, road names, newspapers, advertisements and other such concreteizations. This technique allows the reader to examine the text with diverse co-texts and validate the author's perceptions of the time and milieu covered by the novel. In the opening lines, the narrator refers to his grandmother's sister's visit to England and establishes the narrative framework; "In 1939, thirteen years before I was born, my father's aunt, Mayadebi, went to England, with her husband and son, Tridib." (3) We gather that Mayadebi was born in 1910 and Tridib in 1931. The novel also telescopes the political ferment in Bengal and the upbringing of the grandmother Tha'mma, who was born in 1902 and Mayadebi in the revolutionary decades of the present century. After details of Mayadebi's visit to England, the narrative shifts forward in time to 1960 when Tridib first shared his experience with the narrator. Thus the narrative spills back and forth in time. However all the major episodes are held in simultaneous focus nonetheless to illuminate the major burden of the novel.

Chronologically, the story begins with a passage of time in colonial India when the narrator was not born. The year 1939 is historically significant for the outbreak of the Second World War and the upheaval caused by that epochal event. The Tridib-May component of the story and Mayadebi's visit to London is told to the narrator, twenty-one years later.

Tridib narrates the events to an inquisitive eight-year-old boy. The romantic relationship that develops through correspondence between May and Tridib is significant. Amitav Ghosh explores this mysterious and quaint relationship and the abiding intimacy between the Price family and Tridib's family. It is seen as transcending the shadow lines of nationality and cultural boundaries. The search for invisible links ranging across the realities of nationality, cultural segregation and racial discrimination is the central theme of *The Shadow Lines.* The author questions the validity of geographical boundaries and celebrates the union of aliens pulled together by self-propelling empathy and attachment. Tresawsen and Mayadebi, Tridib and May, Jethamoshoi and Khalil transcend the prevailing passion of war, hatred and communal acrimony.

The first section of the novel ends, with Ila realising that she infatuates the narrator with her looks and body. The narrator's hopes are shattered when Ila says, "You were always the brother I never had. I'm sorry. If I'd known, I wouldn't have behaved like this. Really believe me." (111) The narrator now knows that his days of secret admiration and hopes are over. Yet as he admits, "I knew she had taken my life hostage yet again; I knew that a part of my life as a human being had ceased: that I no longer existed, but as a chronicle." (112)

Section II: Coming Home

In the second section of the novel, Ghosh returns to the Indian subcontinent, to Calcutta and Dhaka. In this section, the narrator as chronicler tries to understand the various nuances and meanings of political freedom. Nationalism and political freedom acquired different shades of meaning after Independence and Partition. Earlier Indian nationalism was a weapon utilised by the freedom fighters in their struggle against foreign rulers. However, this struggle could not even ensure the territorial integrity of India. Partition was viewed as the price for political freedom from British colonial rule. After Partition, nationalism in the Indian context changed its meaning to exclude people on the other side of the border, both in East and

West Pakistan. So different viewpoints of Partition, nationalism and political freedom emerge in this section. It may be recalled that in Indian English fiction there are several novels that belong to the genre of the Partition novel. Some of these novels are Khushwant Singh's *A Train to Pakistan* (1956), Attia Hosain's *Sunlight on a Broken Column* (1961), Manohar Malgaonakar's *A Bend in the Ganges* (1964), Raj Gill's *The Rape* (1974), Chaman Nahal's *Azadi* (1975), Balachandra Rajan's *The Dark Dancer* (1976) and Bapsi Sidhwa's *Ice-Candy-Man* (1988). The vulnerability of human understanding and life caused by the throes of Partition which relentlessly divided friends, families, lovers and neighbours are sown in these novels. Now post-partition Bengali literature abounds in stories of the hapless victims of Partition. The suffering, anger, desperation and determination of these people are well chronicled. Interestingly Partition is also a dominant theme of Bengali cinema. The films of noted director Ritwik Ghatak, like *Komal Gandhar* and *Subaranarekha* highlight the helplessness of the average individual, however well intentioned to influence the course of events. The individual succumbing to the inevitability of history is evocatively portrayed in the films of Ritwik Ghatak. In Indian English fiction, the division of Bengal and suffering caused by Partition is first highlighted by Amitav Ghosh in *The Shadow Lines*. It is mainly portrayed through the grandmother's story.

The section, "Coming Home" starts with the retirement of the grandmother as headmistress near Deshapriya Park. She had taught in this school for twenty-seven years and had worked as headmistress for six years. The year of the retirement is 1962, when the narrator is ten years old. After a description of the touching farewell ceremony, the rest of the opening chapter of the second section shows the grandmother readjusting to a life of retirement. It is noticed that with age she has become nostalgic of the past. It is an eventful year for the narrator's family. His father is promoted to become General Manager of his firm and the family moves from Gole Park to a house on Southern Avenue, opposite the Lake. Staying in this new house makes the grandmother reminisce about her ancestral home in Dhaka:

> It was very odd house. It had evolved slowly, growing like a honeycomb, with the very generation of Boses adding layers and extensions, until it was like a huge, lop-sided step-pyramid, inhabited by so many branches of the family that even the most knowledgeable amongst them had become a little confused about their relationships. (121)

She enthralls the narrator with stories about her ancestral home and early life. She narrates numerous anecdotes, such as the time when her husband caught a chill while "supervising the construction of a culvert somewhere in the Arakan Hills." (125) This chill led to pneumonia and his untimely death. The grandmother was just thirty-two years old then. In order to become independent she opts to be a teacher and gets a job in a school in Calcutta. Her life changes:

> She had no time to go back to Dhaka in the next few years. And then in 1947, came Partition, and Dhaka became the capital of East Pakistan. There was no question of going back after that. She had never had any news of Jethamoshoi and her aunt again. (125)

Amitav Ghosh presents the grandmother's early life as a story told by her to the narrator. Born in 1902 in Dhaka, she grew up as a member of "a big joint family with everyone living and eating together." (121) But when her father died, the ancestral home was partitioned because of a family strife. Whilst at college for her BA in history in Dhaka, she became familiar with the terrorist movement amongst nationalists in Bengal. She tells the narrator "about secret terrorist societies like Anushilan and Jugantar and all their off-shoots, their clandestine networks, and the home-made bombs with which they tried to assassinate British officials and policemen." (37)

Now the story-teller's grandmother who was born and brought up in Dhaka came to Calcutta, many years before the

Partition of Bengal into East Pakistan (now Bangladesh) and West Bengal which is part of India. So she did not undergo the trauma and physical loss of being uprooted from her place of birth during the turbulent days of Partition. The author shows that people like the grandmother, even though she did not suffer materially, the emotional wound had a big impact. When seventeen years after Partition, the grandmother was going to visit her sister Mayadebi at Dhaka, she realises when filling the disembarkation card that "her place of birth had come to be so messily at odds with her nationality." (132) This dichotomy in the situation upsets the grandmother and the author shows that it is bewilderment shared by many people. Emotionally they could hardly accept the Radcliffe line and in their own minds wondered like the grandmother "whether they would be able to see the border between India and East Pakistan from the plane." (151) When told otherwise, they were more confused and like the grandmother would wonder, "what was it all for then—partition and all the killings and everything—if there isn't something in between?" (151)

Amitav Ghosh also raises this query in this novel. As a liberal humanist, he tries to understand the human loss caused by drawing a line on the map right through the homeland. People suffered intensely due to the Partition of the country. This novel examines the impact of Partition in Bengal. It shows that numerous Hindu families had to leave their ancestral homeland in erstwhile East Pakistan and settle in the suburbs of Calcutta. The fate of Muslim refugees as exemplified by the mechanic Saifuddin is similar. Many Muslim families were also uprooted from Bihar, Bengal and Assam and had to migrate to the cities of the eastern wing of newly-formed Pakistan. The novel cleverly shows that people of the grandmother's generation were often bewildered about how places of birth had become at odds with their nationality. The dichotomy in the situation gave rise to confusion and bewilderment in the minds of people long after Partition became a part of the history of the sub-continent.

The Radcliffe line refers to the division of both Punjab and Bengal by Sir Cyril Radcliffe. a London based barrister.

The burden of carrying out the most complex task involved in India's Partition was given to Sir Cyril Radcliffe in June 1947. As Nehru and Jinnah could not agree on a line, the task of a boundary commission was placed in the hands of a distinguished English barrister. Radcliffe was chosen for his admirable legal reputation and for his ignorance of India. Anyone who knew the country was certain to be disqualified as prejudiced by one side or the other. Radcliffe had two choices. Either he followed population as his sole guide, creating a host of unmanageable enclaves or he followed the dictates of geography and a more manageable boundary. He opted for the latter course of action and thus the Partition of India was a pencil line drawn on a map. Radcliffe had barely a month to make his decisions based on maps, population tables and statistics to guide him. This hasty act of Partition of the country, especially in the villages of Bengal and Punjab condemned numerous people to live as minorities within a hostile majority. Ghosh examines in his novel the subsequent psychological problems, which such an arbitrary division caused. There was crude barbarity and demonstration of the noblest sentiments on both sides of the border. What did political freedom mean to such people? This is the question that the author probes whilst presenting the grandmother's story of her life.

An important reason for the grandmother to visit Dhaka was her desire to see her old house. As is shown in several instances in this novel, the grandmother's vision of her ancestral home is very nostalgic. She is also motivated to visit Dhaka to bring her uncle Jethamoshoi back to India. During the few days she spends in her sister's house in Dhaka, she is restless. Soon accompanied by Mayadebi, Tridib, May Price and Robi, she sets out in the Mercedes car with the driver and a security guard of the High Commission. The car has to stop at a particular point in the by-lanes of Dhaka and they walk to the old house. The house has changed. There is an automobile workshop in what was the luxuriant garden of the house. It is no more a magnificent edifice but is crumbling and inhabited by a large number of people. Their uncle

Jethamoshoi is now called Ukilbabu. He is decrepit and bedridden and is looked after by Khalil, a cycle-rickshaw driver and his family. The old uncle fails to recognise them and speaks ill of his relatives when they are mentioned. Above all he refuses to move to India. His mind is rambling, his memory has faded with age but his pertinent rejoinder when asked to move to India raises several important questions on the nature of political freedom.

Delving into the past, he tells the storyteller's grandmother, "Once you start moving you never stop." (215) He justifies his belief by stating that freedom is a concept created in the mind. He recalls what he told his sons when they took the trains to India, during the years of Partition:

> I don't believe in this India-Shindia. It's all very well, you're going away now, but suppose when you get there they decide to draw another line somewhere? What will you do then? Where will you move to? No one will have you anywhere. As for me, I was born here, and I'll die here. (215)

Amitav Ghosh here shows that there is a 'shadow line' between sanity and dotage, imagination and facts. The old man questions the whole ideology of nationalism, which creates boundaries and causes separation. He also raises pertinent questions on the concept of freedom. The old Jethamoshoi seems more secure and mentally at peace with himself in his ancestral home than the narrator's grandmother who has confused loyalties. By befriending the Muslims in his area and even giving them a place to stay in his huge mansion, the old man seems secure and content. By this idea of inclusion rather than exclusion, the old man achieves a form of communal harmony and peace of mind that is denied to others of his generation like the grandmother. Khalil's family cooks for him and takes care of him. In old age he has found a 'family' to look after him. Critics have often pondered why Amitav Ghosh condemned man-made boundaries and frontiers. Some suggest that maybe the author is advocating larger cultural collectivity, as is shown in the lifestyle of the old uncle. This is a very important section of the novel, as it puts forth various views on nationalism, history and freedom and undercuts the prevailing concepts. No wonder eminent playwright Girish Karnad made the following observation: "The grandmother's visit to the ancestral home, is surely one of the most memorable scenes in Indian fiction. Past and future meet across religious, political and cultural barriers in a confusion of emotions, ideals, intentions and acts, leading to a shattering climax."

The climax occurs as the grandmother and Mayadebi are returning in their Mercedes car from their ancestral home. Jethamoshoi is following them in Khalil's rickshaw. The violence that occurs is narrated but recalled through Robi's narrative on pages 243-47 and May Price's recollections on pages 250-51. When they approach the bazaar area they find the shops closed and the road deserted except for a few stragglers. The mob encircles the car, breaks the windscreen and the driver gets a cut on his face. The car lurches and comes to a halt with its front wheel in the gutter. Then, the security man jumps out and fires a shot from his revolver and the crowd begins to withdraw. After this incident, the attention of the crowd is distracted by the creak of Khalil's rickshaw with Jethamoshoi in it. The frenzied mob surrounds the rickshaw. The sisters could have driven away but May Price and Tridib jump out of the car and try to save Khalil and the old uncle. They get lost in the whirling mob. The mob hacks to death Khalil, the old man and Tridib. Recalling the gruesome deaths, May Price tells the narrator years later, "When I got there, I saw three bodies. They were all dead. They'd cut Khalil's stomach open. The old man's head had been hacked off. And they'd cut Tridib's throat from ear to ear." (251) The horror of the act is branded forever in the memories of Robi and May Price who witness the whole catastrophe from close range.

As in Greek tragedies, the violence comes in a terrible manner as it is conveyed through choric characters, like Robi, May Price and the narrator who is Amitav Ghosh's alter ego. The violence is also dramatised. Even after fifteen years. Robi trembles "like a leaf" (247) when he recalls Tridib's death. The death is a fear that haunts him in his nightmares. In his adult consciousness, Tridib's death signified the futility of freedom. In a dispassionate and analytical manner he relates his plight with that of many others in the subcontinent.

Robi realises that the concept of freedom is a mirage. After Independence and Partition, many idealists believed that the religious communalism would sink into oblivion. But the euphoria evaporated, as nobody seemed to realise the meaning of freedom. Intolerance mushroomed in the name of freedom and this led to killings in Assam, the North-East, Punjab, Sri Lanka and Tripura, all in the name of freedom. Recalling such feelings in front of a derelict church at Clapham in London, Robi says:

> And then I think to myself why don't they draw thousands of little lines through the whole subcontinent and give every little place a new name? What would it change? It's a mirage, the whole thing is a mirage. (247)

In contrast, Tridib's death in the 1964 riots arouses animosity and anger in the grandmother. This personal loss transforms the meaning of border for the grandmother. Previously it was just a confused line, now it is something that defines her nationality. When the 1965 war between India and Pakistan breaks out she views it as a threat to the freedom of her grandson and the future of the nation. The meaning of freedom for her is not a mirage but includes fighting against the Pakistanis who barely twenty years ago were her own countrymen.

The novelist sets up connections between the violence in East Pakistan in 1964 and the violence of the Second World War. He vividly evokes the death and destruction of war-torn London in the first section of the novel. However, this violence is shown as a conflict against an alien power. However the communal riots in the subcontinent described in second section of the novel are seen as "a defiance of artificially created national boundaries." (Hemmadi 299) The nationalism of people like the grandmother causes the breaking up of a larger cultural continuity.

In the second section, the novel moves backwards and forward in time. The narrator recalls his youth and the grandmother's memories. The setting shifts back and forth from Calcutta to London and Dhaka. The chapters in London deal with the narrator's attempts to recall the images of the city as portrayed by Tridib. In these chapters the narrator attempts to visualise and activate his memories.

The Shadow Lines starts with a mention of Tridib and ends with an unveiling of the mystery of his violent death. May Price narrates the events which led to Tridib's death. For years she has been guilty that her reckless act of rushing out of the car to save Jethamoshoi and Khalil caused Tridib's death. She says:

> I used to think: perhaps he wouldn't have got out of the car if I hadn't made him, if I'd understood what I was doing. I was safe you see. . . . I could have gone right into that mob, and they wouldn't have touched me, an English memsahib, but he, he must have known he was going to die. For years I was arrogant enough to think I owed him his life, but I know now I didn't kill him; I couldn't have if I'd wanted. He gave himself up; it was a sacrifice. I know I can't understand it. I know I mustn't try, for any real sacrifice is a mystery. (251-52)

So May Price tells the narrator that Tridib's death remains a real sacrifice, a mystery which cannot be comprehended rationally. The novel ends with the narrator glad and grateful, "for the glimpse [May Price] had given me of a final redemptive mystery." (252) So Tridib's death and sacrifice remains a mystery. As Anjali Karpe says, "The act itself indicates that single individual can never hope to quell a violent mob or restrain forces of communal strife. Individual valour is insufficient to change the tide of events and a single handed effort is doomed to die out, before anything else." (316) This is one interpretation of Tridib's death. But the question that arises is what motivated the normally laid-back Tridib to take such an extreme step whilst Robi the man of action cowered inside the car paralysed with fear. Louis James maintains that Tridib was "drawn by the 'shadow-line' of imaginative sympathy." Amitav Ghosh does not provide any clarifications or clear answers to Tridib's death. So the sacrifice becomes a mystery, an absurdity for the common man who fails to find any meaning in it. Tridib's death thus exemplifies that the quest for meaning continues without finality.

The novel upholds the imperatives that ensure empathy and unimpeded flow of friendship. It mocks the conception of militant nationalism, exclusive national pride and identity. The outbreak of communal strife in Dhaka following the disappearance of the prophet's hair in Srinagar exposes the fragile demarcation of political frontiers. Tha'mma's ideals of nationalism, nurtured since the Swadeshi movement, do not stand the test of time. The author shows that her misplaced sense of pride and drawing national borders with blood is likely to be undone by the inherent logic of separateness. Ultimately the message of the novel is the need for co-existence and humanitarian ties despite cultural and political differences. The narrator with his expanded horizons and imaginative understanding of the world, stresses on the need to preserve memories of sanity and humane feelings for this will help in cultural self-determination and inter-personal communication. According to the author, the media and public memory must keep alive the "indivisible sanity" of communities to prevent a recurrence of insane frenzy. G.R. Taneja in his essay aptly says that the novel is "an eloquent critique of colonial hangover and cultural dislocation in a postcolonial situation as also the psychological make-up of the contemporary man who thrives on violence."

Writing in *The New York Times*, Edward Hoover praises *The Shadow Lines* for its international flavour, cross-cultural influences and remarkable characterisation. He praises Amitav Ghosh's use of memory and about the way perceptions change and become enriched with understanding of the characters' past selves. Commenting on the characterisation in the novel, Hoover says: "It chronicles the stories of two families, one in

Calcutta, the other in London, from the outbreak of World War II to modern times. Engaging characters abound: eccentric Bengali matriarchs, earnest 1930's British socialists and their 1970's Euro-punk counterparts, empire builders and their cynical Thatcherite offspring, languid Indian aristocrats and doomed rickshaw drivers."

Characters intermingle not as members of distinct cultures but as complex individuals in a world where geographic boundaries have truly become "shadow lines." These borders are mirrors that reflect not people's differences but their similarities. They produce images that are both beautiful and—in the case of the riots that become a climactic event in the book—horrific.

Commenting on the complex characterisation of Tridib, May Price and Ila, Hoover says, "Tridib, the character to whom the novel's nameless young narrator is first drawn, is an eclectic young Calcutta intellectual who, though he cannot get started on his own career, has a momentous influence on the lives of those around him. From Tridib, the narrator learns about tropical snakes and Irish myths, about Indian archaeology and London gossip. More important, Tridib fires the boy's imagination with a longing to know everything, not through scholarship but through the use of his extraordinary imaginative powers."

May Price, Tridib's lover, is a member of a family that incorporates both the best and the worst of British society. She is a misfit, a frustrated musician, dedicated to a life of international good causes. Like the London of Salman Rushdie's fiction, though without its nightmarish undertones, the city May inhabits is a microcosm of emigrant third world culture, where synagogues have turned into mosques, where Hindi film posters and anti-racism slogans compete for wall space along alleys smelling of African and Caribbean cooking.

This is the world that Ila, the beautiful, spoiled daughter of an Indian diplomat, embraces for a time. She believes that its bohemianism can liberate her from everything she finds repressive in upper-class Indian society. Raised all over the world and having acquired a cultureless identity, she follows her schoolgirl illusions about British decency into a disastrous marriage. The rejected narrator, who has loved Ila since childhood, believes that the only existence left to him is as a chronicler of the lives around him.

There is a danger for authors as technically gifted as Amitav Ghosh to sacrifice coherence and characterization to literary pyrotechnics, but this never happens here. What is finally most impressive is the eloquence of the author's perceptions about his characters. His narrator develops a gentle, compassionate wisdom as he progresses—through his affection for Tridib, Ila and finally May—from an amusingly naive child to a mature young man.

Ila is described as an upper-class Marxist by Hoover: "The people Ila shared her house with spent their evenings in the kitchen whenever they were in. They consisted of a bearded Irish computer scientist, a girl from Leicestershire who had dropped out in her second year at the North London Polytechnic to work with the Fourth International, and a morose young Ghanaian who was very active in the Anti-Nazi League. They would spend their evenings sitting around the deal table in the kitchen drinking mugs of tea, or sometimes, when they could afford it, beer. Their conversations were almost always severely practical. For hours on end they would argue about which kind of pen was better for drawing posters with, or over how they ought to make the arrangements for lunch or tea at their next picket. There were no explosive arguments nor any shouting as there would have been among like-minded people in Calcutta or Delhi. When they did argue, it was usually about small points of tactics and strategy, and the arguments usually consisted of a series of increasingly oblique statements. "These dialogues were so controlled at first I did not recognise them as arguments at all. But in fact there was a frightening quality about them; a seriousness of intent that was all the more deadly for being so quiet."

They seemed to regard her as a kind of guest, a decoration almost. Nor did they seem to resent in her the signs of cosmopolitanism they were always so quick to criticise in themselves and their other comrades. In a way they were proud of her: they would often ask about her family's wealth, how many servants she had "at home" in India, and so on, and they would listen intently as she told them—with many exaggerations, usually. They would talk of her as "our own upper-class Asian Marxist." This seemed to please them: they had an acute sense of history and perhaps they saw Ila as a link with the Fabians.

The Theme of Partition

Throughout history, fanatics as well as ideologues, pushed to the emotional brink of daring their lives, have taken the plunge, which has triggered off a chain reaction of rigid mental fixations and attitudes. Bapsi Sidhwa's novel *Ice-Candy-Man* examines the inexorable logic of Partition as an offshoot of fundamentalism sparked by hardening communal attitudes. First published in 1988 in London, this novel is set in pre-partition India in Lahore. It belongs to the genre of the partition novel like Manohar Malgonkar's *A Bend in the Ganges* (1964), Chaman Nahal's *Azadi* (1975), and Khushwant Singh's *Train to Pakistan* (1956). However in Indian-English fiction it is the second novel on Partition by a woman author. The other novel is *Sunlight on a Broken Column* (1961) by Attia Hosain. Both these sensitive women writers share similar perspectives on the calamities of Partition. The denouement of both novels is quite similar. Both stress a similar vulnerability of human understanding and life, caused by the throes of Partition which relentlessly divided friends, families, lovers and neighbours.

Ice-Candy-Man is a novel of upheaval which includes a cast of characters from all communities. There are Hindus, Muslims, Christians, Sikhs and Parsis, so a multiple perspective of partition emerges as viewed by all the affected communities. Bapsi Sidhwa uses a narrator to tell the tale. A precocious Parsi girl, eight years old with a handicapped foot narrates the story of her changing world with sophistication and wonder. Lenny is like the persona that Chaucer adopts in his Prologue to *The Canterbury Tales*, rendering credibility by being almost a part of the reader's consciousness. With the wonder of a child she is observing social change and human behaviour, noting interesting sidelights, seeking and listening to opinions and occasionally making judgements. Her childish innocence is like the seeming naive display of Chaucer's persona, a source of sharp irony. The device of the child narrator enables Bapsi Sidhwa treat a historical moment as horrifying as partition without morbidity, pedanticism or censure. The highlight of the novel is that the author throughout maintains a masterful balance between laughter and despair. The subtle irony and deft usage of language creates humour which does not shroud but raucously highlights the traumas of Partition. Sensitively the author shows the human toll of Partition, when a concerned Lenny asks: "*Can one break a country?* And what happens if they break it *where our house is?*" (92)

The Parsi paradox of whether to support "Swaraj" or to maintain their loyalty to the British Raj is also humorously delineated. A piquant touch is given to this dilemma. With the impending news of independence, the paranoid feelings of the Parsis, a minuscule minority get accentuated. The Parsis in Lahore at a special meeting at their temple hall in Warris Road, have an acrimonious debate on the political situation. The meeting is interesting as it expresses the insecurity of the Parsis not because of communal antagonism, but the apprehension of their status at the departure of the British. Already the unstinted loyalty to the colonial power is declining. Col. Bharucha and Lenny's father blame the British for bringing polio to India. So at the meeting, India's smallest minority is trying to redefine their strategy which Col. Bharucha claims as "We must hunt with the hounds and run with the hare." (16)

The ambivalent attitude of the Parsis towards Partition and Independence emerged at the main-hall meeting at the Fire-Temple. Col. Bharucha, the President of the community in Lahore, advocates status quo. He warns fellow-Parsis to shun the anti-colonial movement and nationalist agitation spearheaded by Mahatma Gandhi. His reasoning is based on expediency. If there is "Home Rule," political glory, fame and fortune will be acquired by the two major communities, Hindus and Muslims. He considers Home Rule as a power struggle, saying "Hindus, Muslims and even the Sikhs are going to jockey for power and if you jokers jump into the middle you'll be mangled into chutney!" (36) He also advocates caution, because of the Parsis's long-standing attitudes of loyalty to the British. This attitude stemmed from the Zoroastrian religious belief of loyalty to a ruler and a close relationship between state and community. The other cause for loyalty to the British was purely economic. The Parsis primarily traced their secured status as a prosperous minority to British rule, identified as the "good government" of the African prayer. So loyalty was a self-evident precept to the Parsis. Thus Col. Bharucha does not want any Parsi of Lahore to offend British sensibilities by espousing nationalist causes. In a tone of admonition he says, "I hope no Lahore Parsi will be stupid enough to court trouble—I strongly advise all of you to stay at home—and out of trouble." (37)

The sentiments and ideas of Col. Bharucha represent a prominent social code of behaviour amongst the Parsis. They have always venerated loyalty. Dr. Homi B. Dhalla in his essay, "The Zoroastrian Moral Imperative: Its Relevance in the Late 19th and Early 20th Centuries" published in the Delhi Parsi Anjuman's *Dar-E-Meher* (fire-temple) silver jubilee celebrations souvenir (1986) gives instances of loyalty. He states: "Large gatherings of Parsis have over the years, assembled for public acts of worship or thanksgiving (jashan). To cite a few: on July 16, 1854, a jashan was performed where about 6,000 Zoroastrians offered prayers for Britain during its war with Russia. As a mark of celebration, a mammoth jashan was organized on Queen Victoria's Golden Jubilee on Feb. 16, 1887 and again on June 20, 1897 to commemorate her Diamond Jubilee." Also cited in James Boyd and Firoze Kotwal, "Worship in a Zoroastrian Fire Temple," *Indo-Iranian Journal*, 26, 1983, pp. 308-10. Col. Bharucha was thus just following a Parsi moral imperative.

In her first novel *The Crow Eaters* (1978) Bapsi Sidhwa portrayed the dying businessman Faredoon Junglewalla vehemently protesting against the nationalist movement and exhorting his offspring to remain loyal to the British Empire. Col. Bharucha has a somewhat similar attitude. However with Independence imminent and Partition inevitable, there is a subtle change in the attitude of the Parsis of Lahore. The patriarchal advice of Col. Bharucha is opposed. Dr. Mody promptly poses a plea for involvement in the freedom struggle. He says, "our neighbours will think we are betraying them and siding with the English." (37) The banker Mr. Toddywalla says that the Parsis should support the Indian community which appears to be in a dominant position or will acquire political power after Independence. So he asks the assembled congregation to formulate attitudes and actions on Independence based on self-interest. Finally the assembled Parsis resolve to remain in Lahore and abide by the rules of the land. Wafting in self-esteem they agree to Col. Bharucha's suggestion, "Let whoever wishes rule! Hindu, Muslim, Sikh, Christian. We will abide by the rules of the land." (39)

Some Parsis in the congregation express apprehension about remaining in Lahore after Independence and wish to migrate either to London or Bombay (where majority of their coreligionists live). However such fears get over-ruled and the herd mentality desire of staying only in Bombay is also rejected. The final resolution is one of adaptability and compromise. The President of the Lahore Parsis Col. Bharucha says, "As long as we conduct our lives quietly; as long as we present no threat to anybody; we will prosper right here,—" (40) Through this animated conversation, Bapsi Sidhwa reveals the implicit, lurking fear of the Parsis, a vulnerable minority losing their identity and getting swamped by the majority communities—either Hindus in India or Muslims in Pakistan. So even amongst the Parsis the smallest minority in undivided India, the Partition sparked off an impulse for migration from their homelands. Bombay was opted for, primarily due to safety in numbers rather than the safeguards of democratic India. Historically however the movement to Bombay, as the novelist also indicates, was minimal. The Parsis remained in urban areas of India and Pakistan, trying to preserve their identity by not meddling in political matters. The advice of

Mr. Toddywalla is followed, "But don't try to prosper immoderately. And remember don't ever try to exercise real power." (40)

Amidst banter, repartee and humour, Bapsi Sidhwa subtly portrays the underlying fears of the Parsis about Partition and Independence. The depiction of their mental turmoil can be compared to John Masters's depiction of the plight of the Eurasians commonly called Anglo-Indians before the British left the sub-continent. In his novel, *Bhowani Junction* (1954), John Masters aptly depicts the identity crises of the Anglo-Indians. For instance, the loud-mouthed and arrogant Peter Taylor had talked of going "Home" to England (which he has never seen) and wore his solar hat all day to be recognized as an Englishman. Even the anglicized Peter Taylor has a foreboding of impending Independence. He asks Victoria in sheer frustration, "What are we going to do." (42) Knowing that they could become neither English nor Indian, Taylor's conclusion is "we could only stay where we were and be what we were." (21) This shows how Taylor and the Anglo-Indian community have become total prisoners of circumstances. Bapsi Sidhwa shows how the Parsis are similar captives of circumstances in the upheaval of Partition.

Adaptability being part of their social code, the Parsis of Lahore adjust to the changing circumstances after Partition. In *The Crow Eaters,* Bapsi Sidhwa had only hinted at the necessity of changing allegiances after Independence but in *Ice-Candy-Man,* the change in attitudes is depicted. Col. Bharucha and Lenny's father curse the British for bringing polio to India. Lenny suffers from polio and the disease is considered as another example of British treachery. Later in the novel, Lenny's mother, Mrs. Sethi and other Parsi women help Hindu and Sikh families escape in safe convoys to India and assist in rehabilitation of destitute and kidnapped women. Lenny's Godmother rescues the Hindu Ayah forcibly married to her former Muslim friend, the seller of ice-candies. The Godmother helps Ayah return to Amritsar, under police escort. There is already a sense of involvement, with the new reality as Lenny's parents, Godmother and Parsi friends try to bring some semblance of sanity in frenzied Lahore.

Charity and social usefulness is a Parsi moral code, based on the teachings of the prophet Zarathushtra. This is amply revealed in Eckehard Kulke's scholarly book, *The Parsis in India: A Minority as Agent of Social Change* (Delhi: Bell Books, 1978). Kulke states that Parsi charities are cosmopolitan and communal as the ancient scriptures and daily prayers extolled philanthropy. Kulke states "This charity system was made possible and furthered by the basic attitude of the Parsis, motivated by their religion, that wealth is fundamentally positive, that it brings, however certain social obligations along with it." So charity is part of the Parsi ethos.

With witty remarks and subtle usage of language, Bapsi Sidhwa presents the impact of Independence and Partition in vivid images. The altered social reality becomes even more striking, as narrated by the innocent eight-year-old Lenny. Independence becomes evident to Lenny when she visits the Queen's Garden: "I cannot believe my eyes. The queen has gone! The space between the marble canopy and the marble platform is empty. A group of children playing knuckles, squat where the gunmetal queen sat enthroned." (236) So within her restricted space, Lenny aptly reveals the fading away of an Empire and its value systems. The theme of separation caused by Partition is also revealed in a simple but vividly poignant observation by Lenny. During her romps at the Queen's Garden she notices the absence of the cosmopolitan gathering:

> The garden scene has depressingly altered. Muslim families who added colour when scattered among the Hindus and Sikhs now monopolize the garden, depriving it of colour. The absence of the brown skin that showed through the fine veils of Hindu and Sikh women, and beneath the dhoties and shorts of the men, has changed the complexion of the queenless garden. (236)

Through the wondering eyes of the precocious Lenny, the novelist shows the disruption of a settled order and traumatic separations of friends, the legacy of Partition.

The impact of Partition is psychologically understood and narrated through the feelings of a child, who is a member of a minuscule minority. The sense of loss is aptly demonstrated as Lenny and her brother Adi wandering through the garden observe, "Adi and I wander from group to group peering into faces beneath white skull-caps and above ascetic beards. I feel uneasy. Like Hamida I do not fit. I know we will not find familiar faces here." (237) The uprootedness of Partition is revealed as Lenny drifts through the Queen's Garden searching in vain for familiar faces and acquaintances. Even in the child there is a feeling of insecurity. She clings to the hands of her Ayah and cajoles her not to marry the Masseur. A Muslim, the Masseur is one of Ayah's numerous admirers and promises to marry and protect her during the throes of Partition. Overhearing this, Lenny desperately urges Ayah not to get married as it would mean separation. Later when Ayah is abducted it is Lenny who urges her family to search for her. Lenny's responses show the dislocation of life during Partition. The partition novels of Manohar Malgonkar, Khushwant Singh and Chaman Nahal focus on Punjab and the dislocation of life and human feelings in that region. So Bapsi Sidhwa's novel is similar to the novels in this genre. The only difference is that the pointless brutality of communal frenzy is parodied as it is unfurled and narrated by the child-narrator Lenny. She and her younger brother Adi watch "the skyline of the old walled city ablaze and people spattering each other with blood." (134) Fire destroys Hindu, Muslim and Sikh houses and shops at Shalmi. "The entire Shalmi, an area covering about four square miles, flashes in explosions." (137) Fire knows no religion. The shrieks and shouts of "Pakistan Murdabad! Death to Pakistan! Sat Sri Akaal; Bolay so nihaal!" of the Sikh mobs when listening to Master Tara Singh at Queen's Garden and "Allah-O-Akbar! Yaaa Ali! and Pakistan Zindabad!" of the rampaging Muslim mobs gives Lenny as many nightmares as when she recollects the roaring of the lions in the zoo. With such subtle comparisons and ironic exposures, Bapsi Sidhwa shows the brutalization which communal frenzy causes Even lovers turn hostile. Ice-Candy-Man, the Muslim lover of the Hindu Ayah, watches Shalmi and Mozang Chowk burn with "the muscles in his face tight with a strange exhilaration I never want to see." The transformation of a fun-loving man who frolicked and acted the buffoon in the park into an ogre due to communal frenzy is aptly revealed by Lenny's horror at the sadism in his face. A vivid image which is a stark reminder of the brutality of the times. This is the way Bapsi Sidhwa handles the delicate theme of partition, through subtle insinuations, images and gestures. So the stark horror of loss, bloodshed and separation is portrayed without verbosity, sensationalism, lurid details and maudlin sentimentality. The sensitive portrayal of the horrors of Partition enhances the poignancy and cruelty of the event without the author ever appearing pedantic or pretentious.

Allegory is another literary device used by Bapsi Sidhwa to depict the trauma of Partition. The child-narrator Lenny is also affected by the violence at Lahore: "The whole world is burning. The air on my face is so hot I think my flesh and clothes will catch fire. I start screaming: hysterically sobbing." (137) The scenes of violence and arson and above all the venemous hatred of friends who had months earlier rationalized about the impossibility of violence, have a frightening impact on the young Parsi girl Lenny. Violence breeds violence and Lenny is also a victim. Her age is directed at her collection of dolls. In a frenzy she acts: "I pick out a big, bloated celluloid doll. I turn it upside down and pull its legs apart. The elastic that holds them together stretches easily. I let one leg go and it snaps back, attaching itself to the brittle torso." (138) The destructive urge overcomes Lenny and she is not satisfied till assisted by her brother Adi she wrenches out the legs of the doll and examines the spilled insides. This violent act by Lenny is an apt allegory on the mindless violence of Partition. With a morbid sense of humour, Bapsi Sidhwa reveals how the violence of Partition has serrated the roots of people of different communities, irrespective of ideology, friendship and rational ideas. In such a depiction, Bapsi Sidhwa resembles the horror portrayed by William Golding in *The Lord of the Files* (1954). Golding indicated that there is a thin line between good and evil in human beings and it is only the structures of civilizations which prevent the lurking evil from being rampant. At the end of *The Lord of the Flies*, boys of Jack's tribe like barbarians got a sadistic delight in hunting Ralph. The situation is saved as a Naval officer reaches the island and by his presence curbs the pointless brutality of the abandoned boys. Golding had written this novel after World War II and the allegorical meaning was evident. In the world of fiction, a grown-up stepped in to curb the atrocities and brutality of the boys, but when countries commit atrocities there is no restraining power. Lenny's destruction of the doll also has allegorical significance. It shows how even a young girl is powerless to stem the tide of surging violence within, thereby implying that grown up fanatics enmeshed in communal frenzy are similarly trapped into brutal violence. Lenny breaks down and cries at her pointless brutality, a sombre message by the novelist that unless there is re-thinking, brutality and insensitivity becomes a way of life, such is the conditioning of communalism.

Another partition novel, Attia Hosain's *Sunlight on a Broken Column* (1961), also uses a narrator-heroine to similar effect. Attia Hosain's narrator-heroine Laila reveals the trauma of Partition through her memories and insights of her Taluqdar family disintegrating. Like in the *Ice-Candy-Man*, the enigma of Partition is sensitively shown. When Zohra, her cousin married in Pakistan, returns to Hasanpur, she quarrels with Laila about protection of Muslim culture and language. The disagreements were no longer youthful verbal quarrels but echoed bigger divisions. Laila surmises the most cruel aspect of partition when she says, "In the end, inevitably we quarrelled, and though we made up before we parted I realized that the ties which had kept families together for centuries had been loosened beyond repair." (303) Like Lenny, the grown-up Laila is also both nostalgic and restless. Laila ruminates and wanders in her disbanded ancestral home Ashiana after Partition. Memories come flooding back. However her nostalgia is controlled. Whilst walking through the rooms of Ashiana, she remembers the past, but does not wish for the old order to return. Her new-found identity and struggle to be Ameer's lover and wife, curbs any desire for a return to the cloistered feudal order. Instead it broadens her horizons of life. She comes to detest dogmatism, either in the name of religion or radicalism. Her views and perspective of life developed after intense personal struggle enable Laila to tackle the loss of her husband Ameer and the trauma of Partition. So both narrator-heroines, Lenny and Laila react against communal responses and the horrors of violence. The mature Laila rationalizes against communal tension whereas the young Lenny instinctively reacts against the horrors of communal violence.

There are other similarities between the two novelists, Bapsi Sidhwa and Attia Hosain. Both realize there are no easy solutions to communal holocausts except intense struggle against dogmatism. Laila's concerted attempts at breaking from traditional customs, the negation of despair and recognition of struggle are upheld by Attia Hosain. Her narrator-heroine does not lapse into a glorification of the past or take refuge in mysticism, epicureanism or jingoism. Similarly Bapsi Sidhwa shows there are no winners in the communal holocausts of Partition. This is revealed by clever juxtapositioning of images. Gramophones and speakers mounted on tongas and lorries pour out the melody of Nur Jehan's popular film song,

> Mere bachpan ke sathi mujhe bhool na jana—
> Dekho, dekho hanse na zamana, hanse na zamana. (159)

Ironically the sentiments of the song are not followed and instead there is turbulence and violence. At the festival of Holi, instead of splattering friends with bright colours, people are splattering each other with blood. Bapsi Sidhwa shows the human loss in Partition:

> Instead, wave upon scruffy wave of Muslim refugees flood Lahore—and the Punjab west of Lahore. Within three months seven million Muslims and five million Hindus and Sikhs are uprooted in the largest and most terrible exchange of population known to history. The

Punjab has been divided. (159)

Bare facts present the horror of the greatest communal divide in history. Bapsi Sidhwa aptly shows the inexorable logic of Partition which moves on relentlessly leaving even sane people and friends helpless and ineffective. Jagjeet Singh with a furtive group of Sikhs visited a Muslim village Pir Pindo under cover of darkness to warn them of an impending Akali attack. Pir Pindo is attacked at dawn and swamped by Sikhs. Men, women and children are killed. Similarly Sikh families are attacked in Lahore. The neighbour of the Sethis, Mr. and Mrs. Singh leave with their two children and a few belongings. Other goods are left behind with Lenny's parents. Sher Singh the zoo attendant flees from Lahore, due to insecurity, after his brother-in-law is killed. Similarly the student fraternity of King Edward's Medical college is disrupted. Prakash and his family migrate to Delhi and Rahool Singh and his pretty sisters are escorted to a convoy to Amritsar. In Lenny's household the gardener Hari is circumcised and becomes Himat Ali, and Moti becomes David Masih, the politics of compromise and survival. Ayah's lover the Masseur's mutilated dead body is found in a gunny sack. The money lender Kirpa Ram flees leaving guineas and money behind. Even middle-class families like the Shankers flee in haste. Partition is shown as a series of images and events depicting human loss and agony. The dislocation of settled life is aptly revealed by Lenny's understanding of the demographic change in Lahore. In awe she observes, "Lahore is suddenly emptied of yet another hoary dimension: there are no Brahmins with caste-marks—or Hindus in dhoties with bodhis. Only hordes of Muslim refugees." (175) Lahore is no more cosmopolitan. Even the Sikhs have fled. The child-narrator senses the difference and pain caused by the huge exchange of populations.

Bapsi Sidhwa also subtly delineates the psychological impact of the horrors of Partition on the lives of people. The communal frenzy has a distorting effect on people and leads to feelings of suspicion, distrust and susceptibility to rumours. Even the children, Lenny, Adi and their cousin are intrigued and suspicious of any minor deviations from normal behaviour. Mrs. Sethi and Aunt Minnie travel all over Lahore in the car but do not take the children with them. Deprived of long drives, Lenny and her cousin are intrigued at the movements of their mothers. Ayah enhances the sense of mystery when she states that the dicky of the car is full of cans of petrol. The author shows that in a highly surcharged atmosphere, suspicion and distrust become inevitable. The Ayah is also suspicious about the movements of cans of petrol by the two Parsi ladies. If she suspects they are distributing petrol to the arsonists she does not state so. The three children are stupefied by this revelation and let their imagination run wild. Finally they come to the same conclusion. "We know who the arsonists are. Our mothers are setting fire to Lahore!—My heart pounds at the damnation that awaits their souls. My knees quake at the horror of their imminent arrest." (173)

Bapsi Sidhwa cleverly parodies the feelings of suspicion and distrust of the children for their mothers. The imaginary fears of Lenny, Adi and their cousin are a source of humour but also a grim reminder of how rumour becomes institutionalized in a highly surcharged atmosphere. The children only fantasize about their mother's dangerous acts but the author shows how rumour preys upon the frenzied minds of men vitiated by communal hatred. On the radio there is news of trouble at Gurdaspur, which the Ice-Candy-Man and his friends at once interpret as "there is uncontrollable butchering going on in Gurdaspur." (148) There are further rumours of a train full of dead bodies coming to Lahore from Gurdaspur. The Ice-Candy-Man returns panting after a frantic cycle ride and adds to the horror, by describing atrocities on women and stating that the dead are all Muslims. The acquaintances of Queen's Garden believe this rumour and harbour revenge against Sikhs. They now look with hatred on long standing friend Sher Singh, compelling the latter to flee from Lahore.

The role of rumour in both the nationalist movement led by Mahatma Gandhi and the traumas of Partition is best explained in Sumit Sarkar's book, *Modern India* 1885-1947 (Madras: Macmillan India, 1983). In his chapter "The Role of Rumour," Sumit Sarkar shows how peasants and workers responded to institutionalized rumours.

In the vitiated communal atmosphere, insanity prevails as ordinary men lose their rationality. Such a degradation is best exemplified in the rage of Ice-Candy-Man who says: "I'll tell you to your face—I lose my senses when I think of the mutilated bodies on that train from Gurdaspur . . . that night I went mad, I tell you, I lobbed grenades through the windows of Hindus and Sikhs I'd known all my life! I hated their guts." (156)

Revenge becomes the major motivation for the Ice-Candy-Man and his friends. The role of rumour and the consequent pattern of violence as depicted by Bapsi Sidhwa is compact and realistic. It is also very contemporary as similar patterns of violence are depicted by Amitav Ghosh in his novel *The Shadow Lines* (1988). Using the narrative technique of unnfurling events, by reading old newspaper reports, Amitav Ghosh shows how communal violence spread in Calcutta and cities of erstwhile East Pakistan in 1964. As he stresses, rumour took over. The poisoning of water, the trains of dead bodies, all incredible rumours, further vitiated the communal frenzy and increased the violence. Amitav Ghosh's novel is very contemporary and relevant as it shows how communal fanatics thrived on the spread of rumours which intensified feelings of anger and triggered off violence. The bland newspaper reports and memory technique of Amitav Ghosh remove the impact of time. It is implied that the riots are contemporaneous. The 1964 Calcutta riots could be the 1984 Delhi riots, the 1987 Meerut riots or in recent times the 1989 Bhagalpur killings. They all follow a similar pattern, suspicion, distrust and rumour activating conditioned minds, all sources of terrifying communal violence.

Very perceptively Amitav Ghosh shows how different cultures and communities are becoming antagonistic to a point of no return. Hence in *The Shadow Lines* he effectively uses political allegory to stress the need for a syncretic civilization to avoid a communal holocaust. Bapsi Sidhwa's concerns are also similar. The message in Bhisham Sahni's novel *Tamas,* that "those who forget history are condemned to repeat it," is applicable to *Ice-Candy-Man* also. Sidhwa's novel written at a period of history when communal and ethnic violence threaten disintegration of the subcontinent, is an apt warning of the dangers of communal frenzy. Bapsi Sidhwa shows that during communal strife, sanity, human feelings and past friendships are forgotten. At the Queen's Park in Lahore, friends and colleagues had argued endlessly about the impossibility of violence against each other and of fleeing from their homeland. Yet ironically, whilst the elders—Masseur, Butcher, Ice-Candy-Man, Sher Singh and Ayah—gossip about national politics the child-narrator senses the change in the days before Partition: "I can't put my finger on it—but there is a subtle change in the Queen's Garden." (96) The admirers of Ayah, in the pursuit of love temporarily sidetrack communal feelings and "Hindu, Muslim, Sikh, Parsi are as always, unified around her." (97) The others without such motivations are deliberately sitting with members of their own community, huddled together preserving cultural and religious identities. The Brahmins form their own circle of exclusivity. Burkha-clad Muslim women and children have their own group. The saddest fact as observed by Lenny is that even the children do not mix whilst playing.

Lenny attempts social interaction with a group of Sikh children but Masseur tries to pull her away. Sikh women ask her name and the name of her religion. When the child states that she is a Parsi, the Sikh women express amazemant at the discovery of a new religion. It is then that Lenny instinctively realizes the social divide between communities. Rationalizing her feelings she says, "That's when I realize what has changed. The Sikhs, only their rowdy little boys running about hair piled in topknots, are keeping mostly to themselves." (96) The author implies that the events at Queen's Garden are a reflection of a crystallization of feelings at a larger scale in Lahore and other cities of India. Cultural and religious exclusivity leads initially to indifference and later to contempt which becomes the breeding ground for communal violence and bigotry. With a subtle parody, Bapsi Sidhwa conveys the dangers of social exclusivity. The Ice-Candy-Man, in striking attire, enters the Queen's Garden, "Thumping a five-foot iron trident with bells tied near its base." (97) He is in the guise of a holy man and chants "Ya Allah!" With his ash-smeared face and eccentric manner he pretends to be Allah's telephone. The author implies that in an atmosphere which encourages religious bigotry, even charlatans emerge as holy and godmen. The difference between appearance and reality is slim. The Ice-Candy-Man pretends to talk to God on telephone. The scene is ludicrous and a source of rich humour. However amidst laughter the real meaning of such clowning emerges. The Ice-Candy-Man's antics provoke amusement but it is a pointer to the duplicity of people in the name of religion. Their sheer gullibility is exposed in a scene vividly described:

> Suddenly he springs up. Thumping his noisy trident on the ground, performing a curious jumping dance, he shouts: Wah Allah! Wah Allah! so loudly that several people who have been watching the goings-on from afar, hastily get up and scamper over. Sikhs, Hindus, Muslims form a thick circle round us. I can tell from the reverent faces around me that they believe they are in the presence of a holyman crazed by his love of God. And the madder the mystic, the greater his power. (99)

The message is clear. If charlatans can arouse such fervour, then obscurantism needs little prodding to slide into bigotry.

The secular group, Ayah's admirers maintain a facade of unity by cracking ribald jokes on community characteristics. However they also become vicious and prey to communal frenzy in the near future. The Ice-Candy-Man is part of the frenzied mob which abdicates Ayah and keeps her in the brothels of Hira Mandi. So even the passion of love is powerless against religious bigotry. Later in the novel, the Ice-Candy-Man attempts to make amends. He forcibly marries Ayah, changes her name to Mumtaz, and recites love poetry to her. But even here love is shown as powerless. Ayah has a revulsion for her newly-acquired Muslim identity. With the help of Lenny's Godmother she is taken to a Recovered Women's Camp and then sent to her family in Amritsar. The Ice-Candy-Man, now a "deflated poet, a collapsed pedlar" follows her to Amritsar in vain. Their relationship is serrated forever, one more victim of communal frenzy and Partition. Love does not conquer all, when communal and obscurantist passions are aroused.

With a sprinkling of humour, parody and allegory Bapsi Sidhwa conveys a sinister warning of the dangers of compromising with religious obscurantism and fundamentalism of all categories. Otherwise a certain historical inevitability marks this historical process. Though her novel is about the traumas of Partition, Bapsi Sidhwa like Amitav Ghosh reveals that communal riots are contemporaneous and that those who do not learn from history are condemned to repeat it.

Contrasting Strands of Political Nuances

In *The Shadow Lines*, the overall focus is on the meaning and shades of political nuances in contemporary life. The universal urge for political freedom, the response to violence and strident nationalism are some important aspects of contemporary life in the sub-continent, stressed in this novel. The vision of life presented is a dynamic desire to find a harmonious and complete relationship with the rich diversity of the modern world. The quest for political freedom, the violence in modern life, the role of rumour in riots are all aptly delineated in this novel.

It is basically a memory novel, which skilfully weaves together personal lives and Bangladesh. The focus is on story telling. Coil within coil of memories unfurl in the narrator's story. Conventional chronological narrative is not used. The narrator is a young boy who at the start of the novel listens to the variety of stories by his perceptive and scholarly cousin Tridib. These stories create new vistas of experience for the narrator, a young school boy in Calcutta. However the novel never becomes too esoteric. Amitav Ghosh, with his subtle humour and awareness of contemporary politics, ensures that private turmoil and crises are mirrored and intermeshed in public turmoil and crises. Amitav Ghosh uses this technique to unveil the political theme in the novel. The first instance of different strands of political nuances in this novel appear in the memories of the grandmother of the narrator about her old hometown Dhaka. The grandmother is a displaced person and had to leave her ancestral home Dhaka and settle in Calcutta after Partition. She returns to Dhaka and her homeland in 1964. Dhaka is a different city yet in her mind; the place of her childhood remains as real as ever. Her memories are passed on as vivid stories to the narrator. The idyllic vision of the ancestral home at Dhaka is shattered by political events like communal riots in both India and Pakistan in 1964. The political theme of this novel gets highlighted as the narrator shows the contrasting responses to violence and concept of nationalism that are revealed by his grandmother and Tridib.

Most of the grandmother's vision is nostalgic. There is no rancour about Partition and Muslim refugees occupying her ancestral home. Yet this is a novel which acknowledges the restlessness and political turmoil of the times. The communal riots in 1964, in both India and Pakistan, lead to the untimely death of Tridib, by an impassioned mob, in old Dhaka. The death of her nephew changes her perception. She talks now of fighting for freedom, "We have to kill them, before they kill us." (237) Her home in Dhaka, which was like a pastoral retreat, a golden vision, is now a reminder of death and communal violence. The idyllic vision is shattered. The desire now is changed. To use the phraseology of social psychology, the grandmother also now thinks in terms of 'us and them.'

The death of Tridib is the climax of the political theme in the novel. The overall focus is on the meaning and nuances of political freedom in contemporary life. Communal strife and the irresistible urge of nationalism, are also highlighted by the author. Characteristic of many Indian novels in English in the 1980s, politics national and international, is the most important theme of Amitav Ghosh's *The Shadow Lines*. Political freedom, communal strife and nationalism, important aspects of contemporary life in the subcontinent, are some of the strands which make the scope of this novel formidable. Like in his previous novel, *The Circle of Reason*, there is immense zest in story telling. The narrative technique of uncoiling memories and private turmoil mirrored by public turmoil, creates curiosity and makes the style interesting. The vision of life presented is a dynamic urge to find a complete relationship with the rich diversity of the modern world.

Political insights never obtrude or impede the flow of the story. They become an intrinsic part of the story, because of the memory technique. This is what makes the novel distinctive. For instance, the grandmother lying in bed, during her final illness, is told a story about a communal experience Ila underwent in London. The private crisis mirrors public turmoil. The grandmother's response to Ila is not sympathetic. She tells the narrator,

> Ila has no right to live there. . . . She doesn't belong there. It took those people a long time to build that country . . . years and years of war and bloodshed. Everyone who lives there has earned his right to be there with blood. . . . War is their religion. That's what it takes to make a country. (77-78)

The grandmother is not in a state of hallucination. Her insights are sharp and full of clarity. In her conversation, she reveals an alarming prospect, that feelings of nationalism can only develop through the process of war and sustained bloodshed. The novel moves backwards and forwards in time, which makes political issues more realistic. When the narrator had told Ila about the ranting grandmother's reaction, the latter a University graduate in history had promptly categorised the response as that of "warmongering fascists." The narrator aptly rejects such easy generalisations and recalls the more worldly wise Tridib's observations.

> All she wanted was a middle class life in which, like the middle classes the world over, she would thrive believing in the unity of nationhood and territory, of self respect

> and national power: that was all she wanted—a modern middle class life, a small thing that history had denied her in its fullness and for which she could never forgive it. (78)

So as Tridib had observed, the grandmother was not a fascist, but a modern middle class person not living in a world of fantasy and self-deceptions. The grandmother was nurtured in an environment of police raids in the colleges and universities of Dhaka. It was the time of British rule and the terrorist movement in Bengal in the first few decades of this century, "clandestine network and home-made bombs." Her motivation was a desire to be free and so feelings of nationalism got linked to self-respect and national power. So the grandmother can never fathom Ila's desire to live in London, rootless but free of middle class constraints and taboos or May's urge to collect money for worthy causes like famine relief in Africa. There are also Ila's radical friends in London, who picket on politics issues. Dan the Trotskyite who wrote anti-Nazi pamphlets and Tresawsen who edited a left wing newsletter. Another facet of nationalism is revealed in Nick Price, who later marries Ila. Nick gave up a lucrative chartered accountant's job in Kuwait because of outdated management practices and interfering Arab business partners. He still clings to Britain's colonial past, as it provided greater opportunities for exercising power and travel. The grandmother's desire to even kill for freedom, May's internationalism, Nick's colonial hangover, Ila's Trotskyite friends picketing for political causes and Ila striving for personal freedom, are either strands of nationalism or political commitment which the novel brings forth. By exploring connections, distinctions and possibilities, Amitav Ghosh shows that in a changing world, different strands of nationalism and ideology will exist and even compete. The force of nationalism in the quest for freedom or an ideology is often a source of violence. So the 'shadow line' between people and nations is often mere illusion. The force and appeal of nationalism cannot be wished away, just as death by a communal mob in the bye-lanes of old Dhaka. Robi an IAS officer, in charge of a district, philosophises to Ila and the narrator near a derelict church in Clapham, London.

> You know, if you look at the picture on the front pages of the newspapers at home now, all those pictures of dead people—in Assam, the north-east, Punjab, Sri Lanka, Tripura—people shot by terrorists and separatists and the army and police, you'll find somewhere behind it all, that single word; everyone's doing it to be free. (246)

This is the hallmark of the novel, it recognises and acknowledges the violence in our lives. There is state terror, there is majority communalism and minority communalism violence. The novel makes no distinctions, takes no sides. Amitav Ghosh shows that even characters like the grandmother and Ila, who do not indulge in violence are on the fringe of it. The grandmother, even though afraid, was willing to run errands for the Bengal terrorists and kill the English magistrate at Khulna during her student days. There is a certain cruelty in the way Ila breaks from her family to adapt to the more cosmopolitan life style of London. The quest for political freedom in *The Shadow Lines* makes the novel very contemporary.

The complexities of majority and minority communalism are also very sensitively handled by Amitav Ghosh. Using the memory technique, he links two events, riots in Calcutta and mob violence in Dhaka which led to Tridib's death. The violence in Calcutta started on 10 January 1964, the day the first cricket test match of the 1964 series against England at Madras commenced. The narrator, by recalling wicketkeeper batsman Budhi Kunderan's maiden Test Century, is able to focus on other eventful happenings on that day. The schoolbus was nearly empty because of a rumour circulated that the whole of Calcutta's water supply was poisoned. The dozen old schoolboys in the bus, do not doubt or question the authenticity of the information. As the narrator remembers, even the young minds were conditioned to assume and believe that it was 'they' the Muslims who had poisoned the water. The most poignant expression of the communal divide is shown in two actions. The narrator disowns his best friend, a young Muslim boy, named Montu: "I lied, I haven't met Montu for months." (200) Before reaching school "We unscrewed the caps of our bottles and poured the water out." (200) Amitav Ghosh, with his sensitive use of language and unique narrative technique, highlights that such irrational behaviour was not confined to that particular incident. He shows that in the highly surcharged atmosphere of suspicion and distrust, rumour has become institutionalised. The narrator is recalling these events as a research student in the 1980s. The author very subtly conveys that events in the novel are also contemporaneous and can be linked to similar incidents in the 1980s.

Amitav Ghosh stresses that due to social conditioning, the role of rumour in riots or mass movements is deep rooted. The young schoolboys willingly believe that a certain community has poisoned the water in Calcutta. Later as a research student, reading newspaper reports in the Teen Murti House library in Delhi, about the 1964 events the narrator recalls the motivations for riots in Calcutta.

> In Calcutta rumours were in the air—especially that familiar old rumour, the harbinger of every serious riot—that the trains from Pakistan were arriving packed with corpses . . . with refugees still pouring in, rumours began to flow like floodwaters through the city and angry crowds began to gather at the stations. (229)

The author's views on the impact of rumours are authenticated by the distinguished historian Dr. Sumit Sarkar, Professor of History at Delhi University. In his scholarly book, *Modern India 1885-1947*, Dr. Sumit Sarkar projects the role of rumour in the growing popularity of the Gandhian movement. He shows the effectiveness of rumour in any mass movement especially during periods of acute strain and tension.

> From out of their misery and hope, varied sections of the Indian people seem to have fashioned their own images of Gandhi, particularly in the early days when he was

> still to most people a distant, vaguely-glimpsed or heard-of tale of a holy man with miracle working powers . . . peasants were giving vague rumours about Gandhi a radical, anti-zamindar twist. (181)

Sumit Sarkar notes that the currency which Gandhi's name acquired in the remotest villages was primarily due to the impact of rumour, perpetuated by a desire to be represented by a saviour from above. In the section. "The Role of Rumour," Sumit Sarkar reveals that peasants would imagine that Gandhi would end zamindari exploitation. For instance agricultural labourers in U.P. believed he would provide holdings for them. Assam tea coolies left the plantations en masse in May 1921, saying they were obeying Gandhi's orders and hoping for a better deal. Gandhi became a historical necessity. Even local achievements like illegal eviction being restricted in Pratapgarh, due to a peasants' struggle is attributed to Gandhi.

Awareness of the growing internationalisation of the world is highlighted by the author. He shows the coming together of different societies and culture, which has also emphasized their distinctions. *The Shadow Lines* aptly reveals that the cultural divide, communal struggle and misunderstanding is in a state of crisis in India. The political allegory, the contemporaneousness of the motivations for riots is very sensitively handled. The rumour of water being poisoned by a particular community and of a train full of dead bodies, is not confined to particular incidents of certain decades but has become a recurring feature. In the novel, Amitav Ghosh reveals that on 27 December 1963 two hundred and sixty-three years after the Mu-i-Mubarak, believed to be a hair of the Prophet Mohammed, was brought to Kashmir, it was stolen. The newspaper reports, read by the narrator, indicate that "there was not one single recorded incident of animosity between Kashmiri Muslims, Hindus and Sikhs." (225) The targets of the rioters were properly identified with the government and the police. The purveyor of sanity was the wise leader Maulana Masoodi "who persuaded the first demonstrators to march with black flags instead of green and thereby drew the various communities of

Kashmir together in a collective display of mourning." (226) Amitav Ghosh rightly regrets that in the hysteria that prevails in the subcontinent now, the sane and secular Maulana Masoodi has been forgotten.

Using the narrative technique of unfurling events, by the reading of newspaper reports, it is shown that in both wings of Pakistan, there were protest demonstrations. Certain disgruntled bigots hinted at attacks upon the identity of the Muslims. However on 4 January 1964 the Mu-i-Mubarak was recovered by the officials of the Central Bureau of Intelligence.

The protests in Pakistan subsided. Only in Khulna, a small town in the distant east wing of Pakistan, a demonstration turned violent. "Some shops were burnt down and a few people killed." (226) Headlines in newspapers of 7 January 1964 were, "Fourteen die in frenzy off Khulna." (228) Riots spread from Khulna to the outskirts of Dhaka. It is now that rumour took over. The poisoning of water, trains full of dead bodies, all incredible rumours, further vitiate the communal frenzy, and add to the violence. However what makes the novel very contemporary and relevant is the subtle implication by Amitav Ghosh that the lessons of history have not been learnt.

The deplorable violence unleashed upon the Sikhs in Delhi, from 31 October to 4 November 1984, shows history repeating itself. The report of the Citizens' Commission (1985) indicates that the motivation for the Delhi riots, after the assassination of late Prime Minister Indira Gandhi, followed a familiar pattern, insidious spread of rumours. The report prepared by five senior and responsible citizens of Delhi says,

> The basic provocation [for the riots] was provided by the spreading of rumours, some of them of a most incredible nature. . . . On the night of 1/2 November numerous citizens received telephone calls or were told otherwise that the city water supply had been poisoned, by Sikh extremists Allegations circulated like wildfire that truckloads and a train full of dead Hindus had arrived from Punjab and that Sikh students danced the Bhangra on hearing of Smt. Gandhi's death. (Sikri, 36)

The difference between fiction and reality is thus shown as marginal. *The Shadow Lines* shows how rumour mongerers thrived and intensified feelings of anger, which triggered off violence in Calcutta in 1964. Amitav Ghosh's greatest triumph is that the depiction of communal strife in Calcutta and erstwhile East Pakistan, and its continuation in contemporary India, is very controlled and taut. There are no moralising or irrelevant digressions. Lucidity and compactness is achieved primarily by his unusual narrative device.

Violence is never described. It is depicted in several ways. The cause of the riots of 1964 and the violence at Khulna are presented as newspaper reports. The narrator reads these reports, at the Teen Murti House Library, sixteen years later, after a discussion with his friend Malik. A mature, research student, the narrator is still shocked by the needless violence, the motivations which triggered off the violent incidents and the sudden realisation that this was how his cousin Tridib died. The news item narrative technique, with its emphasis on facts, eliminates any digression or gory details. Sheer stark reality is presented, which adds to the horror of the event. Also the bland newspaper reports, just concerned with detail, remove the impact of time. It is implied that the riots are contemporaneous. The 1964 Calcutta riots could be the 1984 Delhi riots or the 1987 Meerut riots. They all follow a similar pattern, suspicion, distrust, rumour activating conditioned minds, all sources of terrifying communal violence. The newspaper reports technique hints at a continuity of the lurking danger of communal strife, which can be sparked off by both marginal and recalled major events. The violence in Calcutta is not narrated, but is presented as the memories and images of the narrator. Again the role of rumour and overall distrust is stressed, facets which have a bearing on communal trouble in the current decade also. Such treatment adds to the immediate relevance of *The Shadow Lines*.

Precise details of the death of Tridib are conveyed by May to the narrator, years later at a dinner in London. May narrates the story to exorcise her feeling of guilt, that she was responsible for Tridib's untimely death. The narrator, being a young boy, had been told that Tridib's death was due to an accident. On learning the truth, both May and the narrator realise they cannot rationalise the motives for Tridib's sacrifice. As May says, "any real sacrifice is a mystery." (252) As a political action, Tridib's reckless act is not redemptive. He had saved May and could have returned to the safety of the car himself. Plunging into the berserk mob just leads to his death. As a political act, it is revealed that individual valour or action cannot stem the upsurge of communal strife. Tridib dies as he lived, an iconoclast, a mystery.

The absence of pessimism, despair and ambiguity makes *The Shadow Lines* a very convincing and effective work of art. The author boldly tackles political themes both national and international. The meaning of political freedom in the modern world is shown as complex and without any easy solutions. For human survival, a new perception of relationships must emerge. On the national level, Amitav Ghosh shows how different cultures and communities are becoming antagonistic to a point of no return. This is revealed as a major issue in contemporary India. The author realises that with the dominant tradition slowly regarding itself as the only legitimate source of India's complex culture, communal antagonism will grow. Hence in the novel he effectively uses political allegory to stress the need for a syncretic civilisation, to avoid a communal holocaust. Above all, the use of imagination and the memory technique make *The Shadow Lines* a compact novel. The narrative is controlled, is not too digressive and does not give the impression of a collection of stories yoked together. Imagination and politics are the binding force of Amitav Ghosh's second work of fiction.

An Overall Assessment

Amitav Ghosh's unique novel *The Shadow Lines* resists easy classification. There are several critical interpretations of this absorbing book. The complex narrative, with its time shifts, is a tremendous achievement. The book is incisive and funny, yet touching, profound and humane. It depicts India and its paradoxes perfectly. The horror of communal disharmony is brought out through the eyes of a child, during a bus journey to school and back during a riot, through a moving and mesmeric haze of incomprehension. The author deftly and imaginatively brings to the fore the absurdity of fanatical violence.

The book is an experience, absolutely amazing. Ghosh switches the narrative in time and space with phenomenal ease. This is a very ambitious book. It is about how boundaries are formed and how identity is created, how notions of nationalism and nations are perpetuated and accepted. It is about journeys through time and through ages. It is about a longing for the past and about unrequited love. Every sentence is carefully crafted and full of metaphor and meaning. This is not a book. It is a journey.

This is a brilliant narrative with the capacity to make the hair stand on end. It is an unprecedented landmark in the same league as Khushwant Singh's novel about Partition, *Train to Pakistan* and succeeds in bringing out the senselessness of violence. Amitav Ghosh's book is a powerful story of adolescent love and its contextual rape in a turbulent political and religious milieu. An exceptional emotional journey from Calcutta to London! The emotions of human beings placed in an unfamiliar cultural ethos are portrayed with exceptional skill and honesty. The complete gamut of human emotions from religious fanaticism to dormant sexual impulses flies across the canvas of this book against the backdrop of two families—one British, one Indian. The depths of these two cultures with their attendant dogmas and inherent beauty is thrown right into the reader's face—making him smile and wince at the same time.

It is also basically a memory novel that weaves together the past and present, childhood and adulthood, India, Bangladesh and Britain, Hindu and Muslim divisions, story and events through the coil within coil of unfurled memories. The novel establishes its socio-historical situation by a careful observation of concrete social reality. As such it can be regarded both as a social document and a political novel. In many ways this novel is a bildungsroman, tracing the growth and development of the narrator from childhood to maturity. It is also part of the recent development in Indian fiction to experiment with the non-fiction novel, a trend initiated by Salman Rushdie's *Midnight's Children* (1980). Like Rushdie's novels on the subcontinent, Amitav Ghosh in *The Shadow Lines* undercuts the ideology of nationalism by questioning official history. The concept and ideology of Nationalism is constructed on the basis of official history. In Ghosh's novel, the fictive nature of history is exposed by juxtaposing it with memory, that both creates and invents. This aspect demonstrates that history and along with it the ideology of nationalism are inventions. In Ghosh's novel, nationalism is viewed as a perennial source of violence. The alternative that the novel suggests is globalism, a popular contemporary viewpoint, especially amongst liberal democrats and socially conscious writers like Amitav Ghosh. An example from the novel will highlight the idea of globalism which the author is trying to convey. Tridib in his letter to May expresses a desire to meet her "in a place without a past, without history, free, really free, two people coming together with the utter freedom of strangers." (144) This desire of Tridib can be interpreted as a wish for dismantling the world order based on nation states. The novel however does not deal with the complexities of globalism.

Ghosh's novel can also be interpreted as a postmodernist work of fiction like Farrukh Dhondy's *Bombay Duck* (1990). Now what is postmodernism. Christina Howells, in her essay "Postmodernism in Literature," describes it as a term "used to denote a multitude of styles and attitudes which exist as a response to high modernism, and partly as a result of post-industrial mass production and late capitalism." She admits that it is a term very difficult to define. In philosophic terms, postmodernism questions fixed meanings and eternal truths. In fiction, postmodernism has manifested itself in an experimentation and eclecticism which has focused on the nature of fictionality and of writing itself. Postmodernism can be attached to almost any work that questions the boundaries and possibilities of the fictional enterprise. Postmodernist also refers to works that attempt to collapse arbitrary borders between genres and to question what constitutes the nature of the genre and that refers directly or by allusion to other texts. Some famous contemporary novelists who incorporate these themes and approaches in their work are the Italian novelist Umberto Eco (a professor at the University of Bologna) in his novels *The Name of the Rose* (1980) and *Foucault's Pendulum* (1989) and Salman Rushdie in his novels *Midnight's Children* (1981) and *Shame* (1983). Angela Carter and Martin Amis have also experimented with postmodernisn in their literary works. Now let us try and understand the postmodernist aspects in Amitav Ghosh's novel *The Shadow Lines.*

Postmodern theory has questioned the separation of history and literature by stressing on the similarities rather than the differences between the two modes of writing. Linda Hutcheon observes that in post-modern theory both history and literature are "identified as linguistic constructs, highly conventionalized in their narrative forms, and not at all transparent either in terms of language or structure; and they appear to be intertextual, deploying the texts of the past within their own complex textuality." (105) *The Shadow Lines* demonstrates some of the above mentioned traits of postmodernism. The novel undercuts history by exposing it as a human construct. The best example of this, in the novel, is the narrator's survey of the newspapers regarding the riots of 1964. The riots, which occupy a unique place in the narrator's personal history, find no significant mention in the newspapers. The newspapers, for years, carry detailed news "of the Congress conference, of the impending split in the Communist party, or wars and revolutions," (228) whereas the riots "by the end of January 1964 had faded away from the pages of the newspapers." (230) The discovery reveals how history is constructed to suit the agenda of the ruling classes. The novel demonstrates history as an invention by juxtaposing it with a memory that can invent: Tridib had once advised the narrator that "we could not see without inventing what we saw, so at least we could try to do it properly. We had to try because the alternative wasn't blackness—it only meant that if we didn't try ourselves, we could never be free of other people's inventions." (31) Consequently memory in the novel substitutes "history" with a "personal history" and in doing so it challenges any claims to "truth" of "grand narratives" or "master narratives," such as those of history. The "grand narratives" of our culture serve to mask the contradictions and instabilities, to unify and order any contradiction that is inherent in any social organization or practice. Postmodernism, however, undercuts any idea of totality by exposing the gaps/ fissures in the "grand narratives." *The Shadow Lines* refuses to smooth over the contradictions in history by unmasking the gaps or fissures in History:

> Every word I write about those events of 1964 is the product of a struggle with silence. I know nothing of this silence except that it lies outside the reach of my intelligence, beyond words—that is why this silence must win, must inevitably defeat me, because it is not a presence at all; it is simply a gap, a hole, an emptiness in which there are no words. (218)

In this way *The Shadow Lines* reveals an "ironic discontinuity at the heart of continuity" (Hutcheon 11) and attempts to liberate people from the meta-narratives that control their lives.

Several other labels can be attached to *The Shadow Lines*. This novel also belongs to the long tradition of fiction that includes *Don Quixote*, *Tristram Shandy* and Salman Rushdie's *Haroun and the Sea of Stories*, all novels which examine the role of imagination in creating and evoking reality. Amitav Ghosh's novel has a symbiotic relationship with fact. In his novel these themes are examined by the use of the geographical metaphor and the journey motif implicit in its title. Incidentally the title is derived from Joseph Conrad's work *Shadow Lines*. So it can be said that Ghosh's novel sets out to discover the relationship between imagination and reality. Renowned postcolonial critic Edward Said also talks about such connections when talking about the novel. Said says. "stories are at the heart of what explorers and novelists say about strange regions of the world." (12) So Amitav Ghosh's approach has a close affinity with certain novels of Graham

Greene like *Travels with my Aunt* and *The Captain and the Enemy* which are likewise concerned with the relationship between imagination, perception and rendering of human experience in everyday life.

In Ghosh's novel, imagination is not just a part of reality, it creates its own reality. Rumour can start a riot. It is seen in the novel that the story of the loss of the Prophet's hair (the Mu-i-Mubarak) in faraway Srinagar can lead to murderous attacks on Indian Hindus in Dhaka. Such is the impact of rumour that numerous people in Calcutta believe that the water supplies have been poisoned and friendships of many years are broken. Imagination is thus seen as a means to link people together. The physical fact of geographical boundaries between nations is not of real importance. The novel shows that the border drawn between the two Bengals has pulled them even closer together. Events in Srinagar triggered off a riot in Dhaka and its aftermath had an immediate impact on Calcutta. The narrator aptly expresses this feeling of bonding and closeness between Calcutta and Dhaka when he says, "so close that I, in Calcutta had only to look into the mirror to be in Dhaka, a moment when each city was the inverted image of the other, locked into an irreversible symmetry by the line that was to set us free—our looking glass border." (233)

The role of rumour and imagination is also evident if we examine *The Shadow Lines* as a social document or a political novel. Written in 1988, when in India different cultures and communities were becoming antagonistic to a point of no return, Amitav Ghosh very sensitively handles the complexities of majority and minority violence. Using the memory technique, he links two events, riots in Calcutta and mob violence in Dhaka which led to Tridib's death. The violence in Calcutta started on 10 January 1964, the day the first cricket Test match of the 1964 series against England at Madras commenced. The narrator, by recalling wicketkeeper batsman Budhi Kunderan's maiden Test century, is able to focus on other eventful happenings on that day. The school bus was nearly empty because of a rumour circulated that the whole of Calcutta's water supply was poisoned. The dozen odd schoolboys in the bus do not either doubt or question the authenticity of such information. As the narrator remembers, even the young minds were conditioned to assume and believe that it was 'they'—the Muslims—who had poisoned the water. The most poignant expression of the communal divide is shown in two actions. The narrator disowns his best friend, a young Muslim boy named Montu, "I lied, I haven't met Montu for months." (200) Before reaching school, "we unscrewed the caps of our bottles and poured the water out." (200) Amitav Ghosh shows that in the surcharged atmosphere of suspicion and distrust, rumour became institutionalised. The narrator recalls these events as a research student in the 1980s. The author subtly conveys that events in the novel are also contemporaneous and can be linked to similar incidents in the 1980s.

Amitav Ghosh stresses that due to social conditioning, the role of rumour in riots or mass movements is deep rooted. The young schoolboys willingly believe that a certain community has poisoned the water in Calcutta. Later, as a research student reading newspaper reports in the Teen Murti House library in Delhi about the 1964 events, the narrator recalls the motivations for riots in Calcutta:

> In Calcutta rumours were in the air—especially that familiar old rumour, the harbinger of every serious riot—that the trains from Pakistan were arriving packed with corpses with refugees still pouring in, rumours began to flow like floodwaters through the city and angry crowds began to gather at the stations. (229)

The political allegory, the contemporaneousness of the motivations for riots is very sensitively handled. He shows that the coming together of different societies and cultures also emphasised their distinctions. *The Shadow Lines* aptly reveals that the cultural divide, communal struggle and misunderstanding is in a state of crises in India. The rumour of water being poisoned by a particular community and of a train full of dead bodies, is not confined to particular incidents in certain decades but has become a recurring feature. In the novel Amitav

Ghosh reveals that on 27 December 1963, two hundred and sixty three years after the Mu-i-Mubarak, believed to be a hair of the Prophet Mohammed was brought to Kashmir, it was stolen. The newspaper reports read by the narrator indicate that "there was not one single recorded incident of animosity between Kashmiri Muslims, Hindus and Sikhs." (225) The targets of the rioters were properly identified with the government and the police. The purveyor of sanity was the wise leader Maulana Masoodi, "who persuaded the first demonstrators to march with black flags instead of green and thereby drew the various communities of Kashmir together in a collective display of mourning." (226) Amitav Ghosh rightly regrets that in the hysteria that currently prevails in the subcontinent, upright individuals like the sane and secular Maulana Masoodi have been forgotten.

From newspaper reports, the narrator learns that in both wings of Pakistan, there were protest demonstrations. Certain disgruntled bigots hinted at sinister plans to undermine the identity of Muslims. However on 4 January 1964 the officials of the Central Bureau of Intelligence (CBI) recovered the Mu-i-Mubarak. The protests in Pakistan became muted and gradually subsided. Only in Khulna, a small town in the distant east wing of Pakistan, a demonstration turned violent. "Some shops were burnt down and a few people killed." (226) However newspaper headlines on 7 January 1964 exacerbated the situation as they stated: "Fourteen die in frenzy off Khulna." (228) This process led to the escalation of riots from Khulna to the outskirts of Dhaka. Incredible rumours further vitiated the atmosphere, increased communal frenzy and added to the violence. However, what makes the novel very contemporary and relevant is the subtle implication by Amitav Ghosh that the lessons of history have not been learnt. The deplorable violence unleashed upon the Sikhs in Delhi from 31 October to 4 November 1984, shows history repeating itself. The report of the Citizens' Commission (1985) indicates that the Delhi riots, motivated by the assassination of the late Prime Minister Mrs. Indira Gandhi, followed a similar pattern, the insidious spread of rumours.

Amitav Ghosh explores the dialectic of history and fiction, of imagination and facts in his book. The author uses established notions of history and historiography to serve his own novelistic concerns. The role of memory in the field of historiography and the undercutting of history through the construction of other narratives/histories are some of the important concerns of the novelist. These concepts are also examined in detail in essays in this volume. Juxtaposing it with memory exposes the fictive nature of history. After all, memory both creates and invents and the author suggests that history and the ideology of nationalism are also inventions. So Amitav Ghosh in *The Shadow Lines* can be seen as undercutting the ideology of nationalism by questioning official history. This concept is also examined in detail in an essay in this book.

Using the narrative technique of unfurling events, by the reading of newspaper reports, the narrator tries to understand the milieu, which led to Tridib's murder. The narrator tries to scan the old newspapers for detailed information on the nature and causes of the communal riots in Bengal in 1964. Much to his horror he discovers that the Calcutta newspapers of 1964 had in the days preceding the riots given very little hints of the impending trouble in erstwhile East Pakistan. They had also barely mentioned the loss of the holy relic from the Hazratbal shrine in Kashmir that triggered off protest movements in both Pakistan and India. The narrator now understands the concept of distance, a theme the author subtly introduces in this novel. The narrator realises that the newspapers like common men and women had believed in the power of distance. "It was after all a Calcutta paper, run by people who believed in the power of distance no less than I did." (227) Srinagar is after all about 1200 miles away from Calcutta and Dhaka was in another country, so the newspaper editorial board had underplayed the theft in Srinagar and subsequent communal disturbances in Dhaka. "And when I looked back at the editions of 1, 2 and 3 January they were the same." (227) So now the narrator understands why his father permitted the family to travel to Dhaka. Obviously the narrator's father had no inkling of the communal crises in erstwhile

East Pakistan. "So looking back at the paper that my father had read that morning, I knew that he could not be blamed for ignoring the stirrings of silence around him: in that paper there was not the slightest hint or augury of the coming carnage; it was replete with the fullness of normalcy." (227) The newspaper focussed on topics of interest to the readers in Calcutta: the conference of the Congress party, the split in the Communist Party of India and wars in other foreign countries. Incidentally, the Communist Party of India (CPI) split into two factions, the CPI and the more radical wing the Communist Party of India Marxist (CPM), in 1964 due to ideological differences. The CPM is currently the dominant party in the Left Front coalition which has been ruling West Bengal without a break since 1977.

The journalists ignored the disturbed atmosphere in Dhaka and so the narrator's father allowed his family to travel to Dhaka. The author says that the journalists must have had an inkling of the troubled atmosphere in former East Pakistan—"for events on that scale cannot happen without portents" (227) but chose to ignore it. The author knows that the journalists were "men of intelligence and good intentions" (228) but cannot wax eloquent on certain events either due to editorial policy or because they are "these other unnameable things so silent." (228) The author subtly shows that such a conspiracy of silence led to the unfortunate death of Tridib as the family travelled to Dhaka without knowledge of the communal tension in that city.

This discovery in the Teen Murti House library enabled the narrator to discover a momentous truth that national frontiers created a false sense of distance and of reality. Dhaka is closer to Calcutta than Srinagar. Yet events in Srinagar are described in greater detail in a Calcutta newspaper than action in Dhaka because both Srinagar and Calcutta are in the same country. The narrator now experiments with a compass on Tridib's old atlas and made some startling discoveries. He now learns the meaning of distance.

His [Tridib's] atlas showed for example, that within the

> tidy ordering of Euclidean space, Chiang Mai in Thailand was much nearer Calcutta than Delhi is; that Chengdu in China is nearer than Srinagar is. Yet I had never heard of these places till until I drew my circle, and I cannot remember a time when I was so young that I had not heard of Delhi or Srinagar. It showed me that Hanoi and Chungking are nearer Khulna than Srinagar, and yet, did the people of Khulna care at all about the fate of mosques in Vietnam and South China (a mere stone's throw away)? I doubted it. (232)

The narrator also discovers that within a radius of 1200 miles from any city in the world as the centre, lay different cities of different countries and that the only event with the power to draw all the various citizens together was war. Ghosh comes to the realisation that "within this circle there were only states and citizens; there were no people at all." (233) The narrator now realises that riots often occur because of gross political manipulation of communal sympathies and nationalist passions. Also he understands that political lines cannot separate people or their common land and realities. Thus he knows now that Dhaka and Calcutta were the "inverted images of one another" that what happened at one place was bound to influence the other. As a liberal humanist, Ghosh has faith in the good will, rationality and common sense of the ordinary people to transcend jingoism and nationalist fervour. The writer observes, "As always there were innumerable cases of Muslims in East Pakistan giving shelter to Hindus, often at the cost of their own lives, and equally in India of Hindus sheltering Muslims. But they were ordinary people soon forgotten—not for them any Martyr's memorials or Eternal Flames." (229-30) Here we get another interpretation of Tridib's death. Explaining this facet, Seema Bhaduri says, "it was the indivisible sanity of people like Tridib on both sides of the border, who often at the cost of their lives, tried to rescue their brethren of opposite religions that really helped to quell the riots." (113) Ghosh acknowledges and approves of such a role and says that the ordinary people demonstrated "that indivisible sanity that binds people to each other independently of their governments. And that prior, independent relationship is the natural enemy of government, for it is in the logic of states that to exist at all they must claim the monopoly of all relationships between peoples." (230) The author feels that states disport themselves on the theatre of war.

Another major theme in this novel is the understanding of the concept of freedom. The novel weaves together the idea of freedom juxtaposing past and present, the personal and the public, the social and the political. Ranging across three generations and moving between two contrasting cultures, the narrative provides a penetrating study of freedom, as an important all-pervading force. The principal characters in *The Shadow Lines* reflect ideas in their own individualistic manner. Tha'mma, the grandmother, glorifies political freedom. Ila is in search of an elusive, personal, social and moral freedom. May and Tridib also strive for a quest that seems elusive.

Political freedom is explored through the character of Tha'mma, the narrator's grandmother. She is the product of a bygone era. Anjali Karpe in her thought-provoking essay, "The Concept of Freedom in *The Shadow Lines*: A Novel by Amitav Ghosh" says that the grandmother is "a strong and independent woman on whom history has conferred a legacy of unflinching faith in the sanctity of political freedom." (307) Historical forces have moulded her character and understanding of the present. Karpe shows that "Political freedom has been the single dominating, over-powering force in her life. Everything else is secondary to the assertion of a stable political order." (308) Her childhood associations were with the terrorist movement against the British in Bengal. She too sought reflected glory and fame by either running errands or cooking for the terrorists. The aim was to be associated with a group of people actively involved in fighting for a political cause. Justifying her fanatical commitment to the cause of freedom, the grandmother often told the narrator, "Yes I would have killed. It was our freedom: I would have done anything to be free." (308)

In her conversation, Tha'mma revealed a grim prospect, that feelings of nationalism can only be developed through the process of war and sustained bloodshed. Lying in bed during her final illness, Tha'mma tells the narrator that Ila had no right to live in Britain as she did not belong there. It took those people a long time to build that country;

> hundreds of years, years and years of war and bloodshed, everyone who lives there has earned his right to be there with blood. War is their religion. That's what it takes to make a country. (77-78)

The grandmother is not in a state of hallucination. Her insights are sharp and full of clarity. When the narrator had told Ila about the raving grandmother's reactions to war and nationalism, the latter was very dismissive. A university graduate in history, she promptly categorised the response as that of "warmongering fascists." The narrator aptly rejects such easy generalisations and recalls the more worldly wise Tridib's observations:

> All she wanted was a middle class life in which like the middle classes the world over, she would thrive believing in the unity of nationhood and territory, of self respect and national power: that was all she wanted—a modern middle class life, a small thing that history had denied her in its fullness and for which she could never forgive it. (78)

So as Tridib had observed the grandmother was not fascist but a motivated middle class individual with a strong sense of national feeling and identity. Her motivation was a desire to be free and so feelings of nationalism got linked to self-respect and national power. She never realised that militant nationalism can be effective in its anti-imperialist phase but gets tarnished when it defines oppositions within and enemies across the border. However Seema Bhaduri in her perceptive article, "Of Shadows, Lines and Freedom: A Historical Reading of

The Shadow Lines" cleverly explains the grandmother's predicament: "With her imagination enslaved to the idea of nationalism, Grandma couldn't see what was so obvious, namely nationalism had destroyed her home and spilled her innocent kin's blood." (108) After the tragic killing of Tridib and Jethamoshoi, the grandmother still did not change her views on nationalism. It was her visit to Dhaka that led to the death of her uncle and nephew. However, instead of remorse she clung even more fervently to her nationalistic faith. She gave away her gold chain to the war effort. Clarifying her stance, she tells the narrator, "I gave it [the chain] to the fund for the war, for your sake, for your freedom. We have to kill them before they kill us; we have to wipe them out." (237) The grandmother could never understand that national liberty couldn't always guarantee the individual's liberty.

Thus the grandmother could never fathom Ila's desire to live in London, rootless but free of middle class constraints and taboos or May's desire to collect money for worthy causes like famine relief in Africa. Various strands of political ideology are depicted in this novel. There are Ila's radical friends in London who picket on political issues: Dan the Trotskyite who wrote anti-Nazi pamphlets and had fought in the Spanish Civil war; Tresawsen who edited a left wing newspaper. Another facet of nationalism is revealed in Nick Price who gave up a lucrative chartered accountant's job in Kuwait because of outdated management practices and interfering Arab business partners. He still believed in Britain's colonial past. We see that the novel brings forth contrasting strands of nationalism or political commitment. By exploring connections, distinctions and possibilities, Amitav Ghosh shows that in a changing world, different strands of nationalism and ideology will exist and even compete. He also reveals that the force of nationalism in the quest for freedom or an ideology is often a source of violence. So the 'shadow line' between people and nations is often mere illusion. Thus the idea of political freedom is an important concept in this novel. It is connected directly or indirectly to all other connotations of freedom. The author also shows that political freedom has different nuances of meaning for different people. There is often just a 'shadow line' between these different ideas of freedom.

The link between concepts of freedom, ideological struggle, feelings of nationalism and the inevitable violence are also explored in this novel. The author shows that the 'shadow line' between people and nations is a mere illusion. The force and appeal of nationalism cannot be wished away just as death by a communal mob in the bye-lanes of old Dhaka. Political realities have to be explored. Robi, an IAS officer in charge of a district, explains to both the narrator and Ila the link between freedom and violence. Talking near a derelict church in North London, he says:

> You know, if you look at the pictures on the front pages of the newspapers at home now, all those pictures of dead people—in Assam, the north-east, Punjab, Sri Lanka, Tripura—people shot by terrorists and separatists and the army and police, you'll find somewhere behind it all, that single word: everyone's doing it to be free. (246)

This is the hallmark of the novel, it recognises and acknowledges the violence in our lives and shows that in the name of freedom, many innocent people are often either terrorised or victimised. There is state terror, there is majority community violence and minority community violence. There is the destructive force of nationalism also as is seen in the death of Tridib. The happenings in Dhaka prove that war or friendship between nations is a continuing political reality. Also as A.N. Kaul says in his essay, "A Reading of *The Shadow Lines*," the relation between India and Pakistan "is not a simple matter of either/or but of an original cultural unity or oneness now tragically fractured by the forces of a bigoted politics." (304) The novel explores all these different aspects of political reality and uniquely makes no distinctions, takes no sides. Amitav Ghosh shows that even characters like the grandmother and Ila, who do not indulge in violence, are on the fringe of it. The grandmother willingly ran errands for the Bengal terrorists and was willing to kill the English magistrate at

Khulna during her student days. There is also a certain cruelty in the manner in which Ila breaks from her family to adapt to the more cosmopolitan life style of London.

The quest for political freedom in *The Shadow Lines* makes the novel very contemporary. After all, the longing for freedom is universal and a primitive urge amongst human beings. However, as Ghosh shows, the method of realisation of freedom varies with each age. Geo-political sovereignty was a major quest during the age of the grandmother. In the modern age, intellectual independence is under threat with colonisers casting their technological nets for the third world mind. Thus Tridib's insistence upon imaginative freedom is, according to Ghosh, the only way to preserve intellectual integrity.

Besides political freedom, other concepts of freedom are also examined in this novel. As Anjali Karpe explains, "what appears as political stability and order, giving rise to cherished values for Tha'mma, is the very reason for Ila to break and escape." (309) The grandmother feels that Ila's yearning for freedom is merely to lead a life without any constraints of morality. Ila is perhaps the finest example in the novel of the paradox of freedom and its connotations. She has a lot of bitterness and dislike for the conservative norms of social and moral conditions in India. Hence her desire to live a bohemian life in London. Ila has spent all her life in different countries of the world, but is unsure of what she is striving for.

As a child, she yearns to be identified with other boys and girls in the international school where she studies. Sadly for her, she is lonely, a victim of racism. She also faces the emotional trauma of being rejected by those around her. As a mature young woman, she tries to establish herself in the West and adjust to their lifestyle. She loves Nick Price with a blinding passion and their marriage is a culminating experience and a time of bliss for Ila. Yet this bliss does not last long. She soon hears of Nick's infidelity, which completely distresses and disillusions her. She feels both rejected and a cultural outcast. Now Ila's disillusionment reveals numerous aspects of cross-cultural interaction and explores different nuances of social freedom. Through Ila's experiences, Amitav

Ghosh examines the strengths and weaknesses of both the Indian and Western cultures. Anjali Karpe has aptly commented on this predicament. She says:

> India may be conservative and restraining, but there is the final security of institution like marriage. On the other hand, it will never allow the kind of freedom which Ila desires. If England provides that emancipated milieu, it also incorporates the evils of racism and the breakdown of social institutions. (312)

Creditably the novelist does not take sides. No culture is projected as totally good or bad. If there is any covert message in this book, it is that synthesis of cultures is desirable. However, the author honestly questions such a possibility. As is seen in the novel, Ila and Nick Price are not happily married and the relationship between Tridib and May Price ends abruptly and in tragic circumstances. Through Ila, the author poses a very existentialist question. Individuals who become more independent, self-reliant and critical also become more isolated, lonely and lack cultural moorings. So Ila's quest for social freedom is shown as ambivalent. She wants to overthrow traditional forms of authority and restraint, in her search for greater freedom. However, unfortunately for Ila, internal factors block the full realisation of the freedom of her personality. Ila is presented as a character existing in a state of servility to her personal fantasies, which distort her vision. Ghosh thus feels that it is necessary to preserve and increase traditional freedom as well as gain a new kind of freedom which enables the individual to realise their maximum potential. The narrator's voice becomes a befitting summary of Ila's elusive quest for freedom. "I could think of nothing to say; nothing that would console her for the discovery that the squalor of genteel little lives she had so much despised, was a part too of the free world she had tried to build for herself." (188) Ila's lifestyle thus may be a warning against the perils of cosmopolitanism.

Another interesting theme in this novel is the way in

which it questions prevailing precepts and ethics, which people often inherit without questioning. For instance, it shows that the value of political zeal and social freedom is no longer stable, permanent and immutable as Tha'mma and Ila had believed. The apparent stability that is offered by such ideas is illusory. Well-defined concepts are often seen as shallow. The reality of nations and border is seen as superfluous, subject to the whims of officials. Tha'mma is bewildered and aghast to know that violence and bloodshed had not resulted in a physical boundary between two countries. With the death of Tridib, her faith in political authority and ardent nationalism is shaken. A process of questioning begins which leaves her bewildered. During her final illness, her idealism turns into helplessness as anarchic tendencies, within and without her, gather force. Her perceptions about Dhaka have changed. She donates her gold chain to the war effort. During the 1965 war against Pakistan, she hysterically tells the young narrator: "We have to kill them, before they kill us." (237) Th'amma remains in bed weak and helpless hoping for a new order to emerge but is unable to visualise or formulate the kind of new order that should emerge.

Significantly, the novel ends with May and the narrator lying in close embrace after the former has given a chilling account of Tridib's untimely and gruesome murder in the mob-infested streets of Dhaka. May interprets this act of Tridib as a sacrifice and narrates the circumstances which led to his death. Rushing to save Jethamoshoi from the frenzied rioters proves futile. The rescue attempt is unsuccessful and Tridib is hacked to death. The act shows that individual valour is insufficient to change the tide of events or alter political violence or restrain the forces of communal strife. In a way Tridib's sacrifice remains a mystery. However, it provides a thematic balance to the novel. *The Shadow Lines* starts with a mention of Tridib and ends with an unravelling of the mystery of his violent death. May Price knows the futility of Tridib's views and their impracticability in her world. But together they attempt to reach a new level of freedom. Tridib and May had become friends as both followed the ideals of humanitarianism.

Jean Sudrann provides perceptive comments on the thematic concerns of Amitav Ghosh with reference to the May-Tridib relationship:

> As in his first novel, *The Circle of Reason*, where Ghosh pitted rationality against emotion as warring forces within and among people, so here the conflict has been resumed in epistemological terms. Knowledge can set us free, but only if it is bred of heart as well as head. May's love—of the narrator, of Tridib, of the cycle-rickshaw man, of the hate-filled lawyer—which prompts her to reveal her innermost thoughts to the narrator, releases him from the silence which is outside his intelligence into the perhaps equally unspeakable mystery of love.

Thus, the novel insists on the imperatives that assure empathy and unimpeded flow of friendship and mocks at the conception of militant nationalism, exclusive national pride and identity. A major incident in the novel, the outbreak of communal strife in Dhaka, following the disappearance of the prophet's hair in Srinagar, exposes the fragile demarcation of political frontiers. The message of the novel underlines the need of friendly ambience, for co-existence and humanitarian ties across cultures independent of political managers. The sanity, desire for peace and commonsense attitude of people beyond borders has the potential to ensure improved international relations and amity. The narrator with his expanded horizons and imaginative understanding of a world shattered by violence stresses on the urgency of preserving the memories of saner and humane transactions. The author stresses that the media and public memory must keep alive the 'indivisible sanity' of communities to prevent a recurrence of insane frenzies and communal violence.

The meaning of political freedom in the modern world is shown as complex and without any easy solutions. In the novel Amitav Ghosh has shown that historically when different cultures and communities became antagonistic to each other, it led to major problems in Indian society and politics. Using examples from history, the author implies that such antagonisms are a haunting fear in contemporary India also. The author realises that with the dominant tradition slowly regarding itself as the only legitimate source of India's complex culture, communal antagonism will grow.

Hence in the novel, Amitav Ghosh has effectively used political allegory to stress the need for a syncretic civilisation, to avoid a communal holocaust. Above all the use of imagination and the memory technique make *The Shadow Lines* a compact novel. The narrative is controlled, is not too digressive and does not give the impression of a collection of stories yoked together. Imagination and politics are thus the binding forces of Amitav Ghosh's second work of fiction.

Works Cited

Beckett, Ian F.W. "Total War," *War, Peace and Social Change in Twentieth Century Europe*, ed. Clive Emsley et al. Open University Press, 1989.

Bharucha, Nilufer and Vrinda Nabar, ed. *Mapping Cultural Spaces Postcolonial Indian Literature in English.* Delhi: Vision Books, 1998.

Coetzee, J.M. *Disgrace*. London: Secker and Warbugh, 1999.

Dhawan, R.K., ed. *The Novels of Amitav Ghosh*. Delhi: Prestige, 1999.

Ghosh, Amitav. *New Yorker*. 23 and 30 June, 1997. p. 104.

Ghosh, Amitav. *The Shadow Lines.* Delhi: Oxford University Press, 1995. All references to the text are from this edition.

Hemmadi, Usha. "Amitav Ghosh: A Most Distinctive Voice," Bharucha, 299-302.

Hoover, Edward. *New York Times*, 2 July, 1989, Sunday, Final Section 7, p. 10. Online Internet.

Hosain, Attia. *Sunlight on a Broken Column*. Delhi: Arnold Heinemann, 1979.

Hutcheon, Linda. *A Poetics of Postmodernism: History, Theory Fiction.* Routledge, 1988.

Karnad, Girish. Book Review of *The Shadow Lines, The Indian Ex-*

press, 18 Dec. 1988, p. 5.

Karpe, Anjali. "The Concept of Freedom in *The Shadow Lines*," in Bharucha, 303-19.

Kaul, A.N. "A Reading of *The Shadow Lines*," in Ghosh, 299-309.

Kaul, Suvir. "Separation Anxiety: Growing Up Inter/National in *The Shadow Lines*," in Ghosh, 268-86.

Kirpal, Viney, ed. *The New Indian Novel in English: A Study of the 1980s*. Delhi: Allied, 1990.

Masters, John. *Bhowani Junction*. New York: The Viking Press, 1954.

Mukherjee, Meenakshi. "Maps and Mirrors: Co-ordinates of Meaning in *The Shadow Lines*," in Ghosh, 255-67.

Plato. *The Republic*. Middlesex, England: Penguin, 1955.

Rajeswari, Sunder Rajan "The Division of Experience in *The Shadow Lines*," in Ghosh, 287-98.

rjb@giasbmol.vsnl.net.in from Mumbai, India, 10 Oct. 1992. Online Internet.

Sarkar, Sumit. *Modern India 1885-1947*. Madras: Macmillan India, 1983.

Sidney, Philip. *Defence of Poetry*, ed. Dorsten Jan Van. Delhi: Oxford University Press, 1978.

Sidhwa, Bapsi. *Ice-Candy-Man*. London: William Heinemann, 1988.

Sikri, S.M., former Chief Justice of India, Badr-ud-Din Tyabji, former Commonwealth Secretary, Rajeshwar Dayal, Govind Narain and T.C.A. Srinivasvadaran, compiled. Delhi 31 October to 4 November 1984, Report of the Citizens' Commission, January 1985. Delhi: Citizen's Commission, 1985.

Sudrann, Jean. "Goings and Comings," *Yale Review*, 79 (1990), 414-38.

The Shadow Lines: An Outline

PALLAVI GUPTA

The *Shadow Lines* is broadly divided into two parts: "Going Away" and "Coming Home," which are in keeping with the major preoccupations of the novel. The novel is narrated by an anonymous character who refers to himself as 'I,' and the mode of narration indicates that the narrator is ostensibly relating the experiences of a past which involves his "father's aunt's" son Tridib, his cousin Ila, his uncle Robi, his grandmother Tha'mma, May Price and others.

The first part, "Going Away," begins on a note of recollection as the narrator pens down his relation to Tridib, the latter's leaving for England in 1939 with his parents, and the muted love-hate relationship which his grandmother shares with Tridib, whom she considers a good-for-nothing. The narrator gives a very detailed picture of his childhood spent on the fringes of Tridib's multifarious personality in the Gole Park episodes. The Prices—close friends of Tridib's parents in England—are introduced in Tridib's conversations with his Gole Park cronies, in particular May Price, an oboe player, whom Tridib has known since childhood. The narrator meets her when she visits Calcutta and then again when he goes to London to work on his Ph.D. thesis. It is this meeting which reveals that Tridib and May have been corresponding with each other since 1959 and accounts for Tridib's precise knowledge of the Prices, specially May, whom he had reconstructed for his Gole Park friends from a photograph she had sent him.

After Tridib and May, Ila is introduced. Having met off and on, the narrator and Ila have one point of reference—Tridib.

However, the narrator's fascination with and memories of Tridib far exceed that of Ila's. His world peopled with his imagination of places and Tridib's memories of places is the opposite of Ila's which is crowded with factual experience of places that she has visited, but without any treasured memories except for the schools in which she has studied.

The narration, at this juncture shifts to the near past and we see Ila, Robi, and the narrator in a pub in London. Their conversation meanders between incidents of the past—the Snake episode in Colombo—and debates on imagination. The narrative flashes back to the narrator's past and then to Tha'mma's as she recounts for him the felt experience of the national struggle for freedom. Back in the pub, the narrator reminds Ila how she herself had invented London for him once, and then relates a long incident to her which had occurred when they were both eight-year-old: the picnic where they met as children, proves to be an event which bonds them as children and Ila shares her admiration for Nick Price—May's brother—with an evidently jealous narrator. He does meet Nick Price in London, seventeen years later, when Ila arranges a meeting with the Prices. The narrator, in the course of the visit, pieces together the puzzle from bits of his memories of what Ila and Tridib had told him about the Prices, their home, and London.

On arriving at Mrs. Price's house—44, Lymington Road—the narrator is escorted into the same room into which Tridib and his parents had entered seventeen years earlier. The changeless quality of the room enables the narrator to identify the pictures on the wall and give a body to the memories which Tridib had shared with him. Ila's memories serve as guides for the narrator when it comes to exploring the house, much to the bewilderment of the onlookers, and the racism to which she has been subjected as a child in London, not only by the children in her school, but also, sadly, Nick Price who avoided her because he did not want to be seen with an Indian.

At this point, the narrative shifts to the time when Tha'mma is battling her final illness and vehemently argues against Ila's staying in London. The narrator is then studying in a college in Delhi and has come home on leave. In Tha'mma's vocabulary, you belong to that place which you have helped build, and so Ila has no business being in London. The argument which ensues between Tha'mma and the narrator ends with the latter justifying Ila's residence in a foreign land.

The scene shifts to the time when Ila comes to visit Calcutta. As both Robi and the narrator are there for their holidays, they decide to party in order to celebrate Robi's departure. This meeting also reveals that Ila has come to mean much more to the narrator than just a cousin' but he is unable to articulate his feelings for her. But the party proves to be a disaster as Ila's absolute morality is unable to distinguish the difference between drinking and dancing in a pub in London and doing the same in a nightclub in Calcutta. It is also this incident which is the narrator's answer to his grandmother's earlier question with regard to Ila. It is Ila's need to be free from the cultural bond which does not allow her to be herself or to be free which makes her reject her own country.

The narrator's return to Delhi is followed by Tha'mma's demise and the receipt of a letter by the Dean of his college from Tha'mma. The letter accusing him of visiting women of ill-repute in Delhi makes the narrator realize that his grandmother knew of his erratic visits to prostitutes and of his unrequited love for Ila.

Back in London, the narrator decides to visit Ila and confess his love to her; but Ila's absolute imperviousness to his feelings prevents him. He goes to meet her at the accommodation she shares with three others—an Irish computer scientist, a girl from Leicester who works with the Fourth International, and a 'morose,' young Ghanaian who is very active in the anti-Nazi league. For her flat-mates, Ila is "a kind of guest, a decoration almost." (97) The narrator meets Nick here, on and off, and the day he goes to visit her she declares that he is badly in need of clothes. She suggests that they visit 'Brick Lane'—"a place where there are lots of cheap retail shops run by Indians and Bangladeshis." (98) Brick Lane surfaces as another piece of the complex jigsaw puzzle which the narrator has in his memory. The 'London Jamme Masjid' turns out to be the place which housed a synagogue when Alan Tresawsen—Nick's uncle—lived here during the War. The story of Alan and his three friends—Dan, Mike, and Francesca—which begins when the narrator visits the Prices for the first time comes full circle as he reveals to the astonished Ila and the disgruntled Nick that his uncle had been killed here in a bomb attack. The narrator's inquisitiveness regarding Nick's job in Kuwait earns him Ila's ire and she summarily closes the door on him, for a fortnight.

They meet again at a dinner given by the Prices on Christmas Eve, and much to the narrator's bewilderment, Ila enquires as to where he had disappeared. The secret of Ila's previous burst of anger is revealed when May asks Nick to "tell the truth" (109) and accept the reality of losing his job in Kuwait on charges of embezzling money. The mood of the party changes thereafter as Nick insults May and remains so throughout the dinner. As there is a blizzard blowing outside, May invites the narrator to spend the night with them. As Ila also is persuaded to stay, she and the narrator share a room, and the incidents of the night make Ila realize the narrator's feelings for her. Though she pities him, she cannot reciprocate his love for her, and the narrator realizes "the inequality of [their] needs," (112) and pushes this aspect of himself into the past.

The second part "Coming Home" begins on a note of reminiscence and like "Going Away" is characterized by a recollection on the part of the narrator. However, unlike the beginning of "Going Away" in which the narrator is relating events which had occurred before his birth and hence smacks of reportage, the opening of the second part is from a past in which the narrator has himself figured. The event, dated 1962, is Tha'mma's retirement at the age of 60 from the post of Headmistress of a girl's school. The tearful affection with which the staff and students alike bid farewell to her arouses the narrator's jealousy as he "had always taken it for granted that it was [his] own special right to love her." (115)

Tha'mma's retirement from the public sphere brews trouble at home as she starts paying attention to things she had never bothered about before: she nags her daughter-in-law, imagines that she is going bald and begins an impossible ayurvedic treatment, and persists in plaguing the new headmistress at the school. Her lack of activity affects her mentally and she starts losing her zest for living. 1962 is a good year for the narrator's family as his father is promoted to the post of General Manager and they shift from their "cramped little flat in Gole Park" to "a new house on Southern Avenue." (119) The change of residence induces Tha'mma to talk about her house in Dhaka. The house shared by Tha'mma's father and his elder brother falls apart when their grandfather dies. The wives quarrel and the brothers follow suit, and, eventually the house is divided with such exactitude that even the father's nameplate is bisected. While Mayadebi's renowned beauty earns her the Shaheb—Tridib's father—Tha'mma is wedded off to an engineer in Burma. The narrator's father is born in Burma and at the age of ten, loses his father to pneumonia. Tha'mma is lucky to possess a bachelor's degree in history which enables her to obtain a job in Calcutta. Though she yearns to see her old "upside-down" (125) house in Dhaka, the partition puts an end to it.

Winter sets in and Tha'mma enlarges her circle of acquaintances in Southern Avenue. One day she discovers "Minadi" whose "family used to live down the lane from us in Dhaka." (128) This meeting gives Tha'mma a chance to connect with her disjointed past and her forgotten relatives—ones whom she had never wondered about. Aided by Minadi's servant, they visit Tha'mma's cousin's widow in Garia, and Tha'mma discovers that her father's elder brother, Jethamoshai, is still alive and living in the same house in Dhaka. This bit of news awakens the Samaritan in Tha'mma and she starts thinking of a mission of "rescuing her uncle from his enemies and bringing him back where he belonged." (137)

It is about this time that May receives her fourth letter from Tridib telling her that he would like to meet her "as a stranger—in a ruin . . . in a place without a past, without history, free, really free." (144) The pornographic contents of the letter, in the form of a childhood experience during the war, make May very angry.

For Tha'mma there occurs a happy coincidence as the Shaheb is posted to Dhaka and soon she is invited to visit Dhaka. For Tha'mma it is a "coming home" to Dhaka. At about the same time May is expected to arrive in Calcutta and Tridib asks the narrator to accompany him to the station.

Forward in time, Ila marries Nick, and this is the first time that the narrator speaks to May about her visit to Calcutta. An inebriated narrator is offered shelter by May in her apartment at Islington and he tries to force himself on her. A hangover and the events of the previous night bring forth a penitent man but May's maturity in handling the situation makes things quite normal once again. May's schedule demands that she go out "collecting money for one of [her] several worthy causes," (162) and the narrator accompanies her. Collecting money together, they go down memory lane, to the time when May had visited Calcutta and the time they had spent together with Tridib. Unable, then, to understand the nature of Tridib's and May's relationship, the narrator had considered it a loss of privilege; but now, he realizes that they had been in love.

A few days before he returns to Delhi, he receives a call from Ila, who has returned from her honeymoon with Nick. Her over-solicitous concern for the narrator amazes the latter, as does her readiness to do little odd-jobs for him. Ila's need for him transports the narrator to the time when they were both eight-year-old, and Ila had just finished telling him her imaginary story about her experience of racism. Tridib's timely intervention is welcomed when he offers to tell them a story to mollify a howling Ila. The story which he tells them, has in turn been told to him by Snipe, Mrs. Price's husband, when Tridib was nine-year-old. The story is meant to be a birthday present as well as a reward for numerous visits to the chemist on Snipe's behalf. The story is about Tristan and Isolde, but neither the narrator nor Ila can recall it in the present. However, one thing becomes evident to the narrator—

Ila's tears as an eight-year-old and her tears now are both related to Nick Price. An outraged and heartbroken Ila tells him, eventually, that Nick has been cheating on her but makes it very clear that she would never leave him. Soon the narrator discovers that "she had invented her own ways of punishing [Nick]," (189) which are primarily put into action by humiliating him in front of his mother by casually remarking about his deficiencies. While observing Nick, the narrator is transported back to the time when May had come to Calcutta, and on being asked about Nick, had remarked, "he's not like us." (189)

3rd January 1964 is the date set for Tha'mma's departure to Dhaka and a day before that Tha'mma receives a letter from her sister, Mayadebi, in which the latter reports the happy discovery of Jethamoshai and their home. The house, it is discovered, has been converted into a workshop for a mechanic called Saifuddin. Tha'mma, Tridib, and May depart for Dhaka on the appointed day and are received by Mayadebi and Robi at the airport. Tha'mma's enthusiastic plans about rescuing Jethamoshai from his enemies are postponed for a week by the Shaheb who diagnoses 'trouble' to come in that area. (197) On this side of the border too, the narrator recalls the presence of 'trouble,' in the form of rumours regarding the poisoning of Calcutta's water supply. An ordinary school-day turns into a horrible nightmare for the narrator as he vicariously participates in the frenzy of a city gone mad.

On the other side of the border, the events are reported through Robi's memories. The day for visiting Jethamoshai arrives and the family sets out. The group is composed of the two sisters Tha'mma and Mayadebi, Tridib, Robi, May, the driver, and a security guard. They discover that while the courtyard has been taken over by the mechanic, the house is occupied by Khalil, a rickshaw-puller, and his family. It is Khalil who takes care of Jethamoshai and is completely devoted to the old man. The senile condition of Jethamoshai's mind prevents him from recognizing them as his relatives, and what he remembers of them is not very flattering for them. Jethamoshai offers a new perspective on the question of being a Hindu in a Muslim-dominated area, by rejecting his sons' offer in the past, and his nieces' offer now to quit his "home." While Saifuddin insists that they take the old man along, with or without his consent, Khalil pleads that he be left with them. Eventually, it is decided that for his safety he would have to be moved. However, he is to be escorted in Khalil's rickshaw as he would only step out on the pretext of going to the court. The plan is that Khalil, in his rickshaw, is to follow their car and deliver him to his relatives. The expectancy of trouble hovers over them and soon enough they run into trouble in the form of rowdy and armed boys and strategically lit bonfires.

The narrative breaks off at this point and the narrator confesses his inability to speak of the events of 1964 as they "lie outside the reach of [his] intelligence." (218) It takes him fifteen years to figure out the connection between the events that had taken place in 1964 in Dhaka and Calcutta, which occur accidentally, while he is attending a talk on the China war of 1962. Speaking of bygone days to his friends, he gets into an argument with them and on going over old newspapers discovers that riots had occurred on both sides of the border, but had received too scant attention to become headlines. In his memory, he recalls Tha'mma's frenzied desire to donate her chain and her blood for the sake of her grandchild and his freedom. He also recalls his mother pacifying him and telling him, "She's never been the same you know, since they killed Tridib over there." (237) One and a half years after Tridib's death, the truth dawns on the narrator of the cause of Tridib's death. While he had been told earlier that Tridib had "an accident in Dhaka," (239) for the first time, he has an inkling that Tridib's death had been caused by reasons other than an accident.

Seventeen years later, the truth of Tridib's death is revealed to the narrator by Robi, who was an eyewitness to the murder. Robi's memory sparked off by a chance remark of a waiter, makes him relive the excruciatingly painful memory of the day Tridib was killed. The other half of the memory is supplied by May, who has been ridden with guilt, blaming herself for Tridib's death. After relating her guilt to the narrator, she realizes that Tridib's act of going after her into the mob was a sacrifice: and though she does not understand it, she knows that she must persevere "for any real sacrifice is a mystery." (252) The novel ends with a sense of gratitude on the narrator's part to May for having given him the glimpse of "a final redemptive mystery." (252)

Some Recent Trends in Modern Indian Fiction: A Study of Shashi Deshpande's *That Long Silence*, Shashi Tharoor's *The Great Indian Novel* and Amitav Ghosh's *The Shadow Lines*

SHAKUNTALA BHARVANI

The last decade has yielded an abundant harvest in the field of fiction. Expatriate writers, Bharati Mukherjee, Gita Mehta, Ruth Prawer Jhabvala and Rohinton Mistry, too, have been in the limelight; to this list may be added the names of Anita Desai and Nayantara Sahgal, who live in India but have greater appeal to the sophisticated Westernized reader. But it is not possible to discuss so many writers in an overview so limited, thus I will concentrate on theme, language and innovative technique in three recent Indian novels in English: Shashi Deshpande's *That Long Silence*,[1] Shashi Tharoor's *The Great Indian Novel*[2] and Amitav Ghosh's *The Shadow Lines*.[3]

I

Shashi Deshpande's achievement lies in the depiction of her central character, the introspective and inward probing Jaya. She is representative of girls brought up in middle-class families in post-Independent India, a time when most parents strove hard to provide their children with English education and exposure to Western modes of living and thinking. Parents inculcated in their girls a certain duality, sometimes quite unconsciously: on the one hand an impulsive desire to be emancipated and liberated, and on the other, an almost instinctive urge to be traditional and conservative. The woman of today, therefore, speaking in the language of psychology, has a near-schizophrenic personality: one side staidly "accepts" while the other craves to "speak," to think and express the life of the mind. *That Long Silence* presents Jaya caught in this dilemma: first, trying to be a fit wife to her husband and secondly, struggling to express the kind of emotions women experience, but seldom express in a male-dominated chauvinistic society.

This is not to state categorically that Deshpande is a militant feminist; her work merely reflects the resulting turmoil and vexation. As she herself states: "Innermost feelings come out in my writings. The kind of emotions we know women have but never come out."[4]

The smooth course of Jaya's existence has been disrupted due to her husband's business problems. He moves into an unfashionable Bombay apartment in Dadar relinquishing all company perks. Jaya finds herself free from the round of high-order entertainment. She ponders on her far from successful writing career and her past memories. In the process of doing this she probes inward, thus emerging from her long moments of silence.

The novel is difficult to read as several characters appear and disappear and seem to serve no ostensible purpose. Statements such as, "Deshpande's style needs a lot more exercising and experimentation" and "The plot, too, would be better structured if some of the fringe characters were left out"[5] are valid criticisms. This is the case, too, with Deshpande's earlier novel *Roots and Shadows*, where even a family tree on the introductory page does not really make for a clearer concept of the novel. But Deshpande's convincing portrait of Jaya, with her veneer of middle-class respectability, is commendable. The questions that haunt her, for example, would never haunt a woman from the sophisticated razzle-dazzle jet-set in which divorce and free love are the in-thing; but they certainly bother Jaya who is brought up to regard even film and pop-music as frivolous. I quote a few lines from the last few pages to illustrate the quality of Jaya's thinking:

> What have I achieved by this writing? The thought occurs to me again as I look at the neat pile of papers. Well, I've achieved this. I'm not afraid any more. The panic has gone. I'm Mohan's wife, I had thought, and cut off the bits of me that had refused to be Mohan's wife. Now I know that kind of a fragmentation is not possible. (191)
>
> While studying Sanskrit drama, I'd learnt with a sense of outrage that its rigid rules did not permit women characters to speak Sanskrit. They had to use Prakrit—a language that had sounded to my ears like a baby's lisp. The anger I'd felt then comes back to me when I realize what I've been doing all these years. I have been speaking Prakrit myself. (192-93)

Virginia Woolf's Mrs. Dalloway or Anita Brookner's heroines could not have been more eloquent on the imbalance in such human relationships.

Though Deshpande's work has not created waves, it certainly needs to be taken note of. Born in Dharwar in Karnataka, she is the daughter of the Kannada playwright and Sanskrit critic, Shriranga. She lives in Bangalore, has two children and her husband is a pathologist. Her earlier four novels are: *Roots and Shadows* which was judged the best novel of 1982-83, *The Dark Holds No Terrors* and two detective novels *If I Die Today* and *Come Up and Be Dead*. At present she is working on a script for Govind Nihalani on man-woman relationships, for which Kishori Amonkar will set the music. *Roots and Shadows* is also being screened by director Prema Karnath.

II

Shashi Tharoor in *The Great Indian Novel*, with superb verve, vivacity and a style eminently readable, adapts the *Mahabharata* story to project the recent political history of India.

The ancient epic is retold not by the rishi Vyasa of old but by the venerable and cantankerous politician saint Ved Vyasji to Ganapathi (the scribe, amanuensis and silent bystander). For those familiar with Rajagopalachari's *Mahabharata*, it is necessary only to read the first few pages to realize that Tharoor's is a masterful parody amounting to "a comic epic in prose" which is grotesque and even offensive in parts.

It is little difficult to understand the traditional Indian psyche without understanding our great epic. The Kauravas and Pandavas are archetypal figures, and their experiences are possible patterns of a universal nature. They are relevant today, and refresh our memory at each stage. This is exactly what *The Great Indian Novel* succeeds in doing.

Like Gita Mehta's recent novel *Raj* it is certainly historical, but it is much more. Like Golding's *Lord of the Files*, it is sociological and satirical as well, for it describes history and society of the India of Mahaguru Gangaji, who presents of course, Mahatma Gandhi. The struggle for Independence, the practice of non-violence and satyagraha, the indigo-march, Nehru and "Priya Duryodhani" are part of the scene. Most of the characters are ludicrous, thinly-veiled historical figures, but the identity of several is chameleon-like and shadow-vague. The presentation of the historical ethos of this period is credible and naturally so, for after graduating from St. Stephen's College, Delhi, Tharoor took a doctorate from the Fletcher School of Law and Diplomacy at Tufts University, USA. Since May 1978, he has worked in Geneva and Singapore for the United Nations High Commissioner for Refugees.

Shashi Tharoor's novel is written in pristine Queen's English with an almost Wodehousian tongue-in-cheek manner. The first 100 pages take the reader by surprise at Tharoor's audacity and extremely cavalier attitude to the *Mahabharata* story and his grossly cynical-critical attitude to Indian life and politics. After this, interest wanes as the analogy is stretched and far-fetched. But is it Tharoor's style which reminds the reader how far ahead the Indian novel in English has progressed. A polished sophisticated elegance of a man about town who is Indian in sensibility—and totally at home with words he can mould and bend at will—this is the most distinctive achievement of Tharoor's *The Great Indian Novel.* I quote one example: "But you see, I'm getting ahead of my story again, Ganapathi. You mustn't let me. I haven't yet told you about Kunti, Pandu's faithfully infidelous wife, and how she fulfilled her husband's extraordinary request for progeny." (86)

III

The Shadow Lines by Amitav Ghosh is a remarkable novel by any standards as it transcends the narrow categorization of an Indian novel. The story centres around Tridib, the narrator's uncle. No less vivid and memorable are the portraits of the narrator's grandmother, his cousin Ila and the English girl May Price. The novel creates a wonderful scene of relationships—uncles and aunts are interspersed easily and without any confusion in the course of the narrative, as are also different locations—Calcutta, Dacca, London. We learn that Tridib was born in 1932, had been to England with his parents in 1939, where his father, an important diplomat in the Foreign Service, had received medical treatment. May Price (with whose family they shared a close relationship) had begun a long correspondence with Tridib in 1959. Tridib died in a riot in 1964, while May was on a visit to India.

It is not, however, such events that make up the vital texture of the novel: we are made aware of them only incidentally. What holds our attention is the delicate thread out of which the narrator creates a larger-than-life portrait of Tridib, who used his imagination not to fantasize but to expand his sense of meaning and erase the narrow barriers of lines and partitions. The narrator fondly reminisces: "Tridib . . . who had given me worlds to travel in and eyes to see them with." *The Shadow Lines* takes the reader into the consciousness of several characters, particularly the narrator's grandmother, Ila's parents and May Price. Each consciousness emerges in light and shade, etched with its own individual quirks and idiosyncracies; each cnaracter is caught between shadow lines in the wasteland of prejudice, dogma and a narrow nationalism. *The*

Shadow Lines ends with the mystery of Tridib's voluntary death—a death symbolic of his sacrifice for humanity.

Time past merges fluidly with time present. At the very start of the novel we have the narrator, a young boy, gazing with respect and admiration as Tridib "makes-up" a story for his group of friends at his *adda* at Gole Park—with a view to impress them about his English connections. This is followed by a long digression about the narrator's own visit to England and his meetings with May Price after Tridib's death. The pendulum swings to the present again at this stage: we are back to the narrator's childhood with his cousin Ila and her mother, nick-named Queen Victoria. Within the first two pages, there are several time-switches, the movement seems natural and easy, making no special demands on the reader. This deft handling of time, in which the "expanded" moment embraces within it, present and past time, gives the novel a Proustian richness and complexity. It is clear that with Ghosh the Indian novel in Englsih has surpassed the rigid barriers of time, place and action, thus making most earlier Indian fiction seem dated and simplistic.

The literary and cultural atmosphere of Calcutta's teashops is quite naturally evoked, and is as easily recognizable as the cigarette which smoulders near Tridib's ashtray when he is engrossed in intellectual activity of a higher kind. The riot and the subsequent events that lead to his death filter through to the reader as the narrator records his research experience while he is sitting one afternoon in 1979 in the Teen Murti House Library, New Delhi. The riots have always remained a mystery to him as he records: "Every word I write about those events of 1964 is the product of a struggle with silence. It is a struggle I am destined to lose." (218) Among the records of January 1964, he reads about the disappearance of the "sacred relic known as the Mui-i-Mubarak"—a hair of the prophet Mohammed, from the Hazratbal Mosque. The cause of the riots, not clear to him earlier, now impinges on his consciousness and he realizes that communal riotss which had been sparked off in Kashmir had spread to Pakistan, Bangladesh and Calcutta. He looks at the atlas which once belonged to

Tridib, Tridib whose imagination surmounted all barriers and borders. He ruminates: "They had drawn their borders, believing in that pattern, in the enhancement of lines, hoping perhaps that once they had etched their borders upon the map, the two bits of land would sail away from each other like the shifting tectonic plates of the prehistoric Gondwanaland. What had they felt, I wondered, when they discovered that they had created not a separation, but a yet-undiscovered irony—the irony that killed Tridib." (232) As the narrator reads on, he passes on from uncertainty to certainty, he is born anew as it were.

The title of the novel is symbolic of barriers and partitions. Individuals stand divided, as do families, nations and countries. Tridib who had tried to teach the narrator "to use his imagination with precision" meets his death because of the violence of nationalism, ironically enough when he is trying to guard his friend, the English girl, from blind Hindu-Muslim hatred. Ghosh subtly suggests that shadow-lines divide, tear, embitter human beings; this artistically leads to the sudden revelation or Joycean epiphany experienced by the narrator towards the end of the novel. It is a novel with a message and a philosophy—this is unfolded in an intricately and colourfully woven piece of tapestry by a sensitive and skilful artisan.

This probing deep into the consciousness of his characters and at the same time studying them as members of a social community certainly does not come as a surprise. Ghosh, born in Calcutta in 1956, a graduate from Delhi University, is a Social Anthropologist with a D.Phil. in the subject from Oxford. He is also the author of *The Circle of Reason*.

Not very long ago the novelist expressed himself in a language to which he was alien but not quite, a language he had mastered grammatically and correctly as a second language. Uneasy and yet appropriately, he took for his theme and background the Raj, colonial India and post-Independent India. He wrote about his country, either in an idealized manner, or in one which would appeal to a foreign reader. He simplified the complexities of Indian life and culture; his language was English but in thought and sensibility he hovered between two worlds. The trio of the twentieth century—R.K. Narayan, Raja Rao and Mulk Raj Anand—laid the foundation of Indian literature in English, but the "Indianness" of their images can certainly be questioned.

These three novels indicate a major advance. The authors have successfully harnessed a foreign language to a sensibility that is essentially Indian as well as modern.

NOTES

1. Shashi Deshpande, *That Long Silence* (Virago, 1988; Penguin, 1989).
2. Shashi Tharoor, *The Great Indian Novel* (Penguin, 1989).
3. Amitav Ghosh, *The Shadow Lines* (New Delhi: Ravi Dayal, 1988).
4. Ratna Rao Shekhar, "Shashi Deshpande: *That Long Silence* Breaks," *Society*, Bombay, Dec. 1989.
5. Usha Hemmadi, "A Middle-Class Tale," *The Indian Post*, Sept. 17, 1989.

Shadow Lines: Cross-Cultural Perspectives in the Fiction of Amitav Ghosh

LOUIS JAMES

> The novel is the only developing genre and therefore it reflects more deeply, more essentially, more sensitively and rapidly, reality itself in the process of its unfolding. Only that which is itself developing can comprehend development as process. The novel has become the leading hero in the literary development of our time precisely because it best of all reflects the tendencies of a new world still in the making; it is, after all, the only genre born of this new world and in total affinity with it.[1]

Bakhtin was writing in a European context, but could have been addressing with even sharper relevance that of new literatures in English. Bakhtin identified the novel as the "open ended" literary form of the modern age, reflecting and bringing together many languages ("heteroglossia"). These languages are not simply linguistic, but socio-ideological" idioms and forms, voices from different strata of cultural experience.

Amitav Ghosh's work introduces a number of "languages," including those of the Indian folk-tale, the *Mahabharata,* journalism, and the memory patterns of the extended family, radically de-constructing traditional novel forms. In a genre associated in Europe with "realism," Ghosh explores Vedic concepts of Maya (illusion) and transcendence to question the possibility of Western realism. In the opening section of *The Circle of Reason,* the village capitalist, Bhudeb Roy, organizes a festival to Saraswati which Ghosh identifies rather loosely as "the

Hindu Goddess of Learning."[2] He has a six-foot image built, with spinning electric lights behind the eyes and a silver-foil halo. During the ceremony the rationalist Balaram leaps onto the platform with defiling sandals and tears off the dyed cotton hair, revealing the clay underneath. "This is not Saraswati, Learning," he cries to the electrified crowd, "it is Vanity." At a deep level, the image of Saraswati *is* "Vanity," for in the Vedic tradition she is a feminine principle and aspect of nature, and only becomes "knowledge" in flowing through the enlightened devotee—Bhudeb Roy is certainly not enlightened. But Balaram is equally benighted—he "exposes" the image not because this misrepresents the tradition, but because it does not represent his concept of Westernized rationalism.

Towards the end of the book there is another festival, the reenactment of Chitrangada's appearance to Arjuna. In the story, taken from the *Mahabharata* via Tagore, the warrior princess Chitrangada is granted the gift of physical beauty for a year in order to attract Arjuna. She becomes his lover, but Arjuna, not knowing the transformation, is drawn by hearsay to Chitrangada's other self. After the year, Arjuna sees her without her beauty, and understands the illusion of the physical. (382) The two episodes are alike and yet opposites. In the first, a religious image is unmasked, showing the crude substance beneath; in the second, physical reality is dissipated to reveal the spiritual.

In both, the real significance of the ritual has been missed. In the first, traditional belief has been prostituted as a means of publicity by the grossly materialistic Bhudeb Roy; in the second, the original legend has been sentimentalized by Tagore and is being played on a gramophone record, in a language the participants cannot understand, in an alien country. Chitrangada is being played by a prostitute, Kulfi. This does and does not invalidate the myths. Misused and misunderstood, the two episodes do have a meaning—the first in the cycle of conflict within which Alu begins his quest for a higher meaning; the second, in the movement that redeems Kulfi (who is given a full ritual burial), and turns Alu back to India. Only through illusion can truth be found.

The concern with the cyclical process of the activity of life underpins the whole book. Reality is Maya, illusion, but only through Maya can reality be understood. The three sections of the novel follow the three Vedic Gunas—Sattva, Rajas and Tamas,—the three aspects of nature ('prakriti') without which no action is possible, taking the development from rising awareness of "Reason," through "Passion," to "Death" or entropy. The process also brings together the divergent stylistic levels of the book—that of an exuberant folk-tale, of the emergence of a human community, and the dialectic between Indian and European consciousness in an alien predicament.

The opening sections focus on a village near the future India-Pakistan border, where Balaram embodies the impact of nineteenth-century scientific reason on India. For Balaram, the modern age began with Pasteur's development of disinfectant and innoculation, and Madame Curie's experiments with radiation to control cancer cells. With these scientific discoveries Balaram believes superstition and ignorance were done away, and the scientific basis of life established. Armed with this knowledge he wages a heroic war against the corrupt commercialism of his arch-enemy, Bhudeb Roy. Yet the inadequacy of this view is hilariously underlined by Balaram's attempt to answer all problems, including war, with buckets of carbolic acid.

Indeed Balaram's concepts of the "new science" were already out of date, Curie and Pasteur being both creators of a new consciousness and the inheritors of the old. Again Ghosh complicates the issue. For Balaram's reliance on a nineteenth-century pseudo-science, Phrenology, in fact approximates to the Indian "superstition" of popular religion and astrology that he opposes. His search for a new Western vision of reality, reflected in the chapter titled "a Pasteurised universe," brings to mind the Vedic legend of the creation of the world, in which the milk ocean of creation was churned by the gods and demons using a snake to separate the poison from the "amrit" (ambrosia). Shiva drank the poison, purifying (pasteurising) the universe. However the outcome was that only the gods drank the "Amrit": Ghosh suggests Balaram also has a one-sided strategy.

Into the story comes Alu, his name, literally "potato." Alu gains his name because his head, of such interest to Balaram, is lumpy like a spud. But Alu, who emerges as the real hero of the book, is also basic, unlovely but ever-renewed, a child of the folk, a creature of the earth. While Balaram pursues his intellectual war against Bhudeb Roy in a landscape scarificed by the internecine India-Pakistan conflict, Alu becomes a master-weaver. Weaving is a central image of the book, bringing together its many paradoxes and opposites. A craft, using the cotton indigenous to India from prehistoric times, it is a paradigm Indian culture. Yet as a mechanical process, it embodies the commercial exploitation that undermine all human societies. "When the history of the world broke, cotton and cloth were behind it; mechanical man in pursuit of his own destruction . . . millions of African and half of America were enslaved by cotton." (57)

When a misdirected flare ignites Balaram's defensive arsenal, Alu escapes with a sewing machine and Balaram's *Life of Pasteur*. Pursued south to Kerala by the police detective Jyoti Das, who becomes a figure of death as the book progresses, Alu crosses the Indian ocean to the imaginary Gulf State of Al-Ghazira with a boatload of Indian women, destined for the town's brothels by Zindi. Sexual, predatory and physically dominating, Zindi is an ambivalent figure of womanhood whose machinations continue whatever quest idealism may pursue. Al-Ghazira is an oil state, a chaotic meeting of the traditional folk, the old tyranny of the Emirs, and the Western pressures of colonial administration and post-colonial exploitation.

A huge economic centre has risen in the desert as a monument to a progress no one wants: when it collapses, Alu is buried in the dead-centre, the rubble arrested by a fallen beam inches from his nose. When he emerges after days of meditation, it is with the inspiration that money, not germs, are destroying civilization. The vision is as flawed as that of Balaram, and when the revolutionary society led by Abu Fahl is crushed by the state, it is with Zindi, Kulfi (an inmate of Zindi's brothel) and an orphan child called Boss that Alu escapes. Following in reverse the routes by which European culture travelled to India, they reach Tunisia, chosen by Ghosh as an instance of a political integration of European and African cultures. Here the trio meet up with an expatriate Indian doctor, Dr. Verma.

The "circle" is closing. For if Balaram came to his vision of reason through biology, attacking deviant microbes with his panacea of carbolic acid, Dr. Verma comes to a Hindu reverence of life also from a basic in microbiology. Dr. Verma even has a *Life of Pasteur*. In it she points out to Alu that the germ both brings death and makes the possibility of life. "It says without the germ 'life would be impossible because death would be incomplete.'" (356) It is Dr. Verma who organizes a dramatic reenactment of the play by Tagore, already mentioned, where the princess Chitrangada, returned to her plain appearance, is seen in her essence by Arjuna. Dr. Verma has to take what Indian actors she can find, and as noted above, when the scene is enacted, within the costumes Kulfi the prostitute takes the part of Chitrangada, while the warrior Arjuna is played by the police-agent Jyoti Das. Kulfi expresses a moment of intense sexual desire and crashes to the ground, clutching her heart, dead.

"Heavenly. Her fathers have gathered her to their heavenly abode" intones Dr. Verma, dressed as Madana, the God of Love. (400) The cycle of death and regeneration is almost complete. After Alu has gone to great lengths to give Kulfi a proper Indian burial, he is told by Dr. Verma that this will give him a reason for going home, and the book ends with Alu, Boss and Zindi, turning back towards India, while the death-bearing Jyoti Das looks towards Europe.

The Circle of Reason is an extraordinarily accomplished first novel. It combines wit, intelligence and creative innovation to explore new possibilities for the novel form in the Indian context. Yet it is not wholly successful. The different narrative strategies pull apart, and the substructure, of knowledge working its way through the stages of the three Gunas, does not sufficiently unite the divergent sections. Moreover the work suffers from being *too* complex for its imaginative integrity: at times one becomes aware of Ghosh's manipulation.

II

In *The Shadow Lines,* Ghosh finds a sharper unifying focus. The novel brings together the forms of the autobiographical novel and the family chronicle, to subvert both. "I am born" begins Dickens' *David Copperfield.* "In 1939, thirteen years before I was born," begins *The Shadow Lines.* Ghosh's novel introduces a family "tree," but it is not the legally-defined family of European society, of Galsworthy's *Forsyte Saga* or Thomas Mann's *Buddenbrooks*—rather, it is the Asian extended family of loyalties, affections and associations. This becomes so complex that even the narrator confesses confusion and the novel is to some extent about the meaning of family relationships in a distintegrating world. "Shadow Lines" of the title refers both to lines of separation, and the invisible links which bind.

There are several lines of family introduced—that of the narrator, based in Calcutta; that of his grandmother's sister, associated with Dhaka, and two further lines bringing into the story Robi and Ila. But the blood relationships merge with those forged by intimacy, as with the British family, linked through domicile in India, of Lionel Tresawsen. The narrator's closest links are with Mayadebi, his grandmother's sister, and with her son Tridib, the enigmatic older friend through which the "I" narrator experiences much of his life.

For if *Circle of Reason* is about "Knowledge," *Shadow Lines* is about "Knowing." The novel moves through an intricate weaving backwards and forwards in time. Narrative sequence is constantly frustrated by the intrusion of memory—memory working not, as in James Joyce's *Ulysses,* as a stream-of-consciousness, so much as remembered family histories, restructured in a search for meaning. Memories sharpen into focus, then blur: "Although I cannot remember when it happened any more than I can remember when I first learnt to tell the time or tie my shoelaces."[3] "I don't know, I can't tell: that world is closed to me, shut off by too many years spent away." (13) Can we ever be sure? One of the most vivid episodes in the novel, a sexual encounter in a bombed theatre, is related by Tridib to May and so taken at third hand by the narrator. But even Tridib cannot be certain of how far his memory has been accurate: "he didn't know whether it had really happened or he had imagined it." Yet this does not invalidate memory. "Reality" for its own sake does not have any specific truth." Ila who claims to be "objective" remembers the cities she has visited by the airport lavatories. (26) Tridib gives meaning to his experience through his imagination, but not wilfully. He teaches the narrator to "use [his] imagination with precision." (29)

Not that the ostensibly "practical" Ila is free from illusion. One of the recurrent motifs in the book is the mental creation of a house from another, secret, place—a vivid expression of the relationship between real and imagined "homes." Arriving in the Tresawsen's house in London, the narrator knows the position of every room. This is because when a child he had been taken to hide in a cellar below Ila's family home in Dhaka, where they had "played houses." Ila had traced out for him an imaginary house, which we discover is identical in form to the London house where Ila had spent her childhood. In the cellar, as they play at having a family, it becomes clear their doll-child represents the earlier Ila. Yet the doll is blue-eyed and flaxen-haired, befriended and protected by the son of the house, Nick Price. In reality Ila was dark, and Nick deserted her: Ila's underground imagination evades reality rather than clarifying it.

The novel gains stature by placing the individual themes starkly in a contemporary context. The shadow lines divide and link peoples and nations. The novel takes place largely on the newly-created Indo-Pakistan border which divides the family and its past. What is this border? Flying over it, the grandmother expects to see some sign. The father laughs—no, it will not be a long black line with green on one side and scarlet on the other. But the grandmother's question is a serious one. If there are no physical signs, where is the difference? Why cannot people as in the past travel from Dhaka to Calcutta without anyone stopping them? What are the 'shadow lines'? (154-55)

Their dual meaning emerges in the final sections of the book when the grandmothers discover a relative, turning senile, left behind in a hostile Dhaka. They go to rescue him—with Robi, May and Tridib. He is trying to escape from the mob when May and Tridib run to his rescue—May is protected by being English, but Tridib, throwing himself to his own death, drawn by the 'shadow line' of imaginative sympathy. Why he should do it is the mystery left by the book. As May says, "He gave himself up; it was a sacrifice. I know I can't understand it. I know I mustn't try, for any real sacrifice is a mystery." (252)

The profoundly personal ending of the book is different indeed in tone to that of Ghosh's first novel. But both end with a ritual, a religious intimation of the cycle and continuation of life. Ghosh's work to-date extends the scope of the novel, not only within its own narrative, but moving outward and beyond the strategies of words, to an exploration of the past and the future of the culture he has inherited.

NOTES

1. Mikhail Bakhtin, "Epic and Novel," *The Dialogic Imagination* (1981), p. 7.
2. Amitav Ghosh, *The Circle of Reason* (New Delhi: Roli Books International, 1986), p. 29.
3. Amitav Ghosh, *The Shadow Lines* (Black Swan edn., Bloomsbury Publishing, 1989), p. 9.

The Shadow Lines and *In an Antique Land*: Some Thematic Considerations

SHARMILA GUHA MAJUMDAR

The two novels under consideration here—*The Shadow Lines* and *In an Antique Land*—deal with history. World War II, our Independence and the partition of the country have provided Amitav Ghosh with raw material against which he studies the historical truths—the meaning of nationalism and political freedom in the modern world—in *The Shadow Lines*. In the first section of the book, called 'Going Away' the story-teller concentrates on London on the eve of, and during, the war, of which he has only a vicarious experience. His knowledge of war was not gained from books but from the experience of his uncle who exercised the greatest influence upon the adolescent story-teller. Tridib taught him how to use imagination and by using this faculty he conjured up certain vivid pictures which by imperceptible degrees merged into a perception of history. In the subsequent sections the author uses the same method to exercise his historical imagination.

In *In an Antique Land* Ghosh has used the mode of the autobiographical traveller's tale to study the past thousand years' history in the context of two continents—Asia and Africa. Naturally the scope of this book is much larger than the former one in both chronological and geographical distribution. But one thing becomes very clear that in both these books, Ghosh's aim is to bring out the unity of human experience notwithstanding the diversity of context.

World War II was generated by militant nationalism and

Ghosh explores the significance of war at two different levels—personal and human. In *The Shadow Lines* the memory of the story-teller shuttles back and forth in time and on his first visit to London he is continuously haunted by Tridib's account of his first visit to London, at 44 Lymington Road where they stayed with the Prices on the eve of the war. In 1939 Tridib's father Saheb, as he was jocularly referred to by his elder sister-in-law, the storyteller's grandmother, took some photographs of Alan Tresawsen, Mrs. Price's brother and his friends. The storyteller recounts in detail what Tridib told him about one of those pictures. It focussed on the tragedy of war as well as on 'exhilaration'—a sense of compassion and fellow-feeling brought about by the shadow of impending death. This sense of exhilaration cut across national borders and both in England and in Germany that was the defence mechanism that people developed to combat the sense of doom. In that picture besides Mayadebi, Mrs. Price and her husband Snipe, there are four others—three young men and a young woman of whom three would be dead within two years. The spectre of war looms large on their lives and "in the foreground of one of those pictures, there is a large, shallow pit. Snipe has been digging that pit for the last two weeks in the back garden. This pit is intended to be the foundation of an Anderson air raid shelter, his second line of defence against the expected German bombs."[1]

With the war hovering on the horizon they knew death was "the most real of their realities." (67) Even before the start of the war they knew that none and nothing of their world would survive. Books, films and photographs are part of history to be studied, analyzed and set aside. But nobody can know the feeling of young, intelligent people who knew they were condemned to death simply because some people have got their priorities wrong.

A couple of pages later there is a vivid description of the house where on that fateful night of September 1940 Dan and Alan died in bombardment. This is a tragedy not only because they were casualties of ruthless nationalism but also because they were people who raised their voices against war-mongering. Ila, who was a member of the socialist movement in Britain, felt proud of being a part of history. She thought Alan and his friends who were witness to the war and fascism, events important in history, must have been as much happy as she was in her political activism. But she never knew that even a small event like a riot did have as much historical importance as a war, as all were results of the politics of hatred, though perhaps on different scales and each provided insight into the personal and human aspects of political violence.

We find a different exposition of the concept of nationalism in a person like the story-teller's grandmother. She was born and brought up in British India. To her, nationalism was a hallowed word, the mainstay of political thinking in the nineteenth and early twentieth century which meant hatred of things British and in her desire to win political freedom she dreamt of killing English officials. She even considered war as a necessary evil which inspired the idea of nationalism and thus strengthened the foundation of a nation. She thought English were a nation because they were reborn in the same pool of bloodshed during wars; blood of their fathers, brothers or sons; while India was yet to emerge as a nation as blood of near and dear ones shed in a war had not baptized Indians. This firebrand nationalism outlived its utility in the late twentieth century and degenerated into a politics of hatred. What was basically a clash of political aspirations was sometimes distorted into senseless animosity. This limited view of nationalism was shared not only by Indians like the grandmother but also by Irishmen like Mike who thought for a person to be rightfully Indian it was necessary to kill Englishmen.

Thus nationalism and war in the European context, nationalism, freedom and partition in Indian context become related things in the author's historical consciousness.

In 'Coming Home' Ghosh comes back to the Indian subcontinent, to Calcutta and Dhaka where he tries to find out the meaning of political freedom. Indian nationalism which was the chief weapon of the freedom fighters in their struggle against foreign rulers could not even ensure the territorial integrity of the country. After partition—the price we are supposed to have paid for our political freedom—nationalism in the Indian context changed its meaning to exclude people on the other side of the border but could not include everybody on this side of paradise. There are several points of view from which Independence, communal riots and partition are seen.

There are people like the story-teller's grandmother who was born and brought up in Dhaka but came to Calcutta long before partition. Unlike so many of their brethren they did not have to feel the pang of being uprooted and to face the daunting task of rebuilding lives from the debris of history. To them 'refugee' was a term of abuse. But even if they did not suffer materially, their emotional wound took a long time to heal and left a deep scar. When seventeen years after partition, the grandmother was going to visit her sister Mayadebi in Dhaka, she was told by her son that at the airport she would have to fill her nationality, her place and date of birth in the disembarkation card she got visibly nervous. As the story-teller realized years later "that she would have to fill in 'Dhaka' as her place of birth on that form . . . and at that moment she had not been able to quite understand how her place of birth had come to be so messily at odds with her nationality" (152) was the reason for her nervousness. This dichotomy in the situation gave rise to confusion and bewilderment in the minds of people even long after partition became a part of the history of the subcontinent. Emotionally they could hardly accept the Radcliffe line and in their own minds wondered like the grandmother "whether [they] would be able to see the border between India and East Pakistan from the plane"; (151) and when told otherwise failed to understand "what was it all for then—partition and all the killings and everything—if there isn't something in between?" (151)

This is the question to which the author addresses himself. The schism in our national life was formalized by drawing a line on the map right through the homeland. Like war this tragedy also brought out the worst as well as the best in human beings on this subcontinent. There have been crude barbarity and also demonstration of the noblest sentiments on both sides of the border. Lakhs of Hindus had to leave their dream behind to swarm to the suburbs of Calcutta. Not a few Muslims like Saifuddin the mechanic had to suffer the same fate. What did political freedom mean to these people? Who can know the feelings of thousands of innocent people who lost their friends and relatives in the communal frenzy?

We take a few minutes off to take a cursory glimpse into post-partition Bengali literature which abounds in stories of these hapless people, their suffering, anger, desperation and determination. Because many Bengali writers of the time came from across the border. I am referring to one such short story by Prativa Basu, significantly titled "Dukulhara"—people who lost their moorings on the other side of the border but failed to strike root on this side.

Bindubasini who lost her husband and son within a year got over her bereavement in course of time, but could never reconcile herself to the loss caused by partition. She was a witness to rioting, killing, groundless apprehension, exodus by villagers. She could not eat, could not sleep, packed bag and baggage in panic and then unpacked at the assurance from her Muslim subjects. But ultimately she had to leave with her widow daughter-in-law and two grand-daughters, one of whom died on their way to India. The other girl and her mother fell prey to flesh-traders while Bindubasini was killed by their accomplice.

The sense of agony and desperation that pervade the story is turned into anger in the grandmother after Tridib's death in 1964 riots in Dhaka. The personal tragedy transformed the meaning of border for the grandmother. Previously she was skeptical about the line, now it becomes something which defines her nationality. When in 1965 war beween India and Pakistan broke out she saw in it a threat to the freedom of her grandson, the future of the nation. The meaning of freedom comes to include fighting away the Pakistanis who barely twenty years ago were her countrymen.

There had also been people like the grandmother's Jethamoshai (father's elder brother) or Saifuddin's father who decided to ignore the shadow line altogether. They did not think it worthwhile to leave their homes just because some politicians were drawing a line somewnere. As Jethamoshai put it, "Once you start moving you never stop. . . . I don't believe in this India—Shindia . . . but suppose when you get there they decide to draw another line somewhere? What will you do then?" (215)

Many years after all this happened, when he tried to revive his memory of the 1964 riots in Calcutta, the story-teller discovered the irony of the entire political process known as our Independence and partition of the country. As a school boy in Calcutta he had a terrible memory of the 1964 riots. Memory of not what he saw or heard but the far more powerful memory of what he felt in his child's perception of the whole thing. The theft of Hazratbal, a holy relic enshrined in a mosque near Srinagar, triggered off communal riots in Khulna, a town in erstwhile East Pakistan. The riots spread to Dhaka and found its echo in Calcutta. As a Ph.D. student he discovered to his consternation that none of his colleagues who were all brought up in Delhi and had even the faintest memory of the riots. One of them was a bit surprised that he remembered a riot in Pakistan so well. For people of Delhi a riot in Khulna or Dhaka is just a piece of news. But not so for somebody in Calcutta. He realized "the simple fact that there had never been a moment in the four-thousand-year-old history of that map, when the places we know as Dhaka and Calcutta were more closely bound to each other than after they had drawn their lines . . . a moment when each city was the inverted image of the other, locked into an irreversible symmetry by the line that was to set us free—our looking-glass border." (233)

Robi's loss in the 1964 riot was no less than many others. He was too young to register anything other than fear; fear that haunted him in his nightmares. In his adult consciousness Tribid's death signified the futility of our freedom. He has developed that objectivity which gives him a dispassionate, analytical outlook. He could relate his plight with those of many others in the subcontinent and knew if they could not outgrow the grandmother's hysterical reaction posterity would never forgive them. The country was freed, somebody drew the line and everybody was led to believe that the monster of religious communalism was laid to rest. They hoped peace, stability, things people associate with the right to self-determination of a nation, would come. But as a member of the post-1947 generation he had seen how the euphoria evaporated. He felt that nobody seemed to know the meaning of freedom. If they did there would not have been so many killings in Assam, the north-east, the Punjab, Sri Lanka, Tripura. People who kill or get killed, do so in the name of freedom. The very concept of freedom is a mirage. Robi's words have the ring of truth that has been borne out by our experience in the subcontinent towards the fag end of the twentieth century: "And then I think to myself why don't they draw thousands of little lines through the whole subcontinent and give every little place a new name? What would it change? It's a mirage, the whole thing is a mirage." (247)

The 1964 riots have been described in *Antique Land* from the other side of the border. The scholar-protagonist's realization does not differ much from the sum-total of that of different characters in the other book. If we remember the unusual provocation for the recounting of riot memories we will at once understand how man's responses to certain things and situations are conditioned by his own history and culture and how tall claims and high hopes borne out by intellectual discourse are belied when the occasions most demand them. In the total Muslim culture of rural Egypt people can hardly conceive of men not circumcised in childhood. For them it is almost as natural as breathing, eating or drinking. So long as people remain outside the purview of the historical process of major cross-cultural conflict and assimilation; so long as they are exempt from undergoing the agony of such a process, physical peculiarities are physical peculiarities, and not symbols. But for a six-year-old who had seen the brutality of riots, the state of foreskin is more than a physical peculiarity sanctioned in a particular culture. It has ever-widening circles of association, completely independent of it, capable of producing an intensely emotional response even in a student of social anthropology. As it happened, Amitav the character, went to attend a marriage at Nabeel's place. He was the only foreigner there. People at Nashawy were always curious about Doctor-al-Hindi. So they started asking him all sorts of questions ranging from the method of disposal of dead bodies to the custom of circumcision in his country. These practices are dictated by religion and in their uni-religious society there is no conflict regarding these things. But to Amitav who has seen Hindu-Muslim riots in the subcontinent where these different practices have been made bones of contentions, these enquiries did not present themselves as innocent curiosity. So he suddenly left the gathering. Nabeel failed to understand why he was so upset about such trivial things. Amitav knows his emotional reaction was conditioned by the memory of a communal riot which he witnessed as the six-year-old son of an Indian diplomat in Dhaka. As he puts it toward the end of the next chapter: "The stories of these riots are always the same: tales that grow out of an explosive barrier of symbols—of cities going up in flames because of a cow found dead in a temple or a pig in a mosque; of people killed for wearing a lungi or a dhoti, depending on where they find themselves; of women disembowelled for wearing veils or vermilion, of men dismembered for the state of their foreskins. . . . I could not have expected them to understand an Indian's terror of symbols."[2]

If the major themes in *The Shadow Lines* were nationalism and political freedom, in *Antique Land* one of the predominant themes is religion—its meaning and practice, the irony inherent in religious traditions—their universality and inter-tradition conflicts that have shaped much of human history. In the wedding-episode Amitav was aware of the punishment of being an Indian; but to be a part of India which has been a melting pot for centuries has its own rewards. The scholar-protagonist of this book gathers parallels in history which reveal the unifying elements in various religious traditions and India is a potent source.

In chapter V of the 'Nashawy' section, there is the story of Sidi Abu-Kanaka, the holy man, whose grave did not yield to the spade of the government engineers who were digging a canal right through the village cemetery. The villagers protested but to no avail. Much to their astonishment and delight the tomb of the much-revered holy man resisted every effort on the part of the government to proceed along the charted line. When the grave was opened the body was found to be still whole and incorrupt and giving a perfumed smell. Convinced of the futility of their effort the authority finally diverted the canal. In gratitude the people of the village built a moqam for the Sidi. There are also stories about how the Sidi wrought miracles to protect the villagers from harm time and again. A similar story is recounted in chapter VI of the 'Mangalore' section; the story of a Bhuta-shrine immobilizing bulldozers that were commissioned to destory it and finally government engineers deciding to divert the project to spare the shrine.

The canonization of local holy men through mystification in folk-imagination is against Islam as Ustaz Sabry points out. The Bhuta-cult is not a part of canonical Hindu practice; it is dismissed by the standard authorities "as mere 'devil worship' and superstition." (264) But one thing is made clear by the two stories; human civilization has moved along the same line even at a distance of a few thousand miles. There is a method in history which may not be as inexorable as physical methods but still powerful enough to establish a pattern in the movement of events.

Preservation of one's religious identity has been the cause of much bloodshed. It is a revelation to know that one's religion may not be such an exclusive prerogative as one may like to think. The concept of exclusivity of one's religion may even be the handiwork of a couple of "enforcers of history." The episode of Amitav's visit to the mowlid of Sidi Abu-Hasira gives us an inkling into the history of development of religious divide. Islam and Judaism have the same semitic origin. They have the same mythological and historical background. They have physical proximity, close linguistic and cultural bonds—factors which in a primitive civilization did forge a kind of acceptance between the two religious groups as is evident from the story of the Sidi who was born of Jewish parents and reportedly converted to Islam when he came over to Egypt. He had followers among both these communities. But "intertwined histories, Indian and Egyptian, Muslim and Jewish, Hindu and Muslim, had been partitioned long ago" (339) and that is why the Egyptian government officials find it so difficult to understand why an Indian who is neither Muslim nor Jewish should have any interest in the mowlid of Sidi Abu-Hasira. To them religion has lost its human face. Socio-political systems do not recognize that human intercourse is a vital part of religion; instead they rigorously classify religious traditions as being mutually exclusive and in a way that best suits the academia, particularly western academia.

The story of the slave of Md H. 6, which initiated this novel comes full circle here. A scholastic search into the derivation of the name of the slave has established him to be a son of one of the several matrilineal communities of Tulunad, i.e. Mangalore in the pre-Brahminical days. Here is also the story of religious assimilation. The local deity of the Bhuta-cult has merged with gods of Sanskritic Brahminical tradition. 'Berme,' the deity of Bhuta-cult becomes 'Bomma' under the influence of 'Brahma' one of the gods in Hindu Trinity; and the slave is named after this mongrel god 'Bomma' which was a common name for boys of the region. Bomma the slave went into the service of Ben Yiju the Jew who migrated from Tunisia via Egypt to India. A trader by profession, he spent seventeen years in the port city of Mangalore. He is a wonderful product of cross-cultural assimilation. Being a part of the Arab-speaking world, the orthodox Jew invoked God by the name of Allah. His relationship with Bomma who practised Bhuta worship was determined probably by the spiritual philosophies of the Muslim Sufi saints and Vachanakara saint-poets of South India. The central metaphor of the devotee being in perpetual bondage to the Lord went a long way in determining various social relationships including that between Ben Yiju and Bomma, a trader and his business agent. Though Bomma was called a slave, their relationship may not have been the same as existing between a master and a slave in the sixteenth-century European colonial system. It was more in the nature of a commitment: "even the most mundane institutions have their life-giving myths and against the setting of that distant backdrop of legend and metaphor, the elements of slavery in the ties that bound an apprentice to a master craftsman, an accountant to a merchant, would have appeared, perhaps, not as demeaning bonds, but rather as links that were in some small way ennobling—human connections, pledges of commitment, in relationships that could just as well have been a matter of a mere exchange of coinage." (263) Man has written history partitioning the past and this has largely been a self-fulfilling process. But the mowlid of Sidi Abu-Hasira which is a small remnant of the world of Bomma and Ben Yiju, probably holds key to the future of humanity.

The most recent developments in the field of religion in India do not escape critical attention in the novel. A newly-prosperous fishing hamlet on the Malabar coast has changed its religious identity from that in the days of Bomma. The villagers who have the benefit of modern education have relegated their Bhuta deity to a lower level and placed Vishnu on the altar. The Bobbariya bhuta the spirit of a Muslim mariner is represented by an image, like a Hindu God. This is how the scholar-protagonist learns the uses of History: "The past had revenged itself on the present: it had slipped the spirit of an Arab Muslim trader past the watchful eyes of Hindu Zealots and installed it within the Sanskritic pantheon." (274) Ironically, on the walls of the newly-built "Hindu" temple there are posters of a "fundamentalist Hindu political organization . . . notorious for its anti-Muslim rhetoric." (273) So this is another side to the story of religion where assimilation leads to confrontation and militancy because these fishing people who had always lived at the periphery of Hindu society try to gain acceptance in the Sanskritic fold by catering to fundamentalism.

Thus the tangent points in the two novels consist in the study of constant interaction between ideas and events and resultant integration and differentiation. Ghosh has drawn parallels between war and riot, Europe and Indian subcontinent to show how all violence whether committed in the name of nationalism or freedom is to be given no other colour. The barriers of nation, country and time dissolve in the consciousness of the author and he reaches a tragic realization of how unscrupulous political forces continue to suffocate human aspirations.

NOTES

1. Amitav Ghosh, *The Shadow Lines* (Delhi: Ravi Dayal Publishers, 1988), p. 60.
2. Amitav Ghosh, *In an Antique Land* (Delhi: Ravi Dayal Publishers, 1992), p. 210.

Theme of Partition and Freedom in Khushwant Singh's *Train to Pakistan* and Amitav Ghosh's *The Shadow Lines*

D.K. PABBY

As the plot of Khushwant Singh's novel *Train to Pakistan* progresses towards its concluding part, one of the main characters viz. Hukum Chand, the magistrate of Chundunnugger, is a disillusioned man as he feels the sting of his helplessness to do much to stop the communal violence that had erupted in the wake of the partition of the country. Political freedom had been achieved apparently through 'non-violent' means but Hindu-Muslim riots had erupted in several parts of India and also in the newly-created Pakistan. Hukum Chand's words of self-introspective rumination quietly proclaim the futility of this political freedom without proper orientation of the people: "What were the people in Delhi doing? Making fine speeches in the assembly! Loud speakers magnifying their egos; lovely-looking foreign women in the visitors' galleries in breathless admiration: 'He is great man, this Mr. Nehru of yours. I do think he is the greatest man in the world today. And how handsome!' Wasn't that a wonderful thing to say? 'Long ago we made a tryst with destiny and now the time comes when we shall redeem our pledge, not wholly or in full measure but very substantially.' Yes, Mr. Prime Minister, you made your tryst. So did many others."[1] The two novels, Khushwant Singh's *Train to Pakistan* (1956) and Amitav Ghosh's *The Shadow Lines* (1988) attempt to grapple *inter alia* with this question of 'the tryst of others' i.e. 'the tryst of the common people' caught between the greed of self-seeking politicians, fanatic religious leaders and their cohorts, power-wielding corrupt bureaucrats and anti-social elements always looking for opportunities to exploit any situation to their own advantage; and the unseemly haste with which the labour government in Britain decided to transfer power. It is on record that Lord Mountbatten, the then Viceroy of India and later the first Governor General of free India, got his reforms commissioner, Mr. V.P. Menon, to draw up the plan for the transfer of power and the division of India in just a few hours. With this plan, he himself flew to London and got Mr. Atlee the Prime Minister of England and his cabinet to accept it in exactly five minutes. The subsequent hasty implementation of this plan without much foresight, far-sightedness and the much-needed preparedness at several levels, led to an unprecedented holocaust of communal frenzy. Before the people could realize the political and social implications of the partition, they were swept off their feet by a wave of violence that swiftly became a tide. Hundreds of people were killed, raped and butchered on either side of the border, and for those who survived the catastrophe, the experience was so traumatic that the memories of those grief-stricken days haunted them for years to come. For millions of people, the independence of the country brought terrible but avoidable suffering and humiliation, a loss of human dignity and a frustrating sense of being uprooted. This is not what they had aspired for in the name of freedom—the partition was a dirty trick.

In *Train to Pakistan*, Khushwant Singh brings to the centre stage the fact of the partition of the Punjab and the question of the subsequent violence on both sides of the border in a very effective, vivid and graphic manner. In a brief preface to the novel, Arthur Lall aptly comments: "Its intrinsic qualities as a novel grip the reader. Throughout, the action sweeps one along. The characters are vivid and highly credible, and Khushwant Singh keeps them going magnificently on two levels: in their quotidian matrix compounded of their passions of love and revenge, their tremendous sense of belonging to a village community, and their insolence and heroism; and then again on the wide stage set by the tornado that breaks on their lives in the shape of the cataclysmic events of the partition of India in 1947." In fact, the novel opens with forebodings of ill omen: "The summer of 1947 was not like other Indian summers. Even the weather had a different feel in India that year. It was hotter than usual, and drier and dustier. And the summer was longer. No one could remember when the monsoon had been so late. For weeks, the sparse clouds cast only shadows. There was no rain. People began to say that God was punishing them for their sins." (1)

Khushwant Singh goes on to describe how the feeling of guilt arose from the maddening violence by the Hindus and the Muslims precipitated by reports of the proposed division of the country into 'a Hindu India and a Muslim Pakistan.' The riots had first broken out in Calcutta and then spread north and east and west engulfing a vast segment of population. Though the novelist does hold the Britishers and the political leaders responsible for the avoidable communal riots, he does not take any sides: "Muslims said the Hindus had planned and started the killing. According to the Hindus, the Muslims were to blame. The fact is, both sides killed. Both shot and stabbed and speared and clubbed. Both tortured. Both raped. . . . The riots had become a rout. By the summer of 1947, when the creation of the new state of Pakistan was formally announced, ten million people—Muslims and Hindus and Sikhs—were in flight. By the time the monsoon broke, almost a million of them were dead, and all of northern India was in arms, in terror or in hiding." (1-2) The massacres and brutalities unleashed by the partition are then juxtaposed against the harmonious bonds of friendship, brotherhood and good-neighbourliness in an obscure, sleepy and tiny village Mano Majra situated near the border and inhabited by only seventy families out of which "Lala Ram Lal's is the only Hindu family. The others are Sikhs or Muslims, about equal in number." (2) Simplicity and calmness of the lives of the Mano Majrans can be gauged from the fact that all the activities of villagers are closely related to and measured in terms of the arrival and departure of various trains from early morning till late in the evening. The shattering of the peace and harmony of this small helmet with the brutal murder of the village money-lender Lala Ram Lal and the daring dacoity at his house by the gang of Malli and his men, is a kind of foregrounding of the communal violence and the anarchic chaos that was to be let loose later. "Ram Lal uttered a loud yell and collapsed on the floor with blood spurting from his belly. The dacoits jumped off the roof to the lane below. They yelled defiance to the world as they went out towards the river. 'Come' they yelled. 'Come out, if you have the courage! Come out, if you want your mothers and sisters raped, Come out! brave men!'" (10)

A close reading of the novel clearly reveals that the dacoity at his house and murder of the moneylender are not merely accidental—these are a prelude to the swelling acts of murder and violence across the frontier which do not remain unretaliated. Though the conversation between the police sub-inspector and the District Magistrate of Chundunnugger about the communal situation in the district town, in the border village of Mano Majra, and the general situation on both sides of the border, is subsumed with gentle irony, it does articulate the general mindset as is clear from the following:

> "Do you know," continued the magistrate, "the Sikhs retaliated by attacking a Muslim refugee train and sending it across the border with over a thousand corpses? They wrote on the engine 'Gift to Pakistan'!"
>
> The subinspector looked down thoughtfully and answered: "They say that is the only way to stop killings on the other side. Man for man, woman for woman, child for child. . . . Here we are on the border with Muslims living in Sikh villages as if nothing had happened. Every morning and evening the muezzin calls for prayer in the heart of a village like Mano Majra. You ask the Sikhs why they allow it and they answer that the Muslims are their brothers." (19-20)

But the calmness of the atmosphere in this 'oasis of peace'

gets shattered when the 'ghost trains' start arriving in Mano Majra. The tense situation is evocatively articulated by the novelist in the opening paragraph of the chapter titled *Kalyug*: "Early in September, the time in Mano Majra started going wrong. Trains became less punctual than ever before and many more started to run through at night. . . . children did not know when to be hungry. . . . Goods trains had stopped running altogether, so there was no lullaby to lull them to sleep. Instead, ghost trains went past at odd hours between midnight and dawn, disturbing the dreams of Mano Majra." (77) And as days passed by, there were more news as well as rumours about the brutalities by the Muslims and Sikhs against each other on this and that side of the border. These obviously led to suspicions between the two communities which had lived together as family members for decades. "Quite suddenly every Sikh in Mano Majra became a stranger with an evil intent. His long hair and beard appeared barbarous, his kirpan menacingly anti-Muslim. For first time, the name Pakistan came to mean something to them—a haven of refuge where there were no Sikhs." (120-21) And the Sikhs too became sullen and angry and some of them started saying "Never trust a Mussulman." The young were particularly unhappy and agitated especially after the arrival of some 'refugees' from across the border. Yet the feeling and spirit of mutual welfare and brotherhood endured and after a long meeting Imam Baksh said: "What have we to do with Pakistan? We were born here. So were our ancestors. We have lived amongst you as brothers." (126) But when the Muslims feel compelled by the circumstances to leave for Pakistan in spite of all the good intentions of the local Sikhs, another aspect of partition/freedom is revealed. Infamous Malli and his gang who had looted the village moneylender and murdered him in defiance of the law, not only now align themselves with the instigators but are also officially appointed 'custodians' of the Muslim property left behind and proceed to loot in broad daylight. On the instigation of the young Sikh boys, quite a few of the Mano Majran Sikhs volunteer to aid and abet the destruction of the train stealthily at night so that the Muslims of Chundunnugger and

Mano Majra among others, would not go alive and safely to Pakistan. The young Sikh, ironically of course, swears by the Gurus and inflames the fellow Sikhs of Mano Majra with the words "By the Grace of God/We bear the world nothing but good will" (152) on his lips. It is, however, the sagacity of the shrewd and wily but good-intentioned District Commissioner who heaps all kinds of abuses on the new political bosses for creating the traumatic situation, that saves the Muslim passengers from being butchered not with the help of the police but with the help of the village Budmash Jugga who was released from the jail and who was told that his beloved Nooran was also travelling by the same train. Jugga, though a dus-numbri (a proclaimed offender) had his mind and heart fired with the noble sentiment of love for Nooran. No sooner is he released than he rushes to cut the thick rope stretched and tied tightly across the railway bridge, after seeking Guru's word from Bhai Meet Singh even without understanding the meaning of that word. In the process of ensuring safe passage of the train to Pakistan, he has to make the supreme sacrifice of his own life: "He went at it with the knife, and then with his teeth. The engine was almost on him. There was a volley of shots, the man shivered and collapsed. The rope snapped in the centre as he fell. The train went over him, and went on to Pakistan." (181) Though some critics have labelled this ending of the novel as 'somewhat melodramatic' due to the lack of sufficient foregrounding of Jugga from a budmash, an anti-hero, into a hero, Jugga's sacrifice can be probably viewed as a form of wish fulfilment for the writer to achieve in fiction what on his own admission, he could not achieve in real life at the time of partition. Referring to the questions raised at the Press Conference after the screening of the film version of *Train to Pakistan* directed by Pamela Rooks at the recently concluded International Film Festival in New Delhi (11-20 January 1998), Khushwant Singh made the following comments which seem to be very pertinent even today i.e. fifty years after the unfortunate tragedy of Partition took place:

Should the partition be forgotten? Has it any relevance to

> us today? My answer to both the questions is an emphatic yes. We must not forget the partition because it is relevant today. We must remember that it did in fact happen and can happen again. That is why I keep reminding people who clamour for an independent Kashmir, Khalistan or Nagaland to remember what happened to Muslims when some of them asked for a separate Muslim state. I keep telling my fellow Sikhs that the worst enemies of Khalsa Panth are Khalistanis, and of the Nagas those who ask for an independent Nagaland. Reminding ourselves of what happened in 1947 and realizing the possibilities of its recurring, we should resolve that we will never let it happen again.[2]

In *The Shadow Lines* the development and growth of Tha'mma's character encapsulates the futility and meaninglessness of political freedom which was otherwise supposed to usher in an era of peace and prosperity for all. During the days of her childhood and youth, she had her sympathies with all those who were fighting for the cause of freedom. In fact, she too wanted to earn small portion of the glory enjoyed by some of her classmate 'terrorists' by running secret errands for them or even cooking for them and washing their clothes. The aim was to be associated with such a group of persons, actively involved in fighting for a 'pious cause.' In response to a question by the narrator, "Do you really mean Tha'mma, that you would have killed him?"[3] we are told thus:

> She put her hands on my shoulders and holding me in front of her, looking directly at me, her eyes steady, forthright, unwavering: 'I would have been frightened. . . . But I would have prayed for strength, and God willing, yes, I would have killed him [the English Magistrate.] It was for our freedom: I would have done anything to be free.' (39)

Her formative years have taught her the need, necessity and desirability of political freedom which is a sort of pre-requisite for economic, social, cultural and intellectual freedom and development. As Novy Kapadia points out, the theme of the novel encompasses all these experiences: "By exploring connections, distinctions and possibilities, Amitav Ghosh shows that in a changing world, different strands of nationalism and ideology will exist and even compete. The force of nationalism in the quest for freedom or ideology is often a source of violence. . . . So the 'shadow line' between people and nations is often mere illusion. The force and appeal of nationalism cannot be wished away (so easily), just as death by a communal mob in the bye-lanes of old Dhaka."[4] Dhaka has been Tha'mma's place of birth, but her nationality is Indian. As a young girl, she had thought of fighting for freedom in East Bengal. But those very same people for whom she had been willing to lay down her life are enemies now in 1964. Feelings of nationalism had after all motivated the fight against the British in Khulna. But in 1964, the group of Indians travelling in the embassy car are the enemies to be hunted down and killed.

However, Tha'mma's disillusionment increases when she has to mention her birthplace on the passport-form during her visit to Dhaka. Home ought to be the place where one was born and brought up, sealed by an emotional bond, where one can claim one's right without a thought and without any hesitation. And if there was a basic confusion on this score—about the very roots of one's origin—an individual's identity would be in question. Leaving Dhaka during the Partition had obviously meant severing old roots and groping for a new kind of stability and identity. Therefore, years later, on her visit to Dhaka, she is distressed to write 'Dhaka' as her place of birth: "She liked things to be neat and in place—and at that moment she had not been able to quite understand how her place of birth had come to be so messily at odds with her nationality." (152)

Finally, the fact that "The border isn't on the frontier: it's right inside the airport" (151) puzzles Tha'mma all the more and she feels that her sacrifice has been in vain: "But if there aren't any trenches or anything, how are people to know? I mean, where's the difference then? And if there's no difference both sides will be the same; it'll be just like it used to be before, when we used to catch a train in Dhaka and get off in Calcutta the next day without anybody stopping us. What was it all for then—partition and all the killing and everything—if there isn't something in between?" (151) Tridib's death bewilders her further. She finds her idealism fast turning into helplessness as the anarchic tendencies within and without her gather force. There is obviously need for an order, a new order, but what kind of an order, remains an unanswered question. Tha'mma lies in bed, weak and helpless. Even as she realizes that war, partition and violence are meaningless if they create no visible borders between two countries; she never accepts and understands Ila's desperate urge to settle in England. Her orientation may be apparently that of a 'warmongering fascist' as Ila terms it, it is nevertheless a harsh truth or at least a harsh partial truth that marks the psyche of the modern nation-states. The likes of Tridib have to die so that a comprehensive view of real freedom may find favour and flourish with the help of personal relationships. Ultimately, the responsibility of achieving and sustaining real freedom rests with every individual as it lies with every nation too within the larger framework. In fact, *The Shadow Lines* questions prevailing precepts and ethics which man inherits blindly. The value of political zeal and social freedom is no longer stable, exclusive, permanent and immutable as Tha'mma and Ila had believed. The apparent stability which is offered by such ideas often proves to be illusory. With Tridib, however, the novel emphasizes the relevance and significance of human relationships. This alone can lead to an attainment of genuine freedom. Man is free to decide on a course of action which is found to affect a whole group of people, a nation, mankind. Every individual shares the responsibility of establishing a code of values which would ensure peace and solidarity for mankind. As Sartre said: "Every one of our acts has at its stake, the meaning of the world and place of man in the universe. Through each of them, whether we wish it or not, we set up a scale of values which is universal."[5]

It has to be remembered that freedom is not just the absence of external pressure, it is also the presence of something else. The struggle for freedom is not without its darker side. If the fight for political freedom aims at ensuring peace for a particular community, it may also arouse and mobilize diabolical forces in man—forces which one would have believed to be non-existent, or at least to have died out long ago. If social and moral freedom is unlimited, it may unleash the numerous problems of excess and the lack of restraint. Taking all this into account, the question that arises is whether there is such a condition as complete freedom? Are freedom for the individual and for the society linked to and compatible with each other? And is absolute freedom a possibility for an individual, a community or for a nation? Should there be sufficient essential preparation, orientation and education of the individuals and of the society to enable them to digest their freedom, realize its full potential and cope with this freedom with dignity and with rationality? Fortunately both the novels *Train to Pakistan* and *The Shadow Lines* raise these significant questions in all their various dimensions and the narratives of the two obliquely explore and subtly answer these questions with the much needed flexibility of interpretation especially with reference to the pluralistic, multilingual, multicultural, multireligious and multiethnic character of the vastly-spread society of India in its widespread regions and teeming with paradoxes and contradictions at several levels.

In conclusion, it can be said that the partition of the Indian sub-continent was the single most traumatic experience in our recent history. The violence it unleashed by the hooligan actions of a few fanatics, the vengeance that the ordinary Hindus, Muslims and Sikhs wreaked on each other worsened our social sense, distorted our political judgements and deranged our understanding of moral righteousness.

The real sorrow of the partition, however, as portrayed in the two novels under review, was that it brought to an abrupt end a long and communally shared history and cultural heritage. The relations between the Hindus and the Muslims were not, of course, always free from suspicions, distrust or the angry rejection by one group of the habits and practices of the other; but such moments of active malevolence and communal frenzy were a rare and transient exception to the common bonds of mutual goodwill and warm feelings of close brotherhood. Even if there were some disruptions on some rare occasions, the rich heterogeneity of the life of the two communities was never seriously threatened. The Hindus never ceased from paying homages at dargahs; the Muslims continued to participate in Hindu festivals; and traders of both the communities continued their usual exchange of goods and services in the bazars, etc. Indeed, one can assert with confidence that the dominant concerns of the Hindu and Muslim intellectuals throughout the nineteenth century and till about 1935, were more with creating free spaces for enlightened thought than with confining people within their narrow religious identities. Organizations which nurtured violent hatred towards each other and incited communal passions did exist, but at the very margins of the solidly and healthily functioning social and cultural order. It is the unthoughtful decision of partition and hollow love of 'nationalism' that let the mischief off and out.

NOTES

1. Khushwant Singh, *Train to Pakistan* (1956; New Delhi: Time Books International, 1989), p. 176.
2. Khushwant Singh, "A Forgetful Nation" in "With Malice towards One and All," *The Hindustan Times*, January 31, 1998, p. 13.
3. Amitav Ghosh, *The Shadow Lines* (Delhi: Ravi Dayal Publishers, 1988), p. 39.
4. Novy Kapadia, "Imagination and Politics in Amitav Ghosh's *The Shadow Lines*," ed. Viney Kirpal, *The New Indian Novel in English: A Study of the 1980s* (New Delhi: Allied, 1996), p. 205.
5. Sartre, *Le Sursis*, qtd. Henry Peyre, *French Novelists of Today* (New York: Oxford University Press, 1967), p. 267.

The Partition of Bengal: A Comparative Study of Amitav Ghosh's *The Shadow Lines* and Sunil Gangopadhyay's *Purba Paschim*

ALPANA NEOGY

In this paper, I am attempting a comparative study of two novels, one written in English, *The Shadow Lines* by Amitav Ghosh and the other a Bengali novel, *Purba Paschim*, by Sunil Gangopadhyay.

Both the novels have as their centre of focus, the Partition of India and the consequent trauma of the East Bengali psyche. Gangopadhyay's protagonist is Pratap Mazumdar, a Hindu from Malkhanagar in East Bengal, and the novel traces his life and times. The narrator of Ghosh's novel is a young boy who grew up in Calcutta and Delhi in post-Partition India. The trauma of Partition continues through three generations. The agonies of displacement, the sense of alienation in the adopted land, the constant dream of a return to one's land—these are the common themes in both the novels.

Fifty years have passed by since India became 'free.' The Bengali diaspora has been dispersed to distant lands. Some have gained successes in new associations and developments. Yet the sense of loss of one's identity, the connection with one's *baari* remains. *Baari* is where one's ancestors have lived for generations. *Baasha*, on the other hand, is a temporary residence no matter how long one has stayed there.[1]

For the East Bengali, 15 August 1947 is the Partition day, not India's independence day, a day that deliberately bifurcated the Bengali community. If the purpose of Partition was to gain freedom, then that freedom is a 'mirage.' Observing the front pages of newspapers which give details of terrorist activities, Amitav Ghosh is driven to ask: "Why don't they draw thousands of little lines through the whole subcontinent and give every place a new name?"[2]

Despair is the dominant note struck by Amitav Ghosh in *The Shadow Lines.* Ghosh brings out the futility of drawing lines across a nation to form two nations, one having an East wing which is separated from its West wing by over a thousand miles.

Tha'mma, the narrator's grandmother, belongs to the generation that had to uproot itself in 1947. When she is all set to go to Dhaka to rescue her Jethamoshai, she inquires if she would be able to see the border between India and East Pakistan from the airplane. "But surely there's something—trenches perhaps, or soldiers, or guns pointing at each other, or even just barren strips of land. . . . But if there aren't any trenches or anything, how are people to know? I mean, where's the difference then? And if there's no difference, both sides will be the same; it'll be just like it used to be before. . . . What was it all for then—Partition and all the killing and everything—if there isn't something in between?" (151)

Subconsciously she has rejected the historical act of Partition. History perhaps could explain the events leading up to this event, perhaps even explain why it happened when it did. It is her memory of her ancestral home (which actually reaches out far beyond any historical fact) which inspires her to go to Dhaka on that tragic mission. Earlier on, when told that Jethamoshai was still alive in Dhaka and that the whole house had been occupied by Muslim refugees from India, she exclaims, "You mean our house has been occupied by refugees?" (135)

This nostalgia for the past, the refusal to accept historical realities, is evident in Sunil Gangopadhyay's Bengali novel *Purba Paschim*[3] published in two volumes, as well. Its vast canvas covers events and occurrences in both East and West Bengal. The novel progresses through the recent history of the two Bengals. Starting in the mid '50s, the novel becomes a living documentation of how political and social change in the two Bengals has affected the lives of the people of Bengal. The novel concludes in the '80s. There is a constant reference to the halcyon days of pre-Partition Bengal. The Nehru days, the Indo-Pakistan war, the rise of Indira Gandhi, the steady economic decline, the increase of revolutionary feelings amongst the youth, the Naxalbari movement, the demands for political freedom in Bangla Desh, the despair of the youth, the murder of Sheikh Mujibur Rehman, all these political facts form the backdrop to this story.

Ghosh's novel, on the other hand, concentrates on one event that triggers off a whole series of events. On 27 December 1963, a relic, believed to be a hair of the Prophet Muhammad, disappears from the Hazratbal mosque at Srinagar in Kashmir. Hindus, Sikhs and Muslims demonstrate throughout the Valley in protest. No animosity existed between the various religious groups in the Kashmir Valley at that time. Indeed, not one incident involving religious discord surfaced after the theft.

Yet, in Khulna, a small town in the distant east wing of Pakistan, a demonstration taken out in protest against the theft, turns violent. Riots spead outwards from Khulna towards Dhaka. Tridib, who had gone to "rescue" his mother's Jethamoshai at Jindabahar Lane, Dhaka, is caught in the midst of one of these riots and is killed. He did not realize that the masses of the subcontinent has "an unregenerate side always prone to violence."[4] Tridib had dreamt of a "better place, a place without borders and countries." When May comes down from England as a stranger, he wants to meet her in a ruin, far from friends and relatives, in a place "without a past, without history, free, really free, two people coming together with the utter freedom of strangers." (144)

The name *Purba Paschim* denotes the two Bengals; in a sense it could denote the Eastern and Western Hemisphere, or the two ends of the horizontal axis. Gangopadhyay traces the genesis of the Hindu-Muslim rift in this novel. A close friend of Pratap Mazumdar, a Hindu student at Rippon College, Calcutta was a Bengali Muslim, Syed Mojammul Haque, affectionately called Mamun who came from a village in Coumilla,

East Bengal. All well-to-do families in East Bengal would send their sons to study in Calcutta in those days. Mamun takes Pratap to this ancestral home one day, knowing full well that his father is a rigid Muslim who would not tolerate even a Hindu shadow to fall on his doorstep. The father takes one look at Pratap's clean-shaven face and remarks, "You look like a Hindu." While the young man shivers in his rain-drenched clothes, he has to answer questions about his home, his father, his profession, his property.

Thereafter, Pratap is permitted to change out of his wet clothes and offered a bowl of puffed rice and a glass of milk. Syed Hakim, Mamun's father, then tells him with deep regret and with the utmost humility that no Hindu could take shelter in his home just as no member of his family could take shelter in the house of a Hindu: this was the unwritten code of the family laid down by *his* father, who had been insulted many years ago at the house of a Hindu brahmin family in Sylhet. He had but entered the brahmin's house when he was asked to go and stand outside. All the potable water of that house was thrown away and the earthen pitchers broken. Pratap, naturally, finds no reason why he should be insulted because some Brahmin, so many years ago had behaved in such a crude fashion.

The prejudices in the Hindu mind, largely due to the strong caste-system, had coalesced through the years. Once Mamun had overheard his friend's mother remark: "Is the boy a Muslim? I had thought him to be a Bengali." As Mamum muses: "If Muslims cannot be Bengalis, then Muslims cannot be Indians too. Only Muslims."

Gangopadhyay attempts to analyse the Hindu-Muslim discord. The prejudices on both sides had hardened their relationships. Mamun believes that both in the field of education and work, the Hindus had been the favoured ones in Bengal. Pratap, very agitated, had replied that he was not even aware that he was a Hindu. Perhaps thc majority Bengali Hindu population, secure in the knowledge of being Hindus, had not fully appreciated the depths of insecurity in the Muslim psyche. But these social differences were not insurmountable,

Gangopadhyay believes.

It was the chicanery of the politicians that permanently divided the land purely on the basis of religion. The Communal Award of 1937 laid the foundation of communalism. In the Bengal Assembly of 250 seats, according to the Award, 117 seats were to be allotted to the Muslim Bengali, 52 to the Bengali Hindus and the rest to the other categories. Under these conditions, there was no way by which Bengal could have a Bengali Hindu government. The Bengali Hindu was the first Indian to acquire western education and the western political system, and also the first to take up the call of freedom. From the Bengali Hindu community had emerged the revolutionaries and the terrorists. Their literature and music had kindled in the masses the desire for freedom. Small wonder then that the British Government felt it necessary to teach the Bengali Hindus a lesson!

The tragedy of Bengal lay in the fact that at the time of Partition she had no leader—C.R. Das, who had dreamt of a Bengal free of communalism where Hindus and Muslims would stand side by side and face the common enemy, the British, had passed away; Subhash Bose had disappeared; and Aurobindo Ghosh had relinquished politics for a spiritual life at Pondicherry.

After Partition, Pratap Mazumdar finds himself a job as a sub-judge in Calcutta and settles down in a small rented flat in one of the poorer colonies. Had he sold off his family estate in East Bengal (and not abandoned it) the money accrued from the sale would have fetched him a mansion in one of the posh localities of Calcutta.

Living in cramped conditions, he and his mother are often swamped by waves of nostalgia as they remember their coconut and mango groves in East Bengal. When it rains in Calcutta, he remembers Malkhanagar. In an enclosed rickshaw in the rain he imagines he is once again in a covered boat in his pond at Malkhanagar. When he sees some fresh *illsh* fish in the market, he buys not one but four of them.

Both Ghosh and Gangopadhyay express a stunned disbelief that Partition could happen at all. For Gangopadhyay it is a cry from the heart—suddenly and in such a cruel manner the Mazumdar family had been cut adrift from a familiar and loved world. The native village is pictured as both sacred and beautiful. Something of value to Bengali culture and the understanding of what home was had been destroyed by the Partition.

Life becomes difficult as the Mazumdar family copes with the changed circumstances. A certain way of life, a certain kind of decency seems to have passed away. Pratap's brother-in-law is a lover of music. The landed gentry had suddenly become "declassed" with Partition. He has spent his youth acquiring a knowledge of music and had not learnt how to earn a living. He gradually fades away unable to cope with the changed circumstances.

Pratap's eldest sister Supriti is introduced to emphasize the tremendous divide between the East Bengali Hindu (the Bangaal) and the West Bengali Hindu (the Ghoti). The Ghotis have always considered East Bengal to be a land of muddy villages and believed that a Bangaal is civilised only when he moves to Calcutta.

Supriti is married to a West Bengali Hindu. After her marriage, she is forced to wipe out the Bangaal lilt in her speech; it takes her even longer to learn the West Bengali idiom. She is never accepted and when her husband is killed, allegedly by the land-grabbing refugees (her "country cousins" according to her in-laws) she is driven out of the family home, penniless.

After Partition, the East Bengali Hindu found that he had very little in common with the West Bengali Hindu. He had a greater affinity of mind with those he had left behind on the other side of the border-line—the East Pakistani Muslim! His food habits were different, his tastes were different, he even spoke differently.

And this confusion about one's identity runs through both the novels. In London, Tutul, Pratap's niece, often meets Bengalis settled there who ask her about her "desh" (that is, one's place of origin). When she replies "Calcutta," she is asked to be more specific in order that she may be identified as an East or West Bengali.

Ila in *The Shadow Lines* rejects everything that is Indian and tries to seek an identity for herself in an alien land. "Do you see now why I've chosen to live in London? It's only because I want to be free. Free of your bloody culture and free of all of you," (88) she yells, as she is dragged out of the hotel dance-floor where she has started dancing with an unknown businessman. Her cousin Robi checks her outrageous behaviour by saying that "Girls don't behave like that here. . . . There are certain things you cant do here; that's our culture." (88) Ila, brought up outside India, travels all over the world with her diplomat father. But she is rootless: she doesn't find a sense of belonging anywhere and fantasizes an existence where she is the cynosure of all eyes. In reality she is lonely and miserable. In an attempt to reject her roots and identify herself with the West, she marries Nick but finds him cheating her for the sake of "variety." Rootless and lost at the end of the novel, she clings to the arms of the writer and Robi, members of her family. Her attempt to adopt an alien culture proves abortive and, at the end, she finds the need to go back to one's family.

Both the novels reject the very concept of Partition. They scoff at national leaders who had believed that problems could be solved by drawing lines across the land. Both Bengals are historically, culturally and geographically one and a division was not a solution to the traditional Hindu-Muslim animosity.

Ghosh believes that freedom in the truest sense is an impossibility even in a "free state." One can be enslaved by memories so powerful that a chance remark can set one's hand shaking like a leaf. There was a time when "sensible, good-intentioned people had believed that once they had etched their borders upon the map, "the two bits of land would sail away." (233) They had created not a separation, but a yet undiscovered irony: "the simple fact that there had never been a movement in the four thousand year old history of that map when the places we know as Dhaka and Calcutta were more closely bound to each other" (233) than ever before.

Sunil Gangopadhyay, through the character of Mamun, reveals the loss of the Bengali Muslim in the newly created land now called East Pakistan to wipe out its Bengali identity. He misses his contact with Shantiniketan, with Murshidabad and with all the culture associated with united Bengal. When he seeks shelter in Calcutta during the Bangla Desh war, he is told not to refer to water as "paani" but to ask for "jal." He remembers a word coined in the earlier days "jalpaani" which was a synthesis of both cultures, Hindu and Muslim. Perhaps herein lay the answer to the problem—find avenues for synthesis. A division of a land purely on the basis of religion was no answer to the problem.

NOTES

1. See Dipesh Chakravarti, "Remembered Villages: Representation of Hindu Bengali memories in the aftermath of the Partition," *Economic and Political Weekly*, Vol. 31, No. 32, Aug. 10, 1996.
2. Amitav Ghosh, *The Shadow Lines* (Delhi: Ravi Dayal Publisher, 1988), p. 247.
3. (Calcutta: Ananda Publishers, 1981).
4. See Nirad C. Chaudhuri, *Thy Hand, Great Anarch* (Chatto and Windus, 1987), p. 806.

The Shadow Lines: "An Intimacy with Elsewhere"

O.P. MATHUR

I have heard the key
Turn in the door once, and turn once only
We think of the key, each in his prison
Thinking of the key, each confirms a prison
Only at nightfall, aetherial rumours
Revive for a moment a broken Coriolanus

T.S. Eliot, *The Wasteland*

Shut up within a suffocating and hedonistic self-centredness, the modern man pays no heed either to the mystery of his inner self or to the vast otherness around him for the regeneration of which a sage like Dadhichi gave his bones. This "intimacy with elsewhere," as A.K. Ramanujan calls it in the blurb of *The Shadow Lines*, is the spiritual filter through which the events and characters of the novel acquire a new meaning and a message which is so well embodied in the paradoxical title itself, for the geometrical razor-thin line has no breadth like that of the shadowy penumbra and cannot be equated with it unless it spreads itself to embrace the space, the otherness, around it. This points to the fact that in this relativistic universe all phenomena are inter-related and that only shadowy and illusory lines divide what we consider to be opposites or at least different reality and imagination ("a place does not merely exist, it has to be invented in one's imagination"[1]). The present and the past (the "urgent contemporaneity of an old newspaper," 227), silence and speech (in most of the novel the narrator's silent remembrance of things past is the spoken word), one country and another, religion and humanism, the commonplace and the saintly. In fact, the lines that divide man from man, nation from nation, are also shadowy.

The intimacy with elsewhere includes both broadening down and broadening out. At the superficial historical and domestic level, the novel covers the period from 1939 to 1964, with a brief meaningful extension into Grandmother's forcefully revengeful reactions against the Muslims at the time of the Indo-Pakistan war of 1965. While Tridib, the protagonist of the novel, is born in 1931, the narrator is born in 1952. But the actual 'events' of the novel start in 1939, while their narration is made about 1979 when the narrator, now a grown-up man of about 27 years, recalls the memories of earlier times encapsulated in his childhood. The main focus is on the early 60s when the narrator is about 10-12 years of age. In 1962, the war with China takes place. In 1963, Maya Debi's husband is posted in Dhaka as Consul General and the Hazratbal incident takes place in Srinagar resulting in communal riots which continue sporadically in Dhaka till early January of 1964 even after the recovery of the Holy Hair of the Prophet. It is in one of such cases of violence that Tridib gets killed. This traumatic event is shrouded in the irony that it happens when it should not have happened. The narrator recalls all these and earlier events through his own memory of his childhood memories which include the memories of others, imagination, hearsay, guesswork, partly his own. The labyrinthine cobweb of this memory novel is woven slowly by him, moving between events and characters, reality and imagination, plain light narration and reflection, amusement and puzzlement, suspense, terror and shock—all culminating in the final stage of 'calm of mind, all passion spent.' The world of his memories and imagination is so well fused at the end with the real world that the transition of memory and imagination with the reality of the present, of consciousness with conscience, is hardly noticed.

The Shadow Lines covers a wide range of devices to drive home its point. Two or three different allegories are used to highlight the flimsiness of lines and the ridiculous irrationality of partitions carved out by them. Ila's making for the narrator a dusty chequerboard of lines (64-71) indicating the different portions of a house, rubbing them off and re-drawing them in a different pattern, suggests the repetitive problem of drawing and redrawing borders on a map, a game that mankind has been playing over and over again through gory centuries, believing that every fresh attempt is final.

> "If we pretend it's a house, it will be a house. We can choose to build a house wherever we like."
>
> "No!" I cried, "It won't be a real house, It can't be."
>
> "Why?" she cried smiling.
>
> Frowning, I puzzled over the pattern in the dust. (70)

Somewhat ironically, tragic dimensions are given to this linguistic word-play when in 1964, much after the Partition and after her husband is dead, Grandmother goes (or 'comes') to Dhaka to her ancestral house to bring to India her uncle-in-law. Now, though this is her first visit to the house, she is not a bride but a widow, her ironical status having been caused by the Shadow Lines of the Partition—lines which her old uncle-in-law, though now in an advanced state of senility, has always been emphatically denying and hence refusing to move to India: "Once you start moving you never stop. That's what I told my sons when they took the trains. I said: I don't believe in this India-Shindia. It's all very well you are going away now, but suppose when you get there they decide to draw a line somewhere? What will you do then? Where will you move to?" (215)

Later in the novel, Robi makes a somewhat similar remark about terrorist violence: "And then I think to myself why don't they draw thousands of little lines through the whole sub-continent and give every little place a new name? It's a mirage; the whole thing is a mirage. How can anyone divide a memory?" (247) Such lines have actually been drawn on the old map of the Indian sub-continent creating two (and later three) countries where only one existed. Pakistan being an "invented, country," (157) the Partition was unnatural and artificial, as was that of East Pakistan from West Bengal, like the division of the ancestral house of Tridib in Dhaka which was partitioned "with a lawyer-like precision":

> When the wall was eventually built, they found that it had ploughed right through a couple of doorways so that no one could get through them any more; it had also gone through a lavatory bisecting an old commode. The brothers even partitioned their father's old name-plate. It was divided down the middle by a thin white line, and their names were inscribed on the two halves—of necessity in letters so tiny that nobody could read them. (123)

The residents of one part of the house try to fantasize about differences from those of the other till they almost begin to believe in their own fantasies of the other part being an upside-down house:

> Every thing's upside down over there. I'd [Tridib'd] tell her [Maya] their meals start with the sweets and end with the dal, their books go backwards and end at the beginning, they sleep under their beds and eat on the sheets, they cook with jhatas and sweep with their ladles, they write with umbrellas and go walking with pencils. (125-26)

In fact, they were mirror-images of each other. The "irony of a looking glass border" (233) made them fight wars like "ourself and our image in the mirror." (204) The image of the looking glass recurs a number of times, possibly suggesting that one man is only a little different from another, though we are all essentially similar. This is in a way related to another suggestion of the oneness of the whole world, the universality of one's home communicated by the novel through a light-hearted play on the words 'coming' and 'going' which can often be interchanged with a slight alteration of the referential context. Children make fun of Grandmother going (or coming?) to her ancestral house in Dhaka for the first time after the Partition: "Thamma, Thamma! I cried. How could you have come home to Dhaka? You don't know the difference between coming and going you see in our family we don't know whether we are coming or going—it's all my grandmother's fault." (152-53) It is, in fact, everybody's fault, for our home, the referential point, is wherever we choose to make it. The artificial divisions of mankind by political borders is also convincingly demonstrated by Tridib's atlas upon which the narrator makes circles with different centres arriving at amazing results pointing to the geographical closeness of the people living 'elsewhere,' i.e. at apparently great, but really short distances from each other about whom we know almost nothing. These cartographical experiments become a means to the understanding of the emotional, cultural and spiritual oneness of man, superseding political divisions marked by the borders often carved by the sword. The compass unites what the sword has divided.

The paradox of the division of humanity between 'here' and 'elsewhere' is emphatically highlighted in the life and death of the protagonist Tridib, who is himself a paradoxical embodiment of the risible and serious. He has eccentricities, amusing (for others) physical ailment like 'Gastric' about which there is an all-round conspiracy of silence, and Falstaffian fabrication of facts which he himself enjoys along with others. Yet these superficial, though lovable, facets of his personality are intertwined with profound intellectual and emotional qualities like those of the Whisky Priest of Graham Greene's *The Power and the Glory*. Tridib is a scholar of wide interests and a lover of all living beings who would not like to see even a dying dog in torment. He remains an island of peace and humanism unaffected by successive waves of violence beating around him—nationalist and terrorist agitations, conventional holocausts and recurring riots like those occurring after the Hazratbal incident which transform even the old Grandmother into a votary of violence and revenge. The protagonist's name can be a slight alteration of 'Tridev' (i.e.

Brahma, Vishnu and Mahesh) and can also be interpreted as even having Christian overtones (the Father, the Son and the Holy Ghost). In Bengali, which is Tridib's mother tongue, the name also means 'God' which, like so many Hindu names after gods and goddesses, may unconsciously or consciously point to the scriptural truth (I am He)—the Divine Power manifesting itself in human beings, the glorification of even the commonplace and the unpromising by making the shadow-lines of divinity surround him with an invisible halo. There is but a shadow-line between the human and the divine. Tridib is an embodiment of the intimacy between here and elsewhere in another respect too. For him there is but a shadow-line between reality and imagination, for, unlike Ila, who lives completely in the present, "shut away from the tidewaters of the past and the future by steel floodgates." Tridib is one of those "who could experience the world as concretely in their imaginations as she did through her senses." (30) He interprets the concrete in terms of the imaginary. This is what inspires him to rethink about the boundaries of nations which artificially divide mankind and to deny them—a denial that makes him find his salvation by getting his throat cut in a foreign country, which he still seems to regard as his own, in an attempt to save his grand-uncle and also Khalil, a rickshawallah whose Islamic faith is of no consequence for him as compared to his status of a fellow-being who had for the same reason provided shelter to Tridib's grand-uncle, popularly known as 'Ukil Babu,' and continued to nurse him even in the state of his advanced senile decay.

Khalil is a foil to Tridib, for in the absence of any other conveyance in the riot-affected Dhaka, he even goes to the extent of taking 'Ukil Babu,' a Hindu, to the Indian embassy in his rickshaw. As could be expected, the rickshaw, while all the others are in the diplomat's car, is attacked by a crowd of Muslim hooligans. May, who is safe because she is an Englishwoman, runs out of the car to save Khalil and Ukil Babu. But instinctively and unthinkingly, Tridib, weaponless, follows. May remains unharmed. But in his vain attempt to save the other two, Tridib gets killed alongwith them. Thus the humanistic values of both Tridib and Khalil cement their willing self-sacrifice in the pool of blood of "that indivisible sanity that binds people to each other independently of their governments." (230)

The influence of Tridib's sacrifice for the sake of his instructive and persistent 'intimacy with elsewhere' is different on different people. It transforms the usually calm and self-controlled Grandmother into a revengeful 'Fury.' Robi is unable "to be free of that memory," the dreams of which haunt him like a nightmare in his sleep. (246) May is eager to share with the narrator her epiphany of Tridib's martyrdom and also to unburden her conscience of the feeling of guilt for Tridib's death, for when she got out of the car, she knew that Tridib would follow her. Having eased her conscience, she says: "But I know now I didn't kill him; I couldn't have, if I'd wanted. He gave himself up; it was a sacrifice. I know I can't understand it; I know I mustn't try, for any real sacrifice is a mystery." (252)

It is this redemptive Christ-like sacrifice for the sins of others which is at the root of Tridib's death, as the narrator also now realizes. It is upon him that the influence of Tridib's sacrifice is most pronounced. He was just a boy when the events of the novel happened, and it is now after his recollection of May's account that, as he is growing into manhood, the real meaning of the events gradually saturates him. Tridib now continues to watch over him (232) and he sees everything fall into a pattern, for, as he says, "Tridib had given me worlds to travel in, eyes to see them with." (20) The narrator therefore must have felt an irresistible urge to acquaint the world with the unspoken message for which Tridib had embraced certain death, and so the narrator uncoils those memories embedded in his childhood, as they come which explain "the irony that killed Tridib." (233) The novel embodies the narrator's continuous, though meandering, discourse on the personality of Tridib and the events happening to him and to all the related persons and on the circumstances that help to fill up the whole picture to make it life-like. They all together gradually build up a complete edifice progressively rising into a spire in the surrounding azure of which time and space have no relevance. The past is alive and is, in its "urgent contemporaneity" (227) on terms of deep intimacy with the present, in fact, with the spiritual resonance of its universal message of "the whole world is a family" and its fine-drawn technique of narration, this highly evocative novel is one of the most important milestones in the onward march of Indian English fiction.

NOTE

1. Amitav Ghosh, *The Shadow Lines* (Delhi: Ravi Dayal Publishers, 1988), p. 21.

The Shadow Lines: A Critical Appraisal

BRINDA VEERAPPA K.

The Shadow Lines (1988), which won Amitav Ghosh the Sahitya Akademi award in 1989, is fundamentally a novel which revives impressions and analyses previous experiences. It combines, with adroitness, private lives and public events in India, England and Bangladesh.

The overall focus is on the significance of political freedom in contemporary life. Characteristic of many Indian novels in English in the 1980s, politics—national and international—is the most important theme of Amitav Ghosh's *The Shadow Lines.* Political freedom, communal discord and nationalism, distinct features of contemporary life in the subcontinent, are some of the strands which constitute the panoramic range of this novel.

The book is in two parts—'Going Away,' and 'Coming Home'—beginning in 1939, thirteen years before the narrator-hero is born, when Mayadebi goes to England with her husband and Tridib. Tridib gives the young boy "worlds to travel in and eyes to see them with," for whom the narrator, as a young boy, is full of devoted admiration, because he enchants the narrator, and holds him spellbound with his immense knowledge and discursive stories about the year he had spent in England during the war. Tridib's stories open up new vistas of experience for the young school boy in Calcutta.

The story, told in first person, is of a growing boy who lives in the shadow of the man he idolizes; and of an individual drawn into history, and social and political turbulence.

The narrator's grandmother, Tha'mma, is pivotal to the narrative structure of this novel. She is a woman of unwavering spirit, who endures perils without fear, struggling and working to give a safe future to her only son. The novel presents an extensive study of a grandmother's relationship with her grandchild. For both the narrator and the grandmother, imagination is an "ideal retreat." The grandmother's memories have been passed on to the narrator as lively, animated stories. There is a clearness in his perception because his grandmother is adept in the art of recollection:

> I could see Kana-babu's sweet shop at the end of their lane with absolute clarity. . . . For me, Kana-babu's sweet shop at the end of the lane was as real as the one down our own lane. (194)

Though the Dhaka of the grandmother's youth has changed, the memory of her house becomes an image in her mind, important enough to live for. Most of the grandmother's vision is nostalgic. Her ancestral home in Dhaka has been occupied by Muslims after the Partition. She feels no malevolence, yet, the novel recognizes the unquiet and the violent political disturbances of the times. The communal outbreak in 1964, in both India and Pakistan, leads to the untimely death of Tridib, an incident which changes the grandmother's perception. Her home in Dhaka, filled with memories of lively experiences, now becomes a reminder of death and communal violence. The idyllic vision is shattered, and the grandmother begins to think in terms of "us" and "them." The death of Tridib is the culmination of the political discourse in the novel.

The grandmother unveils and lays open to view an alarming probability that a sense of nationalism can only develop through the specific process of war and bloodshed. The inner urge that prompts her is a deep, imperative wish to be free, and so feelings of nationalism get linked to self-respect and national power.

> All she wanted was a middle-class life in which . . . she would thrive believing in the unity of nationhood and territory, of self-respect and national power: that was all

> she wanted . . . a small thing that history had denied her in its fullness and for which she could never forgive it. (78)

The private crisis mirrors public turmoil.

The grandmother can never understand thoroughly her sister Mayadebi's granddaughter Ila's desire to live in London, rootless, but free of middle class constraints. The grandmother's response to Ila is not sympathetic. She tells the narrator: "Ila has no right to live there . . . she doesn't belong there." (77)

Ila also contributes to the narrator's voyage of self-discovery: "She and I were so alike that I could have been her twin—it was that very Ila who baffled me." (31) Ila's Trotskyite friends picketing for political causes and Ila struggling vigorously for personal freedom are strands of political commitment and nationalism which the novel brings forth. The force of nationalism in the quest for freedom is often a source of violence. This recognition and acknowledgement of the violence in our lives is the distinguishing characteristic of the novel. Amitav Ghosh shows that even characters like the grandmother and Ila, who do not indulge in violence, are on the periphery of it.

Amitav Ghosh does not use the conventionally conformed chronological narrative. The story moves to and fro, connecting and associating episodes and happenings. The protagonist is almost always present but he is never the initial actuator, nor visibly necessary to the action. But, he is there, always, as a consciousness within which everything emerges and occurs.

Amitav Ghosh prompts certain fundamental questions on imagination and reality. He seems, in fact, to indicate that there is only a 'shadowline' between reality and imagination. The places conceived by the narrator after listening to Tridib's conversation, and pouring over Bartholomew's Atlas are as much intense experiences, as the cities Ila visits. Tridib cautions the protagonist that if he does not learn to see the world through the exactness of his own imagination, he will be forced into constructing and viewing the world through another's invention. It is almost at the very end that the narrator emerges from obscurity, from the shadows of Ila and Tridib. The novel, therefore, is a quest to explore, and to come to terms with his own consciousness, moral surroundings, and intellectual space, which have shaped his consciousness. And he is "grateful for the glimpse" of the final redemptive mystery.

Space is governed implicitly by a reproduction of customary spatial structures. It is a language, perhaps, just like speech. Spatial experience is all-pervasive and powerful. Space, in *The Shadow Lines,* speaks both to and for society by bringing messages from the past and making statements about the present. Traditionally, architecture and space can be seen to be place, time and culture specific. In *The Shadow Lines,* the major challenge facing the concept of space is one of identity. The novel attempts to analyse how space functions to obscure the concreteness of it.

The title of the first section, 'Going Away,' suggests moving away from a space. At the very outset we come across Mayadebi's "going away" from India to England with her family. At once, the concept of space is introduced; geographical space and emotional space. It is a moving away which has a tremendous impact on the narrator as a young boy, though it occurred thirteen years before he was born.

The world of a child can be vivid, almost animate in its imagination, very different from that of adults.

> . . . when Tridib first talked to me about that journey. I remember trying very hard to imagine him back to my age, to reduce his height to mine, and to think away the spectacles that were so much a part of him that I really believed he had been born with them. (8)

Tridib, in his book-lined room, feeds the imagination of the narrator, with stories of the years he spent in London with the Price family, of the original of the catamaran, or the design of the temples at Konrak. The one thing, Tridib says, he wants the young boy to learn is to use his imagination "with precision." (24) Tridib can see Mrs. Price's brother, Alan Tresawsen, with his friends walking down the road to their home—all singing and happily drunk. However, he knows nothing of the world they are going into. He is unable to imagine "the web of trust and affections and small jealousies that must have held it together." (67) He wonders "which was more real, their dirty bathtubs and shared bedrooms or that other reality" (67)—the war in which three of the four of them would be dead, in two years. These graphic descriptions of Tridib's experiences in England form clear, effective pictures in the narrator's mind. His fascination for, and curiosity of England, grows.

Years later, as a twenty-six-year-old, the narrator goes to those places in London Tridib has told him about. Of course, he does not expect to see what Tridib had seen, yet he "could not still believe in the truth of what he did see." The narrator realizes, perhaps for the first time, that imagination and reality are but mirror images of one another. He can see the actuality of the present, but what Tridib had shown him through mental images seemed more real: The Solent Road in London is different from the descriptions Tridib had given him. Though he doesn't expect to see a street which was bombed forty years ago and still look the same, the narrator is cognizant of a reality Tridib had shown him years ago.

The narrator moves from India to England—from one real space to another perhaps in a quest for freedom—cultural, emotional and intellectual. Maybe, the stories told by Tridib confuse the narrator, who begins to deliberate on his real space. Geographically, India is the protagonist's real space, yet Tridib's stories are so fascinating that he needs to find out which his real space is, emotionally. His real space seems to choke him, and he needs to find a space to call his own, emotionally. This dissatisfaction is conceivably the result of the power wielded on the narrator by not only Tridib, but also his cousin Ila, who is of crucial concern in the narrator's voyage of self-discovery.

Ila has travelled the world since she was a child but has been unable to understand the worlds the narrator travels through Tridib. Ila journeys through real geographical spaces, but none of them is her own. They are all only transit points, spaces which she never belongs to. To her, the "Ladies . . . were the only fixed points in the shifting landscapes of her childhood." (20) Ila's quest for a space of her own can be seen from the time she is a young girl: schools are all that mattered to the young Ila—Probably because they are closest to real spaces in her ever-shifting childhood. Real spaces are important to Ila. Even as a child, she seeks, almost struggles, to find one for herself.

Ila lives perpetually in the present. She has no regard for memory—either personal or cultural. Her imagination leads her into error, and her inventions become self-frustrating wish-fulfilments when, in school, she is harried and badgered by the racist Denise. She expects Nick Price to come to her rescue.

> Nick Price knelt down . . . and wiped her face with the sleeve of his shirt. He helped her to her feet . . . and taking her hand in his, he said: Come on, I'll take you home now. (75)

However, the truth is that Nick is ashamed to be seen by his friends, walking home with an Indian. So harshly does Nick's behaviour dislodge the equilibrium of Ila's emotional make-up that she transfers this fantasy to the imaginary life of her doll.

> I tried then to think of Ila walking back from school alone through the lanes of West Hampstead. . . . Ila walking alone in a drizzle under the cold grey sky: Ila who in Calcutta was surrounded by so many relatives and cars and servants that she would never have had to walk . . . as for alone, there we were . . . all waiting to walk with Ila, Ila the sophisticate who could tell us stories about smart girls and rich boys in far-away countries whose names we had learnt from maps. (76)

The pathos of a child's search for a space of her own is brought out by Amitav Ghosh through Ila. Only an invisible line, a shadowline divides real and imagined space, but a child is unable to perceive it. Unfortunately, in Ila, this distressfully inadequate vision doesn't change even when the child attains adulthood.

> Between the physical environment and empirically observable human behaviour, there exists a social system and a set of cultural norms which define and evaluate portions of the physical environment relevant to the lives of the people involved and structures the way people will use (and react to) this environment in their daily lives.[2]

The narrator is impressed by the splendour of Ila's notion of freedom: "free of you, . . . free of your bloody culture and free of all of you," (89) even though "the clamour of vices within" warns him to the contrary. Ila's attempts to break free from her roots, in an attempt to free herself, is a frightful case of a freedom that hurls her to the destructive depths of bondage to another. She marries Nick, who continues to cling to Britain's colonial past and is unable to find himself a space in the present, to make her home in England, freeing herself from India. Yet, she fails to find her real space. Ila's concepts of freedom and home, and her attempts to find a space of her own in an 'alien' space, have ruinous consequences. She is condemned only to "play houses" with Nick, who is openly unfaithful to her. Her marriage to Nick is a failure, yet she clings on, living within her imagined, make-believe world, hardly realizing that the mask she has worn for so long with such finesse, has now become inseparable from her face.

The narrator, having derived his concepts of space from Tridib and Ila, searches for his own space when he grows up, only to find shadowlines. His childhood perception of space, grasped and seen through a child's eyes, a space invented by others, is not his real space. In the narrator, we detect a dissatisfaction with his real space, because of Tridib's and Ila's influences on him. The narrator is not given a name, perhaps, to show that he is not sure of the concept of identity. Probably, his identities clash—politically, he is Indian, but emotionally and culturally, he has still to find himself.

Through the characterization of the narrator's grandmother, Amitav Ghosh makes a touching comment on the lives of many people of the older generations of the subcontinent: of people who have lost their spaces—literal, emotional, and spiritual—because of the Partition. The grandmother's fascination for terrorist heroism during her youth highlights her yearning for freedom. She recalls her desire to work for terrorists who she believed, were fighting for freedom of their land: "I would have been frightened. . . . But . . . I would have killed him. It was for our freedom: I would have done anything to be free." (39)

This yearning for freedom continues well into her declining days because, paradoxically, though in a free country, as far as she is concerned, she is not free. She has been uprooted by the violent ruptures and dislocations caused by historical accidents, along with the indefinitely great number of individuals. Amitav Ghosh powerfully captures the tragedy that has overtaken most people of the subcontinent, a tragedy which is reflected in their deep longing for spaces of their own.

The grandmother's memories of Dhaka, her homeland before Partition, are passed on as colourful stories to the narrator, with a lucidity that makes his imaginative vision very clear.

> She had talked to me so often about that house and that lane I could see them myself—I could hear the buzzing of the flies, and I could see Kana-babu sitting hunched behind his cash-box, scratching his stomach, the same Kana-babu who had once caught their cousin stealing a rosogolla. (194)

The best part of the grandmother's life is spent in Dhaka, an emotionally happy and fulfilling space—space that is real, yet filled with the make-believe of a child.

She moves to Calcutta to work as a teacher upon the death of her husband, initially living in a one-room tenement, and later in a small flat where she 'had always been careful to maintain a titular control' over the household.

India becomes her "Invented country" only because of the partition, a historical accident which has dislocated her geographically, emotionally and spiritually. She continues to stick to her mental space, Dhaka, though decades later "the only worthwhile thing" left for her to do is "rescuing her uncle from his enemies and bringing him back where he belonged, to her invented country." (136-37) Emotionally, however, India cannot be her real space—not yet.

The grandmother is brought up in an environment of police raids in the universities of Dhaka during the British rule, and the terrorist movement in Bengal during the first few decades of this century. Her need to be free, to have a space of her own, are reasons enough to motivate her. But, she has

> nothing but contempt for a freedom that could be bought for the price of an air ticket. For she too had once wanted to be free; she had dreamt of killing for her freedom. It is not freedom she wants . . . she wants to be left alone to do what she pleases. . . . But that is not what it meant to be free. (89)

The grandmother's strong sense of belonging to a space is brought out with her attitude that everyone who lives in a country should have earned his right to be there. Ila, she argues vehemently, has no right to be in England because

> she doesn't belong there. It took those people a long time to build that country; hundreds of years, years and years of war and bloodshed. Everyone who lives there has earned his right to be there with blood. . . . They know they are a nation because they've drawn their borders with blood. (77-78)

She advocates the opinion that it takes war to make a country, and once that happens people forget their differences by birth. She believes "in the unity of nationhood and territory." The provision of territory satisfies people's basic need for identity as opposed to anonymity. Identity relates to a need for a sense of identification with a specific territory. Essentially, it expresses a sense of belonging to a space, and of individual identity. Amitav Ghosh shows that the force of nationalism in the quest for freedom can be a source of violence; a violence that kills Tridib.

Upon moving into a larger house, which seems immense after the cramped little flat, the narrator notices that the grandmother no longer cares for control over the household. The vastness of the new house brings back memories of her huge childhood-home in Dhaka. The past, suddenly, becomes very important to the protagonist's grandmother. Imagination and memory make possible for her the recollection of the concrete reality of her ancestral home and the region about the place. Decades have elapsed and she has stayed away in Calcutta, yet, in her mind, the place of her childhood remains as real as ever. It is a memory, a thought that sustains, soothes, and provides a sense of belonging. She feels the need to go back to her childhood space, ostensibly to bring her old uncle back with her, but in truth, there is a deep desire to go back to that space which once was real, and now remains only in memory to see for herself if the geographical space she still considers her home, is so emotionally too.

Yet, there is a fear within, at going back to a familiar and loved space: a fear of anticipation, of not finding that space which has been enshrined in her mind. "I feel scared. Do you think I will be wise after all these years? It won't be like home anymore." (149) There is, in the grandmother, a passionate eagerness to retain her old space, and therefore, she is not ready to face the reality that may come her way.

The grandmother is unable to understand the concept of boundaries. The idea of boundaries carries a very particular significance and the grandmother wonders if she would be able to see the border between India and East Pakistan from the plane; if

> there's something—trenches perhaps, or soldiers, or guns pointing at each other, or even just barren strips of land.

> Don't they call it no-man's land? . . . if there aren't any trenches or anything, how are people to know? . . . where's the difference then? And if there's no difference both sides will be the same, it'll be just like it used to be before . . . what was it all for then—partition and all the killing . . . if there isn't something in-between? (151)

Little does she realize that the boundary demarcating the two countries is only a 'Shadowline,' that the border isn't on the frontier but in "all those disembarkation cards" she has to fill. The irony hits her hard—her birthplace is Dhaka, which is no longer a part of her country, a place she no longer belongs to, her nationality is 'Indian.' She is unable to comprehend how her birthplace is at odds with her nationality. "In any case her Dhaka had long since vanished into the past. . . . The Dhaka she was thinking of was the city that had surrounded their old house." (193-94)

Amitav Ghosh brings out the pathos of a lost dream. The grandmother has an idea of real space—a space she thinks she belongs to, but, in Dhaka when she looks for her determined space—culturally and linguistically determined space—she finds it no longer there. "Where's Dhaka? . . . this isn't Dhaka." (195) She finds the new hotels, race courses, and the Cinema hall, all wonderful, "But where's Dhaka?"

> This couldn't be it, she cried, It can't be *our* lane, for where's Kana-babu's sweet shop? . . . where's the sweet shop gone? . . . The driver rolled his hands sadly in the air and said: There's no sweet shop here; it's all gone. Now there's only this one. (206)

There are changes, both culturally and linguistically. Her "home" has been occupied by Muslim migrants from across the border, and the grandmother instantly realizes that in real life, there are no determined spaces. There are objectives for a person being in a particular place. These reasons are almost invariably socially defined. To different groups these places are very different, being used for quite different purposes. To the grandmother and Mayadebi, the house holds an idyllic vision of "balconies and terraces, rising in steps out of the ground; the garden where they had once spent their evenings making up stories about their uncle's part of the house." (217) But to Saifuddin, the mechanic, the place has to be put to practical use, "the old portico had sprouted a tin shed," which served as an automobile workshop.

> It was all changed, but now my grandmother didn't care any longer. It wasn't the house she remembered, the house she had built for me in Calcutta, but it was near enough. (208)

The "potential" of an environment can only be made manifest by the users. The individual relates to the need for "personalization": the ability to create for oneself or to put a distinctive stamp on one's personal environment.

Saifuddin demonstrates an aggressive defence of territory through hospitality, bringing "tea for guests from India." (109) Saifuddin, the refugee from India, is cordial to the grandmother, but is very keen on sending the old man away with them, so he can put a claim for the whole house. Hospitality, and invitation to one's territory, is subject to one's control, or ownership of that territory. Thus, the important quality is of control, rather than defence, of the given territory. All along, the grandmother feels no rancour about the Partition or the Muslim refugees occupying her home, but Tridib's death changes her attitude and she develops a hatred for Pakistan. She now talks of fighting for freedom. She sells her most precious piece of jewellery to help fund the war, "for your freedom, we have to kill them before they kill us; we have to wipe them out." (237) India becomes her real space. The grandmother effectively dramatizes the trauma of partition; the lack of emotional, political, and literal space to those who are uprooted by this separation through borders. The borders do not create a separation, only "a yet-undiscovered irony—the irony that killed Tridib." (233) Like Ila, the grandmother also seeks fixed points only to find shadowlines.

It takes the narrator fifteen years to understand and connect the events that kill Tridib in Dhaka, with the events in Calcutta at the same time. He has grown up

> believing in the reality of space; I believed that distance separates that it is a corporeal substance; I believed in the reality of nations and borders; I believed that across the border there existed another reality. The only relationship my vocabulary permitted between those separate realities was war or friendship. (219)

As a child, the narrator's perception of space is always only in the literal sense, the emotional space is beyond his comprehension. "Tha'mma. . . . How could you have 'come' home to Dhaka? You don't know the difference between coming and going." (152) For a child there may be no clear differentiated boundaries, and therefore, the self and the environment fuse. As an eight-year-old, the narrator sees England through the eyes of Ila and Tridib. As a twenty-six-year-old, he feels the need to be free, only to find that real space is always reduced to shadowlines, because it never approximates the imagined space he builds up. The past becomes difficult to imagine: "When I go past Gole Park now I often wonder whether that would happen today. I don't know, I can't tell: that world is closed to me, shut off by too many years spent away." (7) And perhaps, for the first time he is able to grasp that spatial experience links our perceptions of space and architecture, though unconsciously. The nature of environments cannot be separated from people's experience, and images of that environment. As a child, the narrator confuses political and cultural space with geographical space. This is why he is unable to comprehend why

> within the tidy ordering of Euclidean space, Chiang Mai in Thailand was much nearer Calcutta than Delhi is; that Chengdu in China is nearer than Srinagar is. Yet, I had never heard of those places until I drew my circle, and I

> cannot remember a time when I was so young that I had not heard of Delhi or Srinagar. (232)

He measures space with concrete distances. But as a mature young man, the narrator realizes that space cannot be measured on a map, but only by cultural and linguistic identities.

> . . . the places we know as Dhaka and Calcutta were more closely bound to each other . . . after they had drawn their lines—so closely that I, in Calcutta, had only to look into the mirror to be in Dhaka; a moment when each city was the inverted image of the other, locked into an irreversible symmetry by the line that was to set us free—our looking-glass border. (233)

Calcutta and Dhaka, the protagonist realizes, are merely reflections of each other. Within the political construct, the narrator realizes, one's own space and home had political, cultural and inherited psychic overtones.

It is in England that he realizes the truth, when he emerges from the shadows of Ila and Tridib. He returns to India because he is aware of what Ila has lost, and learns what his real home is. "Home" is not a geographical entity, but an emotional, moral and intellectual entity which can be identified in the shadows of one's own inner being.

The narrator's first mature vision is possible when he is unable to accept Ila's concept of space and his hesitation to enter into a space, she is attempting to become a part of: "there's a joy merely in knowing that you're a part of history . . . . we know that in the future political people everywhere will look to us." (104) For the first time, he realizes the truth, and attempts to come to terms with his own consciousness, and the space which has shaped it.

The title, *The Shadow Lines,* itself reflects, in the final analysis, that there is no solid space, either geographically or culturally. The title reflects the existence of various spaces only as abstractions blurring into one another: alien space blurring into native space; cultural space into geographical space. Space, Amitav Ghosh shows, is a pure abstraction built up by psychic, cultural and political constructs. Space has no concrete demarcations, and can be designated only by shadowlines.

Space, in *The Shadow Lines,* perhaps, like all things rare and beautiful, seems difficult to attain.

NOTES

1. Amitav Ghosh, *The Shadow Lines* (New Delhi: Ravi Dayal, 1988), p. 20.
2. Steven Tiesdell, Taner O.C., "Architecture and People," ed. Ben Farmer and Henti Louw, *Companion to Contemporary Architectural Thought* (New York: Routledge, 1993), p. 45.

Like Stepping into a Mirror: *The Shadow Lines*

RAMA KUNDU

A small boy and a small girl are playing 'House' under a huge table in a dusty room. The girl draws a house with her finger on the dust. The boy cannot accept it. He erases a line, draws another. The girl is almost in tears that her house is spoilt. This is one of the many apparently innocuous but very evocative and touching scenes in Amitav Ghosh's *The Shadow Lines*, which is bound to come back to the reader's mind with oppressive intensity after s/he has finished the book; because by then one comes to realize that this is a story about blurred lines across time-space-consciousness—that the writer here interrogates the very basis of such demarcating or dividing 'lines' as may have been drawn up by the metanarratives of historical-cultural continuums.

Firm clear lines distinguishing people from people, and separating place from place, times from times, were the prerogative of a different age. We live in an age characterized by uncertainty, instability, undefinability. so a story, which is truly of our times, can hardly afford the determinacy of strong and distinct demarcation and definitions. This is what one experiences in *The Shadow Lines*. In the novel the signs denoting borders on the map and periods/dates on the calender lose their force as concrete reality. Events take place in different parts of the globe at varying points of history. Yet, as the narrator looks at the destruction, violence, terror, perpetuated in each of the chronotopes—be it war-time England in the

1940s, or riot-scathed Khulna in 1964, or terror-torn India in the 1980s—it seems to be like 'looking into the glass.' It seems as if all the lines so fastidiously imagined and charted by man across time and space, have been but illusory. Again, even the concept of the unique distinctiveness of an individual seems to be but an extension of the above illusion. S/he appears to get merged into other individuals like 'stepping into the mirror.' Similarly the frontier between fictionality and reality, past and present, subject (the narrator) and object (the narrated) surface only to get dissolved again and again.

Amitav Ghosh's novels, which are both Indian and global in perception and treatment, represent a fresh trend in today's postcolonial literature. His novels may be noted for their simultaneous probing into the chronicles of nations and privates lives, the reality of the fictional and the fictionality of the real, the empirical space as projected by the Atlas and the subjective space as surface in the individual's memory and consciousness, specific dates and events the fluid continuity and repetitive sameness of events through time.

It is remarkable how the novelist presents in *The Shadow Lines* the complex pattern of oscillations between and interweaving of the multilayered experience of varied people in diverse chronotopes which ultimately appear to converge into a single text—about strangers meeting amidst ruins—that get restated in a series of apparently varied context, both personal and national. These contexts are, again, distinguished from each other only by illusory 'shadow lines' of borders, calendars, and individual perceptions. Ghosh uses memory and imagination as the narrative devices to interrogate space, time, persona, and overcome the isolability of persons as well as the distance between spaces and times which appear both fluid and concrete. This is the way Ghosh's narrator in the novel struggles to be free of the shadows of racial and cultural metanarratives. It is interesting to see how the author grapples with the multiple "shadows" in the concrete terms of a postcolonial text of our times.

One major device is the evocation of globality. The text is thickly interspersed with countless place-names across the world-map, and the reader is continuously reminded of a vast spatial context. Lands may be broken up by changing borders and frontiers, imposed through war or violence; but they are perceived as one total and single phenomenon.

Owing to the finely managed space-time montage, the story seems to happen in all places at once. As Kaul puts it: "Every corner of it involves all its space and every moment all its moments." (305) The narrator takes care to point out that in his childhood Tridib's parents were always away, either abroad, or in Delhi, because Tridib's father was a diplomat. Tridib's elder brother, who was an economist with the U.N., was also always somewhere in Africa or South-East Asia. People physically move between capitals, countries, continents—Calcutta, Delhi, Dhaka, London, Cairo, Kuwait. Mrs. Price's brother had been hospitalized in Verdun (3) in Germany, on the eve of the war; her father had been a globe-trotter in his days, and had worked in different capacities in Malaysia, Bolivia, the Guinea Coast, Ceylon and Calcutta. The narrator's father goes to Africa on business trip (31), and his uncle happens to be the Indian consul-general in Sofia. (34) Nick and Ila go for their honeymoon to Dar-es-Salaam, and from there to Kenya and Tanzania. Next to the narrator's room in London, there was the American girl from Seattle, who was spending six months in London, before going on to Rome and Paris. (177) Even Nick's secret girl-friends have to come from Martinique and Indonesia. (188)

With equal ease the narrator evokes Calcutta, Delhi, and London—with their respective streets, lanes, shops, restaurants, roadmarks, just as he reminds the reader with perfect ease of America and Benaras, Germany and Dhaka, almost in the same breath. Thus, London becomes vivid as the narrator walks all the way from Charing Cross to Stockwell, or finds himself wandering through Soho or Trafalgar Square, humming a Hindi film song; looks into Brick Lane for the house where Alan and Dan had been killed during the war; passes by Convent Garden, visits the Chinese cafe in Neale Street; accompanies Ila to the small Bangladeshi place in Clapham; remembers Tridib running down to West End Lane to buy papers, and so many other details. These are constantly interwoven in the narrator's memory with locations of Delhi and Calcutta. On receiving the news of his grandmother's death, the boy wanders out of his college, passes Maurice Nagar, Ring Road, the Central Secretariat, the Mall Road (92); also in search of innocent entertainment, he occasionally goes to the Chanakya cinema or the Khyber restaurant at Kashmiri Gate. (93) Calcutta comes alive through such fine touches as "that conversation-loving stretch of road between Gariahat and Gole Park" (8) or the Gariahat fish-market (33) from where the very best 'Ilish' was bought for Ila's mother, as also through the mention of Howrah, Sealdah, Rajabajar, Free School Street, Ballygunge Place, Grand Hotel, and so many other signs.

This Calcutta is, again, resonant with memories of other places. The beautiful greenery of Tridib's ancestral house calls back to Africa; his grandfather had imported rain-forest trees from Brazil and Congo. (45) The huge table in the house was bought in an exhibition in the Crystal Palace of London in the 1890s. Even small articles are supposed to evoke distances. The gifts Ila's parents used to bring back when they came to Calcutta for a holiday included Indonesian leather puppets, or improbable North African stools. Ila's 'Manila' folder contained photographs of girls and boys from various places "two continents away." (22) Even the schoolbag of Magda in Ila's story is purchased in Florence. (73)

In view of the persistent interfusion of spaces, the titles of the two parts of the book—'Going Away' and 'Coming Home'—become ironical; because the impression that emerges from Ghosh's handling of the distances is that one can neither "go away," nor "come home." Possession/dispossession of and belonging to specific spaces become converging, enigmatic experiences. Nearness and distance overlap and interlap into each other as men and women, separated by borders, seas and continents try to reach out to each other, and at the same time even relatives or former fellow-citizens meet as no less strangers amidst ruins of the past.

Apparently, places are to be seen not merely with one's optical eyes. Ghosh's 'internationality' here, to use Steven

Connor's term,[1] differs from, say, Graham Greene's use of varied spatial contexts. His places are to be seen mentally, through imagination or imaginative reconstruction of memory. So place-names could be "a set of magical talismans" to the responsive child as Tridib pointed them out on his tattered, Atlas—Addis Ababa, Madrid, Cuzco, Cairo, Cheops, Algiers, Brisbane—though to Ila, who had been actually to these places, the names evoked nothing. "The places themselves went past her in an illusory whirl of movement, like those studio screens in old films which flash past the windows of speeding cars." (23) Rather in Nick, the narrator finds a kindred spirit, because he wants to "travel around the world like Lionel Tresawsen, to live in faraway places halfway around the globe, to walk through the streets of La Paz and Cairo." (52) His grandmother, on coming to Dhaka after years, insistently asks, "Where's Dhaka," (194) since she misses this truer reality of the city; she misses *her* Dhaka, the place of *her* imagination as conjured by the name.

To her dismay, Grandmother finds herself a foreigner in her own birthplace. Borders are the legacy of history. Borders also shift according to politico-military contingencies. But in the land of imagination, borders are irrelevant. So, Grandmother feels resentful that she should be a foreigner in *her own* city. She finds it hard to get reconciled to the mechanical rules of nationality. She has to 'invent' her country anew. (131) Alan and Francesca had tried to ignore these frontiers in the forties: Alan had got injured while trying to smuggle her out of Germany. The friendship of the four—Alan, Dan. Mike and Francesca—who came from different places, demanding varying loyalties, and lived in the same house in war-time London, could not be spoilt by cultural or political borders, though ultimately war destroyed all the four one way or the other.

In Grandmother's experience, walls and borders had played their role. In her childhood she had seen partition walls coming up in her own parental house, and she felt nervous whenever people said, "We're like brothers." (123) This is representing in microcosm the macrocosmic happenings of history—

the partition that rent Bengal apart. Yet she had tried to reach out to the other side of the wall, both in the family house and on the subcontinental map repeatedly till Tridib was killed by communal violence. Racism is another form of partition wall between peoples which Ila had to face as a child. (76) Grandmother's exclusiveness, as indicated by her emphatic objection—"Ila has no right to be there," (77) i.e., London, shows the obverse face of racism. Tridib's terrible death had made her exclusive to the degree of hysteria; this became evident in her reaction during the 1965 war across the Indo-Pak border, which had scared her grandson.

The same death, however, made the narrator see things in a different way altogether. As the narrator recounts his past notions, it is an admission of past mistakes as well. He had grown up believing in the truth of the precepts that were available to him: "I believed in the reality of space; I believed that distance separates, that it is a corporeal substance; I believed in the reality of nations and borders; I believed that across the border there existed another reality. The only relationship my vocabulary permitted between those separate realities was war or friendship." (218) Later, through the pain and bafflement of personal loss, he glimpses the gap between those illusions of segments and the transcendent reality that percolated through all such dividing nets, and infiltrated the entirety of spaces like the migratory birds flying over frontiers with divine indifference. The narrator's act of drawing the amazing circles (231-34) on the Atlas may be understood with reference to the above realization. It is simultaneously fantasizing and undermining the concept of boundaries which imply the idea of separateness—exclusion—isolation of areas and lands.

After drawing the circles he is struck with wonder that there had really been a time when well-meaning sensible people had thought that "there was a special enchantment in lines." (233) They had assumed that by drawing lines they had pushed violence to the border, that "the two bits of land would sail away from each other like the shifting tectonic plates." (233) Yet the irony, he finds, is that the very act of drawing lines made them more closely bound to each other than ever. So what happened in Calcutta sent its tremors in Dhaka, just as the same tremors shook London and Germany during the war. Coming back from Germany to England, Alan had found it was "like stepping through a looking-glass." (66) And the narrator finds Dhaka and Calcutta "locked into an irreversible symmetry by the line that was to set us free—our looking-glass border." (233) Robi also comes round to the same knowledge through his encounter with terrorism sprouting everywhere, and his fixation with one prolonged nightmare. He has seen people insensately killing each other for what they think "freedom"; the terrorists and separatists in Assam, the North-east, Punjab, Sri Lanka, as well as the army and the police, shooting each other and shooting innocent people, and all citing the cause of "freedom." Robi goes around, carrying his sad silent burden of knowledge that nothing will change even if "they draw thousands of little lines through the whole subcontinent and give every little place a new name" (247); because one cannot divide a memory. The memory goes on working even after fifteen years, and thousands of miles away.

Both space and time appear simultaneously concrete and fluid in the novel. The author's treatment of both, indeed, shows a remarkable flexibility and ambience. There is no linear narration, and no clearly definable specific time-frame. Time and space are perceived as an unbroken continuum only by means of exercising memory and imagination. The author is particular about year, months, and even certain dates. But these signs seem to follow one another in an arbitrary chaotic manner. Thus 1959 is followed by 1940 (17); March 1963 in Calcutta, and 25 September 1940 in London converge and melt into a December night of 1980 in the cellar of the Price house (182); a sequence of 1979 in Delhi slids back to October 1962—the days of the Chinese war; 2 January 1964, the time of the Calcutta-Khulna riots, leads back 27 December 1963, when the 'Hajrat Bal' had disappeared from Kashmir.

Countless examples of such zigzag run through time may be cited from the text. The author weaves a complex pattern of time—a gigantic calendar, as it were—in which various points of past and present are continuously made to intersect and overlap in the most unpredictable manner of an interior monologue. This reminds one of Steven Conner's observation in the concluding chapter of his book on English novel in history. Conner maintains, "The postwar novel of history attempts to understand and represent the vexed and uncertain relationship of the present to its many possible pasts." (199) In thus persistently looking backwards at the various turns of the many possible pasts, the novel inspects its own increasingly complex times through individual recollection as well as the shared exchange of memory. The novelist also seems to have been baffled by an emerging sense of the impossibility of conferring sequence, direction and narratability upon the enigmatic past, and the confusing present in relation to that past.

The viewing and reviewing of the past require a special aptitude. Tridib and the narrator continuously turn back to the past. Incidentally, Tridib is an archaeologist by profession, and the narrator is a history student, and thus both are supposed to be preoccupied with the past. Ila, who lives intensely in the present, cannot understand their imaginative approach to the past. "For Ila the current was the real: it was as though she lived in a present which was like an airlock in a canal, shut away from *the tidewaters of the past and the future* by floodgates." (30) For Tridib and the narrator, on the other hand, the tidewaters of the past rise high and flood their present. They experience the world more concretely in their imagination, since "those experiences were permanently available in their memories." (30) So, standing on the streets of London in the 1980s, the narrator goes back to the war-ravaged London as Tridib had described it in his childhood, and "could not believe in the truth of what I did see." (57) Again, while helping May with her box collection at the end of Oxford Street, he lapses two decades back down memory lane, when May first arrived at Howrah station, and from there slids another two decades down to her childhood in war-time London as Tridib remembered it. (163-65) On the occasion of the Christmas party, Mrs Price invokes the ancestors. As Ila and the narrator, Nick and May gather for the party, she proposes a toast to the two grandfathers,—"Mr. Justice Chandrashekhar

Datta-Chaudhuri and my father, Lionel Tresawsen, for we wouldn't be here together now if it weren't for them." (108)

Grandmother insisted that time was like a toothbrush; it went mouldy if it was not used, and began to stink. (4) In this she seemed to present a contrast to Tridib, who never seemed to use his time, and yet whose "time did not stink." (4) Yet Grandmother herself is sometimes seen toying with time and re-enacting the past in memory which veered round to the "extraordinary history" of the terrorist movement amongst nationalists in Bengal in the first decades of the century. (37) She also talks to the child about her own childhood in Dhaka; on being inquired by her son if they were discussing the Chinese war, the great event of the time, she proudly retorts: "The past is what we talk about" (127); it is her way of re-living a time that is now irretrievable.

People are continuously squeezing in and out of different corridors of time—present, past, remote past, recent past, so many segments of past, which go on crisscrossing each other in so many varied patterns, that one cannot be sure about the specific vantage point of time from which the story is being narrated till the end. One tends to lose the track—which is the present and which is the past! Even at the end the shadow of the past lies long, or, to use the narrator's own term, the 'ghost' lingers, which is but a "presence displaced in time." (181)

Robert Young, in his book *Torn Halves* (1996), explains New Historicism from a fresh angle which corresponds to Ghosh's treatment of the past in *The Shadow Lines*. Young maintains that New Historicism often eschews grand causal or narrative schemes in favour of the tracing of synchronic links between different cultural practices, showing the processes of circulation and exchange among them. (165) It is in this sense that *The Shadow Lines* shows a New Historicist approach to past, so far as New Historicism espouses history as a series of punctual incidents, and tends to see history and culture in synchronic terms, setting aside its relation to any linear processual schemas, and eschewing meaning except insofar as it is made in each instant.

The above perception of time, past and history is reflected in the narrative mode. The narration here is simultaneously an act of remembering, tinged with emotion, as well as a search for meanings both at personal and national levels, which continue to elude. The act of remembering determines the form of the novel—its nonlinear multilayered narrative technique. Instead of mimetic realism, the narrator uses defamiliarising perspectives including mystery, bafflement, indeterminacy. In this context, memory is the only means by which the search for connection is carried on.

Remembering is also a search for identity through the multiple mirrors or glassdoors; the image of mirror rhythmically recurs in the text, and included reflectors of a wide range, from the small handglass to the vast cosmic mirror of the desert that sends inverted reflections in the form of mirages. (247) These mirrors are constituted of personal consciousness as it envisions personal life and national events.

Nick Price had become a "spectral presence" beside the narrator in the mirrors of his boyhood, "growing with me" (50); when Ila, in her anger, declared that she wanted to be free of all of them, he shouted out: "You cannot be free of me because *I am within you* . . . just as you are within me." (89) The mirror image comes back most poignantly on the occasion when he tried to reconstruct the past through the headlines of old newspapers. He felt, "I began on my strangest journey: a voyage into a land outside space, an expanse without distances; a land of looking glass events." (224) This journey is stalled when he stumbles at the point of Tridib's death—his most traumatic memory.

Indeed, from the very opening sentence the narrator has been trying to come to this sequence. and at the same time cannot. He goes on digressing infinitely instead. At moments he would come close to the terrible event, and then again drift away, as if it is too terrible, too impossible to face. Arundhati Roy uses a similar narrative technique in *The God of Small Things* with reference to a very painful sequence; her narrator goes backward and forward in time, veering round the most crucial event (Velutha's death), but fails to summon sufficient strength to blurt it out till near the end. When the narrator of *The Shadow Lines* at last brings himself round to write about Tridib's death, it involves a painful struggle for him. He admits: "Every word I write about those events of 1964 is the product of a struggle with silence. . . . This silence . . . lies outside the reach of my intelligence, beyond words . . . it is not a presence at all; it is simply a gap, a hole, an emptiness in which there are no words." (218) It is an overspreading silence, undefinable by any boundaries; it is the yawning "gap between words and the world." (218) Since he cannot find or construct any meaning of the events he tries to report, the narrator feels, he is overpowered by "the silence of an absolute, impenetrable banality." (218)

It is only at the end that he can describe Tridib's death, and that too at the second hand; because, as he repeats mournfully, "I do not have the strength to listen." (228) The narrator's inadequacy, which is the result of his trauma, epitomizes the shock of violence that has cast its spell on the history of our times; so much so that history has become "enigmatic, broken, and in a certain sense, resistant to being imagined." (Conner 199) The narrator faces this enigma every time he tries to reconstruct the history in his memory which had swallowed up Tridib, or the other segments of history from the 1940s to the 1980s that have insensately destroyed life without any logic.

The task the novelist sets himself is to imagine the unimaginable, and narrate the unspeakable. It is an unthinkable vacancy which simultaneously incites and interdicts. So his narrator must bear witness to that which paradoxically remains barred from witnessing, and continued to think a form of unthinkability.

Fifteen years after Tridib's death, the narrator is still haunted by the impenetrability of its banality. He experiences the sense of living in ghostly aftermath as though history were somehow already finished. It is such a deadness that he has no word for it. As Beckett's Molloy had said: "My life is over and yet it goes on and what tense is there for that." (36)

This has been poignantly true in the narrator's case because, in a way, Tridib and he are inseparable. What he says to Ila could be applied with much more cogency to his relationship with Tridib. "You cannot be free of me because I am within you . . . just as you are within me." (89) Tridib could have said this to him as well.

Tridib had taught him in his childhood to see things clearly without the shadows of inhibitions or illusions. He had told him once that "real desire" for knowing could carry one beyond the limits of one's time, place, and self "to a place where there was no border between oneself and one's image in the mirror." (29) For the narrator, however, this reflection in the mirror revealed Tridib's image as well. In his desire, self-image and Tridib had become merged. Since childhood he had attempted a conscious identification with Tribid. Tridib had left for England at eight. The narrator says, "I *believe* I was eight too when Tridib first talked to me about that journey." He tried hard to define Tridib's looks, and subsequently came to identify himself with Tridib: "I had decided that he had looked like me." (3) A strange bond existed between the two. The boy considered it his "unique privilege to understand Tridib," (170) and deliberately blurred the lines between fictional illusion and reality in order to be Tridib. The carefully maintained anonymity of the narrator may be understood in this light, as also his avoidance of any descriptive details regarding his own appearance.

It may be noted that Tridib is also a narrator; he told the story of his journey to London in instalments; retold the story of Snipe; frequently took to mythmaking (instead of reportage) and fabulation, like Ila about Magda, and Tha'mma about the inverted life in the 'other' part of the Dhaka house. Tridib, who used to make up 'fairy lands' for him by means of his stories, had given him worlds to travel in and also eyes to see them with. Yet he knew that the sights Tridib saw in his imagination were infinitely richer than he would ever see. Hence his aspiration to be *not like* Tridib, but Tridib himself, entering into him, as it were. This explains his love-making to May at the end. The narrator carries Tridib within him, and re-lives his life, imaginings, fancies, perceptions. Once Tridib had told him to "invent" properly; since we could not see without inventing what we saw, it should be done properly; because otherwise "we would never be free of other people's inventions." (31) Later the very act of narrating itself—which involves a sustained exercise of imaginative insight on the narrator's part in order to wrench himself free from historical metanarratives—becomes accomplishing, in a way, what Tridib had told him to do.

The narrator is, as it were, an extension of Tridib's desires, dreams, imagination; so much so that he finally must have Tridib's girl too, and only together with her can have a glimpse of the "redemptive mystery" behind Tridib's death. This is only natural in the glass-door world of the novel. This is in tune with the postmodern perception of character—that s/he cannot portray a fully individuated person.

The narrator not only appears a mirrored image of Tridib, he also serves as a mirror to reflect times, places, people. This is a power he has inherited from Tridib. At the same time he has also inherited the central story from Tridib who had, again, inherited it from Snipe—"an old story, the best story . . . a very sad story, about a man without a country, who fell in love with a woman-across-the-seas." (186) 'Ghosts' of tellers assembled behind the story that underscored the sadness and simplicity of genuine human relationships which were not controlled by country frontiers, or cowered by distances.

Tridib had handed down the simple story to the children as he had been given it by Snipe in his own childhood. But later Tridib had also personalized the story when he wrote to May that he should like to meet her as 'strangers amidst ruins.' What Tridib had wanted was finally realized by his mirror image, or extended self, at least for once; that was fifteen years after Tridib's death, when he met May and found that she too remained pinned down to the shambles of the past, that both of them were struggling under the rubbles of a terrible memory. Their shared sorrow had divested them of all other racial or generational identities, and brought them together 'across-the-seas,' for one night, at the end of the novel.

The Shadow Lines leaves the reader with the sense that reality or history is but provisional; that a world of eternal verities is no longer possible and that at best it could be but a series of constructions, artifices, impermanent structures—like drawing a house in the dust, or writing one's name in water (like Keats), or 'strangers meeting amidst ruins' for one brief interval.

The author captures the historical moment we are living through with its enigma and uncertainty, bafflement and plurality in the postmodernist context of blurred lines and mystery shadows. He sets himself an impossible task—grasping 'shadows.' It is indeed remarkable the way he captures them.

NOTE

1. "Both the reading and readerships of fiction have become more complex, hybrid and mobile in the postwar period than previously. . . . The availability and popularity of contemporary international fiction is increasing. Indeed, large international readerships have been built up for the 'Latin American novel' or the 'African novel.'" (Conner, p. 27).

Bibliography

Samuel Beckett, *The Trilogy*. London: Calder and Boyers, 1959.

S. Conner, *The English Novel in History*. London: Routledge, 1996.

Amitav Ghosh, *The Shadow Lines*. 1988; New Delhi: O.U.P., 1995.

Suvir Kaul, "Separation Anxiety: Growing Up Inter/National in *The Shadow Lines*," *The Shadow Lines*. New Delhi: O.U.P., 1995.

R. Young, *Torn Halves*. U.K.: Manchester University Press, 1996.

The Blurring of Postimperialism and Postcolonialism in *The Shadow Lines*

SHYAM S. AGARWALLA

Aparna Dharwadker and Vinay Dharwadker say that "Ghosh displays, in other words, the same cosmopolitanism in treating postimperial England and postcolonial India that characterizes the current generation of Indian English poets."[1] Amitav Ghosh, fully Indian by birth, and upbringing, creates such singular variations in his novels *The Circle of Reason* (1986) and *The Shadow Lines* (1988) on the theme of the East-West encounter as to transform it altogether.

To understand the uniqueness of the East-West encounter in *The Shadow Lines*, we should examine briefly some fictional works, related to the same East-West encounter, written by Englishmen and Indians. To begin with, *Siri Ram-Revolutionist* by Edmund Candler is about the political agitation by Indians in the early period of the twentieth century. Saros Cowasjee, in his Introduction to this novel, writes: "his [Candler's] attitude towards Indians was that they were an 'inferior' race. Liberty, he believed, was for those who deserve it, and the Indians did not deserve it. In *Siri Ram-Revolutionist*, he comes close to Kipling in his general distaste for most educated Indians, and in his admiration for the British rulers in India."[2] Mr. Candler was Principal of Mohindra College, Patiala, when he wrote this novel. He makes his character Skene speak of India:

You are told that Indians are denied freedom of speech

> and liberty of the Press; but you must remember things are different here. Rumours of cow-killing will stir blood to a white heat, the story of defiled mosque will raise a Jehad. There is all the difference between holding a lighted match to an iron safe and to a haystack. (96)

At the close of his oration, he throws aside the mask and speaks bluntly:

> I hate cant. India is as much the property of the English as the estate of one of your Zemindars is the property of the landlord whose ancestors won it by the sword, or was given it for service. . . . It is quite true that if we left the country each community would be at the other's throat. This is one good reason for our staying. But it is not *the* reason. We are here because it is our country. (98)

Miss Irene Burn's novel *The Border Line* was published in 1916. Her attitude towards the Swadeshi movement is expressed through "the man with a torch" who secretly attends a students' meeting.

> You hate the English folk, yet you speak their language better than your own. You prate of Swadeshi, say you will wear only Indian made loincloths, yet you vaunt your knowledge of the English tongue; you rode here on an English foot carriage along roads made by the English, where the lamps are fed by the lighting wire and not by country oil. (155)

The second phase of Indian nationalism produced in 1922 and the following years some novels written by Englishmen, notably E.M. Forster, Edward Thompson and E.W. Savi. Mrs. Maud Diver makes the 'patriotic' Sir Lakshman Singh say in *Lilamani* that "no worse harm could befall to India than that Great Britain should cease to be paramount power. . . . But in order for being paramount she must be, in best sense, a power; not mere figurehead or rash experimentalist shifting now to this foot now to that."

In Paul Scott's *The Jewel in the Crown* (1966), we find anglicized bourgeois Indians who, in the words of Frantz Fanon in *Black Skin, White Masks*, have become "rigidified in predetermined forms, forbidding all evolution, all progress, all discovery. I call middle-class a closed society in which life has no taste, in which the air is tainted, in which ideas and men are corrupt."[3] Kumar, in speech and thought, is English, in colour he is Indian,[4] his speech is better accented than Merrick's (109) and he has internalized the English way of thinking something his father had chased all his life. Duleep Kumar's pursuit of the English way of life and thought had alienated him from his family and country and had led to a self-imposed distancing from his son. Hari is as much alienated from India as Daphne or Colin, to him England is home, (287) he doesn't know Hindi and he hated the black town as much as "any man fresh out from English would hate it." (191) Hari belongs nowhere, none of the two—the Indians or the British—trust him. Colins fails to recognize him and thus thrusts an anonymity and invisibility on him as if he doesn't exist.

We can examine Edmund Candler, Irene Burn, and Maud Diver, all colonial writers, in oppositional to postcolonial writers, notably Kazuo Ishiguro, a Japanese settled in Britain. In his novel, *The Remains of the Day*, Ishiguro attempts to subvert the myth of benevolent paterialism which was invoked to legitimate the deployment of power by the British ruling class, both at home and abroad. It is suggested, through the character of Stevens, the butler, in Lord Darlington's house, that England's ability to confer order on some unruly parts of the world was strongly predicted on the dignity of its serving classes. Stevens' unquestioning submission to a social order which reflects and supports the model of filial devotion deployed by empire to mask the enforced servitude of its colonies; as Helen Tiffin has noted, "I am your mother and father" was the missionary rhetoric whose standard slippage in India, Africa, and the Caribbean was from God to Queen Victoria and the British government.[5] The transfer of Darlington Hall to genial American, Farraday, is the symbol of final diminished role of Britain on the world stage. It is no longer an imperial power. The discomfiture of Stevens in the new world order and the deliberate parody of P.G. Wodehouse's butler, Jeeves, in Stevens, is the deliberate undermining of Britain as an imperial power by the novelist.

Scott's *The Jewel in the Crown* is symbolic of the double metaphor of colonial discourse—one where the colonizers rape the colonized culture and the other where the colonized rape the white woman. The opening page describes it as the "story of a rape, of the events that led up to it and followed it and the place in which it happened." (9)

The English characters in Amitav Ghosh's *The Shadow Lines* are neither Mr. Skene of Candler nor "the man with a torch" of Irene Burn. The England of the this novel does not arouse fantasies of domination and revenge in the mind of the narrator; it is simply the partial setting for his own experiences of love, discovery and loss. Sex between the characters is also not a metaphor for empire.

The Shadow Lines portrays the friendship (and antipathy) between various branches of an upper-class Bengali family and an English family over three generations. The narrator's family is spread over Dhaka, Calcutta, and London. The narrator's family consists of his grandmother, Mayadebi's elder sister, and his parents, and their three sons, Jatin, an economist with the UN, Tridib and Robi. Ila, Jatin's daughter, is always away with her parents. The narrator's family is settled in Calcutta where his grandmother is a headmistress in a school. On the other hand, the family of Mayadebi, with the exception of Tridib, goes around the world. Tridib lives in his ancestral house in Ballygunge place, who is often seen at a loose end at Gole Park, in an *adda*, with his acquaintances.

The friendship between the Indian families and the English family began when Lionel Tresawsen was in India. Lionel Tresawsen was a globe-trotter, a 'prolific' inventor, highly ambitious, and quick-witted. Later on, in India, he "developed an interest in spiritualism and began to attend the meetings of the

Theosophical Society in Calcutta, where he met and earned the trust and friendship of a number of leading nationalists. . . . He had also begun to attend seances conducted by a Russian medium, a large lady. . . . I was at those seances that he met Tridib's grandfather, Mr. Justice Chandrashekar Datta-Chaudhuri . . . their friendship was sealed across innumerable planchette tables." (52)

This friendship between Tresawsen and Datta-Chaudhuri is strengthened by their heirs. In this connection, 1939 is significant, because the story in the novel starts at this period of time. It is also the Second World War period. This is the period when the British imperialism was at its zenith in India. This is the period which also accelerated the fall of the British empire. The military might of Hitler was challenged by the UK. The British declaration of war automatically brought in India and the colonies, as it had done in 1914.

The membership of the Theosophical Society brings Tresawsen and Datta-Chaudhuri in each other's intimacy. The Theosophical Society was a western attempt to fuse with the springs of Indian spirituality. Founded at New York in 1875 by Madame Blavatsky, Col. Olcott and Williom Q. Judge, the society shifted to Adyar near Madras in 1878. Annie Besant, as President of the society, gathered many prominent Indians around her, and the society opened branches in many cities, all over India. There could be no better place for an Indian than the society to develop friendship with an Englishman, a colonized with a colonizer. The Indian spirituality as opposed to British materialism, places Datta-Chaudhuri and Tresawsen on surer footing. It is the blooming of friendship between their successors, which forms the backbone of the narrative of *The Shadow Lines*. Mrs. Price, the daughter of Tresawsen, and Mayadebi and her elder sister continue to maintain this friendly relation, irrespective of the fact that the year 1939 was the year of Indian slavery. But the spirituality of the Theosophical Society dissolves any trace of antipathy between the colonizer and the colonized. Amitav Ghosh thus prepares us for a friendly English woman and her family.

The family of Tridib "had taken his father there [London]

for an operation. . . . They had to go even though it was 1939 and they knew there might be a war." (12) The English historian A.J.P. Taylor writes: "Hospital beds were kept empty for the air-raid casualties which never came. Even the maternity wards were barred against expectant mothers."[6] Even social services ceased—no free milk, no school dinners. A blackout began. Motor cars were forbidden to use their headlights. Ghosh invites us to suspend our disbelief, to read his novel, of the political scene of England in 1939.

Dan wrote for *Daily Worker*, a left-wing newspaper. Communism was gaining ground in the thirties in England. Many important poets and novelists in England were left-wingers, including George Orwell, who, later on, recoiled from the Stalinist horrors and had written *The Animal Farm*. The publication of *Problems of Soviet Literature* was the first extensive statement of Soviet critical theory to reach English readers. The essential items were clear, though: art should be by and for the workers, it should be propaganda in the class struggle, it should be, in Zhdanov's words, class literature, tendentious and political. For common readers, the *Daily Worker* served the purpose of politics and literature, both. Amitav Ghosh's Dan "was the son of an eminent Cambridge physicist who had done a degree in chemistry. . . . After that he had worked as a journalist for a while, on a number of left-wing papers. . . . There was never any doubt in Tridib's mind that Dan was Tresawsen's political mentor." (62) So, Tresawsen is a Theosophist and a left winger, at least not an imperialist like Winston Churchill.

Amitav Ghosh portrays the affable, friendly, fine, English men and women in *The Shadow Lines*, from 1939 to 1979. Mrs Mayadebi finds a kind of "exhilaration" in the air in 1939. She says to Tresawsen:

> Everyone was so much nicer now; often when she and Tridib were out walking people would pat him on the head and stop to have a little chat with her; the shopkeepers would ask her where and how her husband was, and when he was to have his operation. (66)

But after a few pages, following this "exhilaration," Ghosh shows a true English picture, a white man's disdain for a brown one. "Ila walking alone because Nick Price was ashamed to be seen by his friends, walking home with an Indian." (76) His sister May Price volunteers an excuse: "He was very young, and at that age children want every one to be alike." (76) Edward Said says that Western domination of the non-Western world is not some arbitrary phenomenon but a conscious and purposive process governed by the will and intention of individuals as well as by institutional imperatives. The devotion of Tresawsen to Indian spirituality is a recurrent image in the Western discourse or West's inferior 'other,' for the West always vaunts the East for its spirituality, longevity and stability. In describing these qualities as 'overvalued,' Said suggests that the vision inscribed in such motifs is as distorted as its negative counterpart and similarly produced, above all else, by Western projections onto the Other.

Ila's upbringing and education in England is a matter of contradictory opinions. Her father was with the UN and a university in the North of England. Her mother was called Queen Victoria, who loved to lord over her household servants, like white memsahibs of the colonial India. She was "the daughter of a man who had left his village in Barisal in rags and gone on to earn a knighthood in the old Indian Civil Service." (25) The white memsahibs, in the colonial India, had their life of idleness and frivolity, their scandal-mongering and flirtations, their insensitivity and their rudeness towards Indians. And it was one or more of these traits that the memsahib was portrayed by E.M. Forster, George Orwell, Denn's Kincaid, A.J. Ackerley, and Edmund Candler. Queen Victoria says to her servant: "Shatup Ram Dayal. . . . Stop bukbukking like a chhokra-boy." (25) In Bengal, even today, a pompous, snobbish, showy, woman is derisively called *Rani Victoria*. Pannikar very aptly describes the type of the anglicized Hindus:

> They [the aristocrat middle class] conversed in the morning like English gentlemen about possible changes in weather, in a country where weather hardly experienced

> any fluctuation for months together, wore double breasted suit and tie in hot and sultry Indian summers and learnt to waltz and trot in dancing halls. Their social prestige was measured in terms of the number of invitations to the Governor's banquets and to the tea parties and dinners hosted by lesser English officials. . . . Admission to prestigious schools in England was highly sought after and a degree from either Oxford or Cambridge became the ultimate in intellectual attainment.[7]

This madness for phorenophilia is a common characteristic of the anglicized Bengali elite, soaked in everything English, a lapdog of British imperialism. The Chatterjees of Vikram Seth's *A Suitable Boy* belong to this anglicized upper-middle class Calcutta society. The Subaltern School, led by Ranjit Guha, speaks of this upper-middle class and its role in shaping India's historiography:

> The historiography of Indian nationalism has for a long time been dominated by elitism—colonial elitism and bourgeois-nationalist elitism. . . . Both these varieties of elitism share the prejudice that the making of the Indian nation and the development of the consciousness—nationalism—which informed this process were exclusively or predominantly elite achievements.[8]

A.N. Kaul says: "It is true that for the privileged Datta-Chaudhuris nationality has ceased to have any significance and crossing national frontiers means nothing more to them than a smooth transition through customs and immigration at identical airports."[9] For Ila, India is not her home. She flees Calcutta, feeling stifled by its social environment, and seeks a home in London. She marries an Englishman, buys a house, finds a job, and tries to settle down. Ila lives in London because "she wanted to be free." The postcolonial India has seen thousands of men and women migrating to England and the USA "to be free" from social conventions and mores, all elites, in search of power and position, even marrying foreigners. For them, nationalism is a constraint, a Hindu imposition, a more imaginary construct, which must be resisted as forcefully as possible. Salman Rushdie, Rohinton Mistry, Nirad C. Chaudhuri, Bharati Mukherjee are some writers who have challenged the Hindu construct of nationalism.

The narrator's grandmother, on the other hand, is fiercely anti-imperialist. Tha'mma, brought up on the stories of Khudiram Bose and Bagha Jatin, has lived the nationalist dream and experienced the setbacks and successes that give it its character. Her personal history of anti-imperialism sharpens her sense of nationhood and of the formation of the Indian nation-state. Of Britain, she says to her grandson:

> It took those people a long time to build that country; hundreds of years, years and years of war and bloodshed. Everyone who lives there has earned his right to be there with blood: with their brother's blood and their father's blood and their son's blood. They know they are a nation because they have drawn their borders with blood. Hasn't Maya told you how regimental flags hang in all their cathedrals and how all their churches are lined with memorials to men who died in wars, all around the world? War is their religion. That's what it takes to be a country. Once that happens people forget they were born this or that, Muslim or Hindu, Bengali or Punjabi; they become a family born of the same pool of blood. That is what you have to achieve for India, don't you see? (77-78)

This is militant nationalism, as opposed to non-violent nationalism of Gandhiji, which ignited the mind, heart, and imagination of Bengalis. Even an ardent supporter of Non-cooperation movement, a follower of Gandhiji, Saratchandra Chatterjee, the Bengali literary giant, became an ardent exponent of armed revolution and admirer of Subhash Chandra Bose. He said to S.C. Sengupta: "Do you think a young revolutionary who goes to kill a white man, a limb of imperialism, with a revolver in one pocket and a packet of potassium cyanide powder in another, loves the motherland less fervently than your Mahatma?" Out of this militant nationalism sprouted his famous novel, *Pather Dabi* ('The Claim of the Road'). It is second in importance to Bankimchandra Chatterjee's *Anandamath*.

Ila and her family, like many bourgeoise elites in the colonial India, had enjoyed a considerable clout, name, fame, and money and they continued to do so even in the postcolonial India, without shedding a drop of blood. Suvir Kaul comments:

> To such militant nationalism, and to a nation whose borders are confirmed in war, she exhorts her grandson. These, after all, are the values she learns from her youthful desire to be free, where freedom was forged in the crucible of often violent anti-colonial struggle, and, once achieved, maintained by extending the same antagonistic logic to the construction of the nation-state. War against a common enemy unites, it ratifies boundaries and deepens the ideological and international oppositions necessary to mould an internally coherent national identity, it legitimizes the claim of the state to be the sole agent and authority of violence.[10]

The failure of her faith in the postcolonial India is not only her tragedy but also the tragedy of an entire class: "All she wanted was a middle-class life in which, like the middle-classes the world over, she would thrive believing in the unity of nationhood and territory, of self-respect and national power, that was all she wanted—a modern middleclass life, a small thing, that history had denied her in its fullness and for which she could never forgive it." (78) Fanon, the great African postcolonial political theorist, observes the modern African middle-class by comparing its achievement with its counterpart elsewhere and writes:

> The bourgeois phase in underdeveloped countries can only justify itself insofar as the national bourgeoisie has efficient economical and technical strength to build up a

> bourgeois society, to create the conditions necessary for the development of a largescale proletariat. . . . [In Europe] such a bourgeoisie, dynamic, educated and secular, has fully succeeded in its undertaking of the accumulation of capital and has given to nation a minimum of prosperity.[11]

He also recommends violence as a grim reality. He sees it as creating a social melting-pot in which old shibboleths dissolve and new assumptions take their place: "Violence alone, violence committed by the people, violence organised and educated by its leaders, makes it possible for the masses to understand social truths and gives the key to them." (118)

Fanon goes on to reiterate that violence properly understood and directed can be positive and purifying: "At the level of individuals, violence is a cleansing force. It frees the native from his inferiority complex and from his despair and inaction; it makes him fearless and restores his self-respect." (180) Seen in this perspective, the grandmother is not only relevant to this novel, but is also a postcolonial two-dimensional character in *The Shadow Lines*.

But, as stated above, India could not fully rupture its imperialistic absorption and bond with England. Once again Fanon hits out at both the ex-colonialists and the black elites in a fine pattern of irony:

> The Third World often gives the impression that it rejoices in sensation and that it must have its weekly dose of crises. These men at the head of empty countries, who talk too loud, are most irritating. You'd like to shut them up. But, on the contrary, they are invited to dinner. In fact, we quarrel over who will have them. (136)

Fanon here gives a picture of a postimperialtist ruler. Amitav Ghosh also shows the narrator, Tridib, May, and Price as the facsimiles of the postimperialist feature of his novel. The narrator is unable to digest the militant nationalism of his grandmother. Very often, he defends Ila. For Tridib, May is foreign, sexy and desirable, a figure of romance, from far across the seas. Similarly Ila, living in London, is a figure of romance for the narrator. Both Tridib and the narrator are Indians but they love women, living across border.

Tridib dies in Dhaka, is rather killed by a violent and frenzied mob of Muslims. Ila marries Nick. The narrator marries (sexy) May, once coveted by Tridib. The narrator, of the postcolonial India, accepts the inevitability of the partition of India, believes in political separation and the absoluteness of socio-cultural differences across nations, say, India and Pakistan. The partitioning of the Bose family's home in Dhaka can serve as an allegory of the great Indian partition. The once-familiar house becomes a matter of curiosity for both halves of the house. But England is not a matter of curiosity, either for Tridib, the narrator, or Ila. It is easy for them to journey to London and come back unharmed. But Tridib's death at the hands of a Dhaka mob, the flight of the grandmother, Mayadebi and May from this riotspot, finally seal any bond of affection and love between Dhaka and Calcutta which "were more closely bound to each other than after they had drawn their lines." Amitav Ghosh, like Frantz Fanon, writes that the theatre of war cleanses, cathects the messy violence of the streets. This is how the narrator puts it:

> The madness of a riot is a pathological inversion, but also therefore a reminder, of that indivisible sanity that binds people to each other independently of their governments. And that prior, independent, relationship is the natural enemy of government for it is in the logic of states that to exist at all they must claim the monopoly of all relationship between peoples. (230)

The postcolonial Dhaka frustrates the attempt of the grandmother, Mayadebi, and Tridib to rescue old Jethamoshai from the rioting mob. There is that "Shadow Line" between India and Pakistan, which had been drawn in maps by administrators, who believed "in the enchantment of lines, hoping perhaps that once they had etched their borders upon the map, the two bits of land would sail away from each other like the shifting tectonic plates of the prehistoric Gondwanaland." (233)

Gathering the threads of our discussion, we find the story of *The Shadow Lines* is the story of two upper-class families, one in London and other in India. Prices in London are called the post-imperialist breed. In *A Passage to England*, Nirad C. Chaudhuri quotes his son about middle-class English men and women:

> The English well-bred middle-class type is so very English that it is impossible to get to know their various little ways unless you have lived with them. . . . They are too polite and considerate to think of imposing their habits on foreigners, yet they get upset if people do not conform to English ways in England, a marvellous specimen of human beings, very complex altogether.[12]

Ila conforms to the English ways. Datta-Chaudhuris are the anglophiles. The grandmother could not conform to the English ways and, therefore, condemned Ila's love for freedom and called her a whore. Amitav Ghosh, like Nirad C. Chaudhuri, tells us that the postimperialist England has shed its material superiority, naughtiness, snobbiness, egoism and standoffishness. His conclusion is indigestible. The love of the narrator with May Price and the marriage of Ila with Nick Price lift the shadow lines between the West and the East. But, is it convincing?

Edward Said has written about the ending of E.M. Forster's *A Passage to India* as "a paralyzed gesture of aestheticized powerlessness" in which "Forster notes and confirms the history behind a political conflict between Dr. Aziz and Fielding—Britain's subjugation of India—and yet can neither recommend decolonization nor continued colonization. No, not yet, not here' is all Forster can muster by way of resolution."[13] Benita Perry writes:

> But cannot this finale, which speaks of "cosmic irresolution" rather than domestic resolution, be read as indeter-

> minate, as signalling, amongst other possibilities, the hope in a deferred, postimperialist conditions towards which the novel points but has not the means to articulate—"No, not yet"—and which cannot be fulfilled in the space the novel occupies "No, not there"? And since the novel speaks a reluctant bourgeois Englishness, a failed cosmopolitanism, a sceptical sympathy for Indian nationalism and an unequivocal distaste for the deportment of an imperial hegemony, cannot it be received as enunciating a confessional and destabilized liberalism which having confronted the obscenities of European empire and having suffered a further undermining of already disarrayed values through encountering India's diverse systems of meaning, can only retreat into undecidability.[14]

A Passage to India was written in the mid-twenties of the twentieth century. The undecidability of the colonial elitism is understandable, for India is too vast a country to be understood by one or two visits to her by an outsider. The evidence for metropolitan anti-imperialism does not make for a long or inspiring story. We may also read up instances of affiliation with the colonial struggles and commitment to colonial self-determination, cited in the manifestoes of those groups active during the nineteen-twenties, thirties and forties, and who, in 1954, reformed as the movement for colonial freedom. The marriage of Ila with Nick and of the narrator with May may be seen between the undecidability of Forster and the protagonists of the Movement for Colonial Freedom.

The Shadow Lines, between Forster and the protagonists of The Movement for Colonial Freedom, is partly postimperialist and partly postcolonial novel. It has neither the distancing of the colonizer and colonized of Jane Austen's *Mansfield Park* and Kipling's *Kim* nor Ngugi wa Thiong'o's *Caitaani Mutharabaini* (*Devil on the Cross*) and Raja Rao's *The Serpent and the Rope*. A writer's handling of the material can be effected by his material base in society, that is his class position and standpoint. It does affect his approximation of reality or rather his effectiveness in correctly reflecting reality. Amitav Ghosh had experienced neither a prison term in postcolonial India for attempting to decolonize the mind like Ngugi wa Thiong'o nor Fanonian distaste for imperialism as seen in Adil Jussawalla's poetry. Thiong'o had to suffer a prison term in a free country for propounding decolonization of the mind of African writers, for writing African fiction in one's own native language. Jussawalla, based on the ideas of Frantz Fanon, constructs postcolonial Indian citizen or an intellectual as a "missing person," who is "missing" precisely because his subjectivity and agency have been annihilated by the colonial past and the postcolonial present on the subcontinent. Jussawalla's anti-heroic protagonist has to erase the colonial and postcolonial conflicts and contradictions, which have produced him and which he still embodies. Amitav Ghosh fails on both counts. His attempt at synthesizing the West and the East, through marriage, like Forster, fails. At best, *The Shadow Lines* is a product of a mind and a birth, which is neither wholly western nor wholly eastern. It is an attempt to Indianize westernization by yoking postimperialism of Prices with postcolonialism of Dattas, by violence together. It is a case of overlapping the colonized and the colonial mind-sets and intertwined languages of Orientalism and Occidentalism.

NOTES

1. Aparna Dharwadker and Vinay Dharwadker, "Language, Identity, and Nation in Postcolonial Indian English Literature," in *English Postcoloniality: Literatures from Around the World* (Westport: Greenwood Press, 1996), p. 104.
2. Saros Cowasjee, *Introduction to Siri Ram-Revolutionist* (Delhi: Aronld, 1988), p. 9.
3. Frantz Fanon, *Black Skin, White Masks*, trans. Charles Lam Markmann (New York; Grove Press, 1968), p. 160.
4. Paul Scott, *The Jewel in the Crown* (London: Pan Books, 1966), p. 157.
5. Helen Tiffin, "The Body in the Library; Identity, Opposition

and the Settler-Invader Woman" (1993), p. 7.

6. A.J.P. Taylor, *English History: 1914-1945* (Oxford: The Clarendon Press, 1965), p. 455.
7. R.N. Pannikar, *Culture and Consciousness in Modern India* (New Delhi: People's Publishing House, 1990), pp. 33-34.
8. Ranjit Guha, "On Some Aspects of the Historiography of Colonial India" in *Subaltern Studies*, ed. Ranjit Guha (New Delhi: OUP, 1982), p. 1.
9. A.N. Kaul, "A Reading of *The Shadow Lines*," Amitav Ghosh's *The Shadow Lines* (Cult Edition, New Delhi: OUP, 1995), p. 303.
10. Suvir Kaul, "Separation Anxiety: Growing Up Inter/National in *The Shadow Lines*" in Amitav Ghosh's *The Shadow Lines*, p. 279.
11. Frantz Fanon, *The Wretched of the Earth* (1961; Harmondsworth: Penguin, 1990), p. 194.
12. Nirad C. Chaudhuri, *A Passage to England* (Delhi: Orient Paperbacks), p. 137.
13. Edward Said, "Representing the Colonized: Anthropology's Interlocutors," *Critical Inquiry*, 15, 2 (1989), p. 223.
14. Benita Perry, "Overlapping Territories, Intertwined Histories," in *Edward Said: A Critical Reader*, ed. Michael Sprinker (Oxford: Blackwell, 1992), pp. 28-29.

The Shadow Lines: Nationalism Defamiliarised

RAHUL SAPRA

"Devotion to one's own nation; patriotic feelings, principles or efforts" is how the *Oxford Dictionary* defines nationalism. If Tha'mma, a character in Amitav Ghosh's novel *The Shadow Lines,* were to define nationalism, it would not be very different from the above definition. That there is an undercutting of Tha'mma's nationalism is obvious from a cursory reading of the text. In doing so, the novel raises certain serious issues related to the phenomenon of nationalism. *The Shadow Lines* undercuts nationalism by questioning History, the official version of History, on which the idea of a nation is constructed. However, as far as offering solutions to the problems of nationalism is concerned, the novel refuses to oblige.

For an understanding of the novel's stance vis-à-vis nationalism, one has to begin by analysing Tha'mma's concept of nationalism. What constitutes Tha'mma's nationalism? Hutchinson and Smith observe:

> Nationalism was, first of all, a doctrine of popular freedom and sovereignty. The people must be liberated—that is, freed from any external constraints; they must determine their own destiny and be masters in their own house; they must control their own resources; they must obey only their 'inner' voice. But that entailed fraternity. The people must be united; they must dissolve all internal divisions; they must be gathered together in a single

> historic territory, a homeland; and they must have legal equality and share a single public culture.[1]

Tha'mma's idea of nationalism constitutes of almost all the above-mentioned characteristics. To begin with, it was the lure of freedom from the colonial rule that ingrained the feeling of "nationalism" in her. She tells her grandson how she was fascinated "by the stories she had heard about the terrorists. She had wanted to do something for the terrorists, work for them in a small way, steal a little bit of their glory for herself."[2] She would not have even flinched from killing the English magistrate in the name of freedom: "yes, I would have killed him. It was for our freedom: I would have done anything to be free." (39) The use of the word "our" is significant, for throughout Tha'mma is conscious of the fact that she is a part of a larger community sharing a common interest. Her concept of nationalism would be meaningless if it is not coupled with the idea of fraternity. Her efforts to strengthen the unity of the country range from making girls in her school "cook one dish that was a specialty of some part of the country other than her own," (116) to a craving for a war that would make "people forget that they were born this or that, Muslim or Hindu, Bengali or Punjabi: they become a family born of the same pool of blood." (78) Sacrifice for the country is for her the ultimate unifying force. She argues that Ila can never belong to England for "everyone who lives there has earned his right to be there with blood: with their brother's blood and with their father's blood and their son's blood. They know they are a nation because they have drawn their borders with blood. War is their religion." (78) Consequently, for the country to be united, to define itself, it needs borders. Thus a nation ends up defining itself in opposition to other nations, particularly to its neighbors. The partition of the ancestral house in Dhaka illustrates this point. The house across the partition-line functions as an antithesis to Tha'mma's house. To entertain her sister she invents the myth of an "upside/down house" (125)—a house in which everything opposite to their house happens. The significant point is that Tha'mma "almost came to believe" (126) in her own story—just as in the case of the nation she believes that the opposite happens across the borders. Her brand of nationalism is one which "shuts other people out; which defines 'Us' against 'Them.' To call yourself Australian or Chilean or Sri Lankan is to draw a psychological as well as a physical boundary around yourself and those who claim the same national identity. The fact that 'We' are inside that boundary, or border, necessarily means that 'They' are outside it."[3] Therefore Tha'mma is circumspect of any "Indian" who lives beyond the borders. The fact that Ila is living not in India but England is enough to make her "a greedy little slut" (79) in her eyes. Her endeavour to bring the "poor old man" (136) from Dhaka to India is not born out of any family feelings, for the narrator tells us that unlike his mother his grandmother "had never pretended to have much family feelings; she had always founded her morality, schoolmistress-like, in larger and more abstract entities." (129) It is the abstract entity of nationalism that inspires her to bring the old man to India: "I'm worried about him, poor old man, all by himself, abandoned in that country. Imagine what it must be to die in another country, abandoned and alone in your old age." (135-36) Further, Tha'mma's nationalism sustains itself by a desire to perpetuate the values of common heritage and by striving towards building a better nation. In this regard her view is reminiscent of Ernest Renan's idea of a nation propounded in his famous essay "Qu'est-ce qu'une nation?" in 1882. For Renan,

> A nation is a soul, a spiritual principle. Only two things, actually, constitute this soul, this spiritual principle. One is the past, the other is the present. One is in the possession of a rich legacy of remembrances; the other is the actual consent, the desire to live together, the will to continue to value the heritage which all hold in common. A heroic past is the social principle on which the national idea rests. To have common glories in the past, a common will in the present; to have accomplished great things together, to wish to do so again, that is the essen-

> tial condition for being a nation.[4]

Therefore Tha'mma would force her grandson to exercise for "you can't build a strong nation, without building a strong body." (8) For her Robi's physical strength is nothing but good raw material for nation-building: "Watch Robi, he's strong, he's not like the rest of you in this country." (35)

Thamma's nationalism, according to the theorists, would fall under the category of the primordial view. Paul R. Brass observes: "the primordialist argues that every person carries with him through life 'attachments' derived from place of birth, kinship relations, religion, language, and social practices that are 'natural' for him, 'spiritual' in character, and that provide a basis for an easy 'affinity' with the people from the same background."[5] But the novel shows some serious complications in the above-mentioned view: Tha'mma, an ardent nationalist, is foxed to find her "place of birth at odds with her nationality," (152) for the partition of Bengal has made her a foreigner in her homeland Dhaka. She is forced to realize that no amount of bloodshed can make the borders 'real.' Before flying to Dhaka, she asks her son if "she would be able to see the border between India and East Pakistan from the plane." (151) When her son laughs at her question and taunts her if she thought that "the border was a long black line with green on one side and scarlet on the other, like it was on the school atlas," she tells him, "But surely there's something—trenches perhaps, or soldiers, or guns pointing at each other, or even just barren strips of land. Don't they call it no-man's land." (151) In the process of the conversation, Tha'mma ends up questioning some of the fundamentals of her idea of Nationalism:

> But if there aren't any trenches or anything, how are people to know? I mean, where's the difference then? And if there's no difference both the sides will be the same; it'll be just like it used to be before, when we used to catch a train in Dhaka and get off in Calcutta the next day without anybody stopping us. What was it

> for all then—the partition and the killing and everything—if there isn't something in between? (151)

By highlighting the fact that even after partition there might not be any "difference" between the two regions across the border, the novel questions the ideology of nationalism. One of the fundamental characteristics of the ideology of nationalism is that, as mentioned earlier, it defines itself in opposition to other countries across the borders. Tha'mma initially keeps on asking "Where's Dhaka," (194) but realizes, although reluctantly, that there is nothing upside down across the border. On entering the part of their house that was at one time across the partition, "Mayadebi and grandmother began to laugh, hugging each other. Nothing upside down," (212) said the grandmother. By stressing on identity rather than on the differences across the border, the novel questions the primordial view of nationalism—the view that the grandmother holds. Paul R. Brass observes that from the primordial point of view Hindus and Muslims, due to the cultural differences, were destined to separate into two distinct nations. He states:

> From the primordialist point of view, which was also the view of Muslim separatism, Hindus and Muslims constituted in pre-modern times distinct civilizations destined to develop into separate nations once political mobilization took place. The differences between the two cultures were so great that it was not conceivable that assimilation of the two could take place and that a single national culture could be created to which both would contribute. The contrary view is that the cultural and religious differences between Hindus and Muslims were not so great as to rule out the creation of either a composite national culture or at least a secular political union in which those aspects of group culture that could not be shared would be relegated to the private sphere. From this point of view, Muslim separatism was not pre-ordained, but resulted from the conscious manipulation of selected symbols of Muslim identity by Muslim elite

> groups in economic and political competition with each other and with elite among Hindus. (88)

The narrative undercuts the view based on difference between the created regions in the subcontinent by highlighting the similarities between Dhaka and Calcutta: after Partition the two cities are seen as "an inverted image of each other." (223) However, the point to be emphasized is not that the narrative highlights the similarities, but the way in which it does it. The narrative accomplishes the task of undercutting the ideology of nationalism, by questioning the received/official version of history. The various characteristics of the primordial view of nationalism, as exemplified through Tha'mma, have a common basis or emerge from a common source, that of history. In fact the whole idea of a nation-state revolves around history. The idea of nationalism nourishes itself on past glories:

> Simón Bolivar in Colombia, Juan and Evita Peron in Argentina, Jawarharlal Nehru and Mahatma Gandhi in India, are all used as icons on which to hang the emotions of current nationalisms. In former Yugoslavia, Slobodan Milosevic linked old stories about Croat atrocities with promises of Serbian greatness to fill the emotional and economic hole left by Tito's death. The ultra-right nationalist Vladimir Zhirinovsky continually harks back to Russia's former greatness to harness current discontent.[6]

In *The Shadow Lines,* the narrative undercuts history by juxtaposing it with memory—a memory that can invent and create—and in the process it exposes history as just another invention and not a given. Tridib had once advised the narrator that "we could not see without inventing what we saw, so at least we could try to do it properly. We had to try because the alternative wasn't blackness—it only meant that if we didn't try ourselves, we could never be free of other people's inventions." (31) The narrative of *The Shadow lines* is an attempt to free oneself of other people's inventions: from the meta-narratives that envelop the modern man. History revealed through personal memory not only appears to be more authentic but also exposes the fictive nature of the received History, and thereby exposes the way in which the idea of a nation is constructed. Benedict Anderson in his pioneering work *Imagined Communities: Reflections on the Origin and Spread of Nationalisms*, argues that nation "is an imagined political community." It is "imagined because members of even the smallest nation will never know most of their fellow-members, meet them, or even hear of them, yet in the minds of each lives the image of their communion."[7] He further states that one of the main factors in spreading this idea is the medium of "print-capitalism." (40) He explains this by analysing the role played by the first American newspapers:

> What were the characteristics of the first American newspapers, North or South? They began essentially as appendages to the market. Early gazettes contained—aside from news about the metropole—commercial news (when ships would arrive and depart, what prices were current for what commodities in what ports) as well as colonial political appointments, marriages of the wealthy, and so forth. In other words what brought together, on the same page *this* marriage or *that* ship, *this* price with *that* bishop, was the every structure of the colonial administration and market-system itself. In the way the newspaper of the Caracus quite naturally, and even apolitically, created an imagined community among a specific assemblage of fellow-readers, to whom *these* ships, brides, bishops and prices belonged. In time of course, it was only to be expected that political elements would occur. (62)

The Shadow Lines points towards a similar role played by print capitalism and the media in propagating the ideology of nationalism, of which Tha'mma becomes a victim. However, it is her memory that liberates her, although momentarily, from the constraints of received History. In Dhaka, her memory allows her to see the similarities/affinities across borders, for instead of giving in to the official version of History and seeing

Dhaka as a foreign country, she recollects every detail of the city that had surrounded their old house in Dhaka. The narrator informs us that "people like my grandmother, who have no home but in memory, learn to be very skilled in the art of recollection." (194) But Tridib's death immediately brings back the distinctions between 'us' and 'them.' Suvir Kaul observes that the "crowning irony of *The Shadow Lines* is that almost as soon as Tha'mma realizes the legacy of her birthplace is not separable from her sense of herself as a citizen of India, her nephew Tridib's death at the hands of the Dhaka mob confirms in her a pathological hatred of 'them'."[8] The incident brings Tha'mma out of the space created by her memory and once again pushes her into the web of territorial politics. For the 1965 war with Pakistan, she donates her only gold chain, her husband's gift, to the war fund. The narrator finds her in a hysterical state listening to the war news on the radio and when he asks about the chain, she screams back at him: "I gave it to the fund for the war. For your sake, for your freedom. We have to kill them before they kill us; we have to wipe them out." (237) When in her frenzy she shatters the glass front of the radio and cuts her hand, she wants to rush to the hospital to "donate it [her blood] to the war fund." (237) The powerful effect of the war news on Tha'mma is nothing but an extension of the manner in which, what Anderson calls, print-capitalism/media generates the sense of a community. The sociologist Michael Billig observes that the spirit of the nation is kept alive by the stuff of everyday life. He calls this "Banal nationalism": "It is the nationalism of flags; of national anthems; of rousing language—'our country' or 'our nation'—of processions and celebrations to mark national days or battlefield heroics shrouded in the mists of time."[9]

However, the best example in the novel, which reveals the fictive nature of history is the narrator's survey of the newspapers regarding the riots of 1964. The riots that, over the years, had acquired a significant place in the narrator's memory find no significant mention in the newspapers or the chronicles of that time. His survey of the various documents of the period reveals the startling discovery that "By the end of January 1964 the riots had faded away from the pages of the newspapers, disappeared from the collective imagination of 'responsible opinion,' vanished, without leaving a trace in the histories and bookshelves." (230) The discovery reveals that history is not an impartial record of events but a process of selection, invention and even rejection. While the national newspaper of 11 January 1964 does mention the riots—"*Curfew in Calcutta, Police Open Fire, 10 dead, 15 wounded*" (224)—in the Calcutta newspaper there was not the slightest reference to any trouble in East Pakistan, and the barest mention of the events in Kashmir." (227) The narrator, significantly, points out that the news about the riots was deliberately suppressed: "*they* must have known . . . all the canny journalists; everybody must have known in some voiceless part of themselves—for events on that scale cannot happen without portents. If they knew, why couldn't they speak of it." (227) The newspapers, on the other hand, were full of reports "of the Congress conference, of the impending split in the Communist party, or wars and revolutions." (228) Even though the number of people killed in the riots was "at any rate not very many less than were killed in the war of 1962" (229)—Malik, narrator's friend, thanks to the newspapers, is confident that the riots must have been a "local thing. hardly comparable to a war." (221) Through Malik's ignorance of the riots, the novel exposes the gaps in history. It is these gaps that make the narrator's recounting of the past "a struggle with silence." (218) However, it is only with the help of his memory that the narrator discovers, although after fifteen years, "a connection between my [the narrator's] nightmare bus ride from school, and the events that befell Tridib and others in Dhaka." (218) It is memory that forges links beyond boundaries: the narrator remembers the peculiarity of the fear that he had experienced during his nightmare bus ride, the fear "that sets apart the thousand million people who inhabit the subcontinent from the rest of the world—not language, not food, not music,—it is the special quality of loneliness that grows out of the fear of war between oneself and one's image in the mirror." (204) Unlike the narrator and Tridib who could experience the world "concretely in their imagination," (30) Ila, who experiences the world through her senses, without inventing what she sees, easily gets trapped in the jaws of history: "there's a joy merely in knowing that you're a part of history. We may not achieve much in our little house in Stockwell, but we *know* that in future political people everywhere will look to us—in Nigeria, India, Malaysia." (104)

However this does not imply that memory can compensate for the gaps/fissures in history and generate a picture of totality, for memory has its own limitations: "What is the colour of that knowledge? Nobody knows, no body can ever know, not even in memory, because there are moments in time that are not *knowable*: nobody can ever know what it was like to be young and intelligent in the summer of 1939 in London or Berlin." (68) Though memory has its limitations, unlike History it is not created; it cannot be tempered with nor can it be forgotten: Robi's efforts at forgetting Tridib's death come to a naught when "a chance remark by a waiter in a restaurant" (247) takes him back fifteen years to the moment of Tridib's death. He "would have given anything to be free of that memory" but realizes that no one can "divide a memory." (246-47)

Thus, by juxtaposing received history with personal memory, Ghosh not only exposes the gaps in history but also attempts to portray the idea of a nation as an invention. However, that is not the end of the argument. A.N. Kaul in "A Reading of *The Shadow Lines*" observes that "in viewing nationalism as both an invention and a force of destruction Ghosh has put himself alongside a considerable number of modern western scholars ranging from Elie Kedourie and Hans Kohn to Tom Narin and Benedict Anderson."[10] Kaul argues that to "call nations 'inventions' and to see nationalism merely as 'a source of terrifying violence' is to take a too simplistic view of historical reality." (302) He disagrees with the claim that "*The Shadow Lines* is concerned with 'the meaning of political freedom in the modern world'," (303) because, according to him, the novel evades rather than explores political realities:

> 'Shadow Lines' is a metaphor for evading rather than exploring political realities. How can Ghosh be interested in the real possibilities and the real difficulties of going beyond national divisions—that is, in the possibility of a further historical development of these historical formulations—when for him they scarcely exist. (303)

Whether one agrees with Kaul's view or not, he does raise a significant issue: What is the novel's stance vis-à-vis the political problems in the subcontinent? Is the sole purpose of the novel to suggest the similitude across the shadow line borders? Or does the novel also suggest an alternative to nationalism which has become 'a source of terrifying violence'? The only alternative towards which Ghosh appears to be inclined is that of globalism. Tridib's letter to May expressing his desire to meet her "in a place without a past, without history, free, really free, two people coming together with the utter freedom of strangers," (144) can be read as a wish for dismantling the world order based on nation-states. The novel attempts to demonstrate the mingling of people across international borders; the pairing of characters in the novel is such: Tridib and May, May and the narrator and the families—Datta-Chaudhuris of Bengal and the Prices of London. The circle that the narrators draws on Tridib's atlas cuts across all boundaries and helps him to view the countries within the circle as devoid of their borders. It leads to the amazing discovery that foreign places/cities that appeared to be distant are actually far closer: "Chiang Mai in Thailand was much nearer Calcutta than Delhi. Chengdu in China is nearer than Srinagar is." (232) The discovery implies that the creation of borders creates distances which are actually not there. Further, it is implied that inside the borders one can only be a "citizen" and not a human being: "It seemed to me [the narrator] then that within this circle there were only states and citizens; there were no people at all." (232-33) Thus globalism—the removal of all boundaries—appears to be the only way for the "citizens" to become "people."

However, the alternative of globalism, which the novel

seemingly suggests, is not to be interpreted as a genuine attempt at furnishing a solution, for the novel refuses to deal with the complexities of globalism. Globalism is as fluid and as protean a term as nationalism. If nation is an invention then so is the idea of globalism. The current trend of globalization, from one point of view, is nothing but American culture sold by the media as global culture. By ignoring to deal with the complexities of the phenomenon of globalism, the novel refuses to offer any solutions,—but then who is looking for solutions when offering solutions is not in vogue anymore.

NOTES

1. John Hutchinson and Paul R. Brass, "Elite Competition and Nation-Formation," *Nationalism*, ed. John Hutchinson and Anthony D. Smith (Oxford: Oxford UP, 1994), p. 4.
2. Amitav Ghosh, *The Shadow Lines* (Delhi: OUP, 1995), p. 39.
3. Nikki van der Gaag, "Bullets and Borders," New Internationalist Issue 277, 40 pars. Online. Internet. 5 June, 1999. par. 16.
4. Qtd. in Hutchinson and Smith, p. 17.
5. Paul R. Brass, "Elite Competition and Nation-Formation," *in* Hutchinson and Smith, p. 83.
6. Gaag, par. 11.
7. Benedict Anderson, *Imagined Communities: Reflections on the Origin and Spread of Nationalisms* (London: Verso, 1983), p. 15.
8. Suvir Kaul, "Separation Anxiety: Growing Up Inter/National in *The Shadow Lines*," in *The Shadow Lines*, p. 283.
9. Gaag, par. 12.
10. In *The Shadow Lines*, p. 302.

Two Exiles and One at Home: A Study of *The Shadow Lines*

ALPANA NEOGY

It was Victor Hugo who had described exile as being a long dream of "home." I propose to examine this theme of being an exile or being at home through three generations of women in Amitav Ghosh's novel *The Shadow Lines*. Many people live in their homeland, some in exile. A simple distinction between living at home and being an exile could be determined by geographical location. Many of us, however, are physically at home and yet are mentally in exile. Therefore, the lines that separate homeland from foreign lands may often be lines in our minds.

To be wrenched from home, family, everything pleasant and familiar and to be forced into a New World, this is the defining experience of the exiled one. Tha'mma, the grandmother of the narrator in *The Shadow Lines*, is anxious to emphasize that she is not a refugee, a word that is anathema to her, as she had left Dhaka long before Partition in 1947. Yet she is an exile.

In 1936, she is a young widow in Calcutta with no savings but with a grim determination to work and fend for herself and to send her son through school and college. She is barely 32 years of age, and she can only look back—the best years of her life are behind her.

Her youth had been spent in the ancestral home at Dhaka. Differences between her parents and her uncle's family had led to the division of the ancestral property, everything being divided into equal parts, even the brass nameplate. Yet, divided though it was, this was her home, her familiar world, a world she could identify with, relate to; a location where every street corner had a connection for her either with people or with events.

Calcutta, where she settles down after the death of her husband, is an alien city to her. Even the dialect spoken here is different. She starts living in a one-room tenement in the slums of Bhawanipore and takes up the job of a schoolteacher. And when India is partitioned in 1947, her home in Dhaka is lost forever. Since it was located where it was, it was now in East Pakistan, an alien country. Henceforth, her home was only a memory.

The sorrow of expulsion and the alienation from her land transforms itself into an overwhelming strength, which enables her to cope with life against all odds. A new land is accepted as her nation while she copes with the double tragedy, early widowhood and Partition. It is natural for her to be highly tense, very insecure, always anxious and always afraid to lose control. Everything around her has been so fragile, so tenuous.

Tha'mma achieves much through her own efforts, shunning all help from her relations. She becomes the headmistress of her school and her son gets a job as a junior executive in a company which dealt in vulcanised rubber after he completes his education. Thus it is not surprising to see her reluctant to abdicate her authority over the household even when her son acquires himself a wife. And when she retires, she finds it difficult to give up her twenty-five-year-old habit of going to work and visits her former school everyday. Finally, her son reins her in when the new Principal rings him up and complains!

Like all exiles of her generation attempting to settle down in the newly adopted land, it is the grandmother who sets down the rules at home. Fiercely independent and combative as she is, she is in command. Time is like a toothbrush, she says. It gets mouldy if not in use. And so everyone remains busy in the house with no one ever found wasting time. The narrator's mother, for example, is allowed to listen to the afternoon radio play only once a week.

Yet, even though she makes every attempt to make Calcutta her permanent home, Tha'mma remains nostalgic about her youth in Dhaka. She can never forget her homeland. When she was a student at College, the heroism of Khudiram Bose and Bagha Jatin had fascinated her. She would have liked to participate in the terrorist movement but was unable to do so, as she was a girl. For the freedom of the nation she would have done anything, even killed if necessary, she says. The enemy then was the British and she believed that everything would be just fine once India became free.

Things become somewhat hazy for Tha'mma once India is partitioned. This is not what she had bargained for when she had supported the Nationalist movement. Now "home" is an adopted land and to go to her ancestral home requires the production of a passport and the issuance of a visa. And what seems more absurd to her is that there are no fences, no walls to mark out the boundaries between India and Pakistan. "What was it all for then—Partition and all the killing and everything—if there isn't something in between?" (155) she wonders.

Ironically, it required a few tragic killings—of Tridib, of her Jethamoshai and of Khalil, the rickshaw puller—for her to realise that these boundaries are all in one's mind.

She goes to Dhaka on a rescue mission—to bring her uncle "home" to India. How can he live in a foreign country? As she fills up the disembarkation card before she lands at Dhaka airport, for a while her place of birth seems oddly at variance with her nationality. It is the joy of returning, of seeing her home once again—a common dream of all exiles—which really spur her on in the Dhaka visit.

Once she sets foot in Dhaka, she realises that so much has changed, and none of her friends remained. As the events unfold themselves, her euphoria diminishes. "Where is Dhaka?" (207) she keeps on asking. And her disillusionment again follows the usual pattern of such visits. When exiles return to what was once their home, they are often confronted with the fact that reality is quite different from the nostalgia that had sustained them all this while in exile.

After the brutal murders of Tridib and the others, Tha'mma returns to India and regresses into a combative and dissonant form of nationalism. The enemy now is Pakistan. A precious necklace given to her by her husband (and surreptitiously worn by her lest people say "Look at her—she's been a widow for years and she's still wearing jewelry as though she were a girl" [236]) is given away to the National Defence Fund during the Indo-Pak war of 1965 which takes place soon after Tridib's death. She is ashamed to wear it any longer, she says. She had to give it away. "For your sake, for your freedom. We have to kill them before they kill us." (236-37) "Them" now signifies those who live in her former homeland; and "us" are those who belong to her adopted land.

All these years, even though she had made a conscious effort to accept Calcutta as her home, emotionally her heart had remained in the land of her birth. Tridib's death and the events in Dhaka result in a paradigm shift of the shadow lines of her mind enabling her to reconcile her state of exile with her adopted home.

Coomaraswamy had said: "A single generation of English education suffices to break the threads of tradition and to create a nondescript superficial being deprived of all roots." (*Dance of the Shiva*, 156) I am almost tempted to believe that Ila is a product of such an education. She rejects her roots, her relatives, her cars and servants in India and seeks an identity for herself all alone in an alien land because she wants "to be free." (92) To Ila, freedom means to be able to do just what she wants—to drink beer at a restaurant, to dance with strangers. She revolts when her uncle Robi tells her that in India there are certain things girls cannot do. "That's our culture; that's how we live," (92) he says. To Ila, this is sheer hypocrisy and she finds the double standards of Indian society too difficult to accept. She, too, is an exile but of a different kind. She turns her back to her country out of choice not due to any compulsion. She chooses to be an exile and relocates herself in England.

As a child she would fantasize an existence where she is the cynosure of all eyes. In actual fact she was miserable, lonely and in a moral vacuum. This deception, too, is necessary. How else can she justify her *raison d'être*? How else can she convince herself and her relations that she was successful in her adopted land? And that India was too backward for her?

Ila goes to England believing that by physically living there and by adopting Western ways and style, she would be accepted there. But even though she speaks better English than many English-speaking people, Ila's search for freedom turns out to be an elusive one. Her dark skin (something she cannot shed as she can shed her Indian connections) makes her remain an outsider. "She doesn't belong there. She has no right to be there," (82) exclaims Tha'mma to whom Ila is little better than a "greedy little slut" (83) who has abandoned her country merely for the sake of money and "all the things money can buy—fridges, colour TVs and cars, calculators and cameras, all those things you can't get here." (83)

Ila marries Nick Price in the hope of gaining an identity for herself in England. Perhaps her marriage would make her part of the English mainstream, she believes. But when she finds him cheating on her for the sake of "a bit of variety" (190) she finds it difficult to cope with the situation. She is shattered to discover that "the squalor of the genteel lives she had so much despised was a part too of the free world she had tried to build for herself." (190) Rootless and lost, Ila is left towards the end of the novel, "clinging" (247) to the arms of Robi and the narrator, the members of her family in India.

Nick's betrayal makes Ila realise that there is a mental crossing over involved in the process of adoption of a new home for the exile. Physical relocation is just not enough. A change of perspective, perhaps a shadow of a line, needs to be traversed in order to make "home" out of a state of exile.

Ila had voluntarily sought for herself a state of exile—quite different from Tha'mma's case for whom there was no choice. Ila sought to build for herself a better world but realised that this required a sacrifice of certain principles and norms, that the freedom that she wanted required a certain payment of one's values.

The narrator's mother, in contrast, does not consider herself an exile. India is her home and she does not pine either for Dhaka or for other distant shores. She is content being a housewife, fussing and caring for her husband, her mother-in-law and her son. Relatives—shunned by her mother-in-law—and family were the central points, which gave her world its shape and substance. As her husband goes up steadily in his job, they move up the social ladder—from an apartment in Gole Market area to a more spacious dwelling in the more affluent Southern Avenue. She ensures that there is serenity and the correct atmosphere in the household when her husband returns home from work, tired. As her son, the narrator, says, it was in the fussing and caring for her husband that his mother was able to demonstrate her "effortless mastery of the household arts." (131) Her homeland is where her family is, Gole Market or Southern Avenue. There are no divisive shadow lines in her mind.

If there is any anxiety in her, it is for her son. With a note of hysteria she warned the narrator as she drilled him for his examinations that "if I didn't study hard I would end up over *there* [the slums]; that the only weapon people like us had was our brains and if we didn't use them like claws to cling to what we'd got, that was where we'd end up." (138) Good performance at examinations is of the utmost importance, so important that when Tha'mma dies, the narrator is informed of the event only after his examinations are over. As he says in "the tidy late-bourgeois world I had inherited, examinations were more important than death." (96)

In the mother, one sees that cohesive and reparative identity so imperative in the life of a newly emerging nation. By maintaining a low profile and by not getting involved in any confrontation with her highly charged mother-in-law or by never over-reacting to any situation, the narrator's mother ensures that her family "tasted most fully and richly the subtle rewards of a life that had never strayed from convention by so much as a displaced hair." (131) She is positive in her outlook, believing that there is no substitute for a good education—an education that teaches its citizens to gain cosmopolitan bearings in the wider world. A nation can only be built on a sound foundation when its citizens are given good education, she believes. Her role in the family and in the society around her is clearly defined. Her son compliments her "ability to modulate the volumes and harmonies of our house down to a whisper, while making sure that its rhythms kept ticking over, in perfect time, in much the way that a great conductor can sometimes produce, within a vast tumult of music, one perfect semibreve of silence." (131) She suffers from no angst or nostalgia. She is here and now, neither an exile in terms of where she lives nor one in terms of what she believes.

Who then is an exile? Is it possible to live in a country and be an exile in it? Mentally not be there? Tha'mma remained one for seventeen long years after the Independence of the country which tragically and ironically coincided with its Partition. She too had been divided—physically she was in India but her heart remained in Dhaka. It was only after her revisit to Dhaka that she was able to reconcile the differences and remove the shadows from her mind.

Does physical dislocation make one an exile? Ila exiles herself from her own land and tries to assimilate herself into the Western lifestyle. To the English she is an alien, not one of them. She traverses a tough path as she grits her teeth and prepares to exorcise herself of the shadows in her mind. In her last conversation with the narrator, she says to him: "Nick and I are driving down to Cornwall for the weekend. We're taking a little holiday. Nick wouldn't dream of doing anything that might upset me, really, believe me. You mustn't believe a word I said. I made it all up. That's the truth of it. It's all fine now. We need a little holiday, that's all." (248) And the narrator adds: "She was speaking very fast, in an unnaturally high voice" (249) as she made a compromise with her conscience. The point is this: Ila has burnt her boats as far as her connections with India are concerned. Since she wants to be accepted in British society, she is willing to work for it. For her, physical separation from the land of her birth is not what makes her an exile, but the mental divide that keeps her away from the British mainstream. She will pay any price, even overlook her husband's infidelity in order to cross the shadow line that keeps her from being accepted in her adopted land.

Of Shadows, Lines and Freedom: A Historical Reading of *The Shadow Lines*

SEEMA BHADURI

This paper focuses on Ghosh's treatment in *The Shadow Lines*,[1] of the changing middle class ethos in India during the pre- and post-Independence era. It advances the thesis that the lives of the characters in this novel are determined largely by their idea of freedom and that this idea is, in its turn, shaped by the history of the times.

This paper highlights how in this novel, the failures of nationalism and nationalist governments find voice in the characters's memories and views of the partition, militancy, and the riots. The major characters here move towards a global humanitarianism, coming to grips with the realization that freedom cannot be geo-politically defined or delimited.

Finally, Ghosh's prescription for freedom in the context of the dubious meaning which political independence holds and the distortion of perspectives the individual inevitably undergoes in an increasingly heterogeneous world, is closely scrutinized.

It would be interesting at the outset to look at collectively, three articulations in the novel:

> I gave it to the fund for the war. I had to, don't you see? For your sake, for your freedom. We have to kill them before they kill us; we have to wipe them out. (237)

> I don't believe in this India-Shindia. It's all very well,

> you're going away now, but suppose when you get there, they decide to draw another line somewhere? What will you do then? Where will you move to? None will have you anywhere. As for me, I was born here, and I'll die here. (215)

> Tridib . . . . had said that we could not see without inventing what we saw, so at least we could try to do it properly. . . . We had to try because the alternative wasn't blankness—It only meant that if we didn't try ourselves, we would never be free of other people's inventions. (31)

These three extracts represent the different ideas of freedom underlined by different world-views that, in *The Shadow Lines,* unfold vis-a-vis one another in the commonplace rounds of middle-class life. The ramifications of the nationalist ethos essentialized in the first quote, surface in the lives and memories of the older generation—the narrator's grandmother and her fellow relatives—who lived their prime lives when nationalism rode the world's politics. Evolving from its denouement are the imperatives, in the younger generation i.e. in the narrator and in Robi, Tridib, and May, for yet another world-view, a global humanitarian approach to counter the war, riots and militancy-ridden political atmosphere of the present-day world.

Spanning roughly four decades from the forties to the eighties, the narrative builds on the life and interaction of two families—the one, the narrator's (including Tridib's) and the other, the Prices of London who have been closely associated with Tridib's family throughout this period.

The narrative is an impressionistic rendering of a perceptive middle-class youth's world of these changing times. It evolves in the stream-of-consciousness tradition, through sketchy, disjointed outlines of memories, associations and fancies as they pool into the narrator's mind and consciousness by way of reminiscence, fusing gradually into a coherent pattern of stories mutually interrelated yet disparate, intersecting only laterally, spatialized in their simultaneity the profile of a multilateral world. In the fragmentary pieces—the random diversions of the narrator's memory—is captured the socio-cultural ambience of Calcutta and partly, of London. One finds encoded here the larger patterns of Indian society locked in its internal affiliations and antipathies.[2]

It is a world of memories and reminiscences with the narrator recalling his past associations in order to trace the gradual shaping of his vision under the guiding voice of Tridib who is relationally an uncle doing research in anthropology but functionally a friend and guide full of abstruse knowledge from whom the narrator learns how "to see." For, for the narrator (as for Ghosh) reality lies not in the obvious but in what is evoked and understood by memory and imagination over changing laps of space and time. This novel is all about 'seeing' and 'not seeing.'

To 'see,' as the narrator learnt from Tridib, is to appropriate imaginatively all things seen or heard of—to make the vicarious one's own. It is to embody the world in one's consciousness. It is a multiple vision that emerges, and an acute sense of locale i.e. of the present. End result—in the currents of quotidian living are deciphered the larger drifts of history—national as well as international. To 'see' these currents that hold individual lives in such abeyance for what they are, is to tide them—to be free. And freedom is what almost all the characters in the novel are groping for.

Ghosh's characters have to deal with two types of servility—the one is to ideas spawned by history viz. the ideas of nationalism. These ideas hold sway even after the times to which they were relevant, have passed. The other is servility to one's personal fantasies that distort one's vision, 'Thamma'—the writer's grandma—personifies the first type while Ila, the writer's cousin personifies the second. Thamma essentializes the spirit of European nationalism. She is a typical neo-Victorian figure in her progressive view of the future and her Puritan sense of work and discipline. Nationalism, the product of those times, carries for her the earnestness of religion, informing her every thought and deed. So her grandson must run rather than walk, that he might be strong enough to face the impending challenges to the nation. She opposed any Indian's opting for a life in England on the grounds that the English had earned their liberty and prosperity by incorporating military valour with their religion. Indians she felt, had no right to enjoy what they hadn't earned. (77-78) Her preferences likewise are for men like Robi (Tridib's brother) who have an unintellectual moral impulse and a commitment to action—the type that made the firebrand nationalists of her own youth—the type she admired and had wanted to join. (36-37) Tridib's indisposition to money-earning (he was without a job), his aversion to the Bengali middle-class discipline and snobbery (he frequented street-side talk-shops and guzzled unlimited cups of tea which spoilt his constitution) threatened her Puritanical commitment to work progress and discipline.

But Grandma wasn't the only Indian type to be found during the nationalist period and Ghosh is interested in the totality of impressions of the object/time-span he is depicting. So there is grandma's foil in the anglicized elite, Tridib's father, whom Grandma disparagingly called the Sahib and thought incapable of any achievement.

But here lies Ghosh's pronouncement—Grandma could never get the type of freedom she had dreamt of from India's independence: she had had to eke out the difficult connotations of widowhood in the class-ridden Hindu society that political independence little altered. She became a foreigner to her own home in Dhaka, more foreigner than the English May who didn't need a visa to visit East Pakistan. (195) Besides, her visit there brought the greatest disaster imaginable—her uncle and nephew were killed by rioters close to their home. The responsibility was largely hers—she had insisted on going there and bringing away her uncle to India. Her nonagerian uncle's views on this issue of nationhood and migration, expressed just before he was coaxed into leaving his house, strike at the essential unsoundness of nationalist principles: "I don't believe in this India-Shindia. It's all very well, you're going away now, but suppose when you get there, they decide to draw another line somewhere? What will you do then? Where will you move to? None will have you anywhere. As for me, I was born here and I'll die here." (215)

With her imagination enslaved to the idea of nationalism, Grandma couldn't see what was so obvious, namely, nationalism had destroyed her home and spilled her innocent kin's blood. The extent of her subjectivity can be grasped by the fact that even after this tragedy which affected her mental balance, he gave away her gold chain, the only ornament she had retained with her after her widowhood as a momento of her dead husband. Unable to either reconcile herself to Tridib's death or to understand its fundamental causes, she clung faster for faith to that very idea that had let her down. She tells the narrator: "I gave it [the chain] to the fund for the war. . . . For your sake, for your freedom. We have to kill them before they kill us: we have to wipe them out." (237) She could not understand that national liberty in no way guarantees the individual's liberty.

The new generation in the new era of internationalism must view liberty differently, and one of the easily available methods which the narrator's cousin Ila adopts, is escape—escape to the West, to England. For, to her, freedom means liberty from the restrictive customs that delimit the individual's activities in India. (89) Ila represents the vast majority of the Indian youth who, enamoured of the West, tap impatient heels at their Oriental anchorage. No wonder her mother prefers butler English to plain Hindi while speaking to her Indian maid and has been nicknamed Queen Victoria by Grandma. But freedom is not an external condition merely and Ila is not really free. She is victim to the fantasy her child's mind had built to mentally escape the racial discrimination she has faced in the European schools. She had fancied herself to be a princess whom the white girls didn't like because she was extraordinarily beautiful and intelligent and because all the boys wanted her. She ends up marrying the same Nick who had once let her be beaten by a racist gang from his class. As a child, Ila lived out that fantasy in the form of her beautiful doll Magda for whom she was inordinately jealous. (71-76) She fantasized that Nick, Mrs. Price's son, was in love with Magda. Soon after her marriage however, she discovered that

Nick had been and was ever going to be unfaithful to her. And this, as the narrator puts it, made her realize that "The squalor of the genteel little lives she had so much despised was a part too of the free world she had tried to build for herself." (188)

The longing for freedom is universal and primitive to man but the method of its realization varies with the times. Amitav Ghosh sets his narrative in the current age. The narrator's and Tridib's world is global. Hence, when in Calcutta, the young narrator's mind roamed in the London of Tridib's memories and vice versa, and Delhi seemed about as far from Calcutta as London. It is the present-day world besieged with militants in India (246) and famines in Africa. (162) Every age is distinguished by a distinct set of problems. If geo-political sovereignty was the aim of grandma's age, intellectual independence is under threat in the present with colonizers casting their technological nets for the 'third world' mind. In such a setting Tridib's insistence upon 'seeing' remains the only way to preserve one's intellectual integrity.

The story, or whatever there is of it, eddys around the characters's first hand yet scattered experiences of war, violence and riot, their edges deceptively softened by commonplace occupations love and envy, memories and dreams. The conventional hero of the traditional novel, who leads the action that affects others, is absent. And yet in this age when peoples, cultures, truths, whirl together uncomfortably, one of the most thrilling acts is perhaps to look beyond imposed assumptions, discover realities for oneself and then 'act' in full knowledge and responsibility, as Tridib does in the end. But before coming to that, one must know better what seeing according to Ghosh involves.

Memory and imagination occupy prime place in this business of 'seeing' for memory enlivens the present with the past while the imagination helps to ingest the vicarious, the distant and thereby widen one's world. For those like Ila who cared for neither memory nor imagination, 'the current was the real.' For her therefore, London was only the "busy, bustling town" of the present. Tridib explained to the narrator that even Ila invented places like London, for every place "has to be invented in one's imagination" but as she had all along travelled with her father—a U.N. employee, from country to country, "the inventions she lived in moved with her so that although she had lived in many places, she had never travelled at all." (21) As a result, she identified exotic places like Cairo and Adis Ababa only by the position of the 'Ladies' in the Departure Lounge of the airports for "those were the only fixed points in the shifting landscapes of her childhood." (20)

Ila dismisses imagination as fancy. But Tridib, the narrator says, was an archaeologist not interested in "fairy tales." Imagination must be used with "precision," he said. (24) The faraway must be so vividly recreated as to bring up the feel of the place. Hence the narrator, when in London for the first time, locates with little trouble or help its different streets and the buildings that had stood there during the world war II and also identifies Mrs. Price's house, showing a surprising familiarity with its internal structure. And all this because he had first "seen it with Tridib's eyes [so that] its past seemed concurrent with its present." (31) This historical vision makes to the narrator the bombed and gutted streets that Tridib had seen, seem somehow simultaneous with their present peaceful settlements. (57) And it was the former reality, the narrator realizes, that seemed truer than the latter. Tridib had captured for the narrator something precious. "I wanted to know England not as I saw her, but in her finest hour—every place chooses its own and to me it did not seem an accident that England had chosen hers in a war." (57)

History leaves its mark not only on a place. Every object howsoever trivial, has for Ghosh its relevance to the greater reality of its times. The Citroen parked on an English roadside, the huge table in Ila's Calcutta home—everything becomes an artefact of the times. A simple photograph taken at the Prices' during the II World War encapsulates the entire history of England of the times. There was in it the freshly dug pit to serve as an emergencey trench: there was Alan Tresawsen a free lance journalist writing for socialist papers. Of the remaining figures in the photograph, one was a Trotskyist who had fought the Spanish Civil War and now wrote for left wing papers, another was an Irish nationalist, the third was the academic, Snipe—Mrs. Price's husband, the fourth was Tridib's father—the suited booted Anglicized Indian. Then there was Tridib's mother standing with baby Tridib in her arms, and with the veil on her head. There was also the lady Francesca Halevy who shared the house with the three men. Mrs. Price didn't know who she shared it with. (60-65) There was another photograph—of Lionel Tresawsen, Mrs. Price's father. This photograph is equally significant because he was a globe-trotter, inventor, humanist (51-52)—a Renaissance figure, who summed up the spirit of European History. The need for a historical vision in which memory and imagination are incorporated is essential because, for Tridib every image/situation/personality is inherently complex—its apparent clarity he thinks, is a sign of one's own ignorance. (67) This means that every such image—be it Ila then, or a London street—incorporates multiple layers of reality. For instance, the present always includes the 'presences' from the past. The narrator says that the figures from the past are all around us, "their ghostliness is merely the absence of time and distance . . . a ghost is a presence displaced in time." (181)

"Seeing" with imaginative precision leads one to freedom for it has the force of detachment. To know a thing especially an idea or concept in the totality of its context is to 'place' it; to assimilate it in one's mental framework and thereby to become free of it. Such detachment from things external gradually leads to the coming face to face with oneself, with one's image in the mirror. (29) This union of one's public and private selves is freedom. It means the reconciliation of one's desires which belong to the public field, with one's knowledge and consciousness, which are private. To act then in such a state is to act in free will. Tridib's death while trying to save his granduncle from the rioters in Dhaka is such an act, possibly. Its motives, no doubt, are complex. To the narrator it remains a mystery. (252) And yet, slowly over the years, chance discoveries coupled with his propensity for looking beyond the apparent, for contradicting general assumptions born of the skill of 'seeing,' leads the narrator on to discover the larger truths this act signifies. An analysis in some detail, of Tridib's death is essential for several reasons. It is the only 'act' proper in the novel since it shows independent determination and an awareness of the possible outcome on part of the agent. Besides, it is of great structural significance in the novel. It would indeed be right to look at it as an epiphany, a full illustration of the narrative's major concerns viz. the idea of individual and political liberty in the context of growing internationalism.

It was no doubt clear to Tridib as it was to everyone else in the car that fateful hour that his going out unarmed into the murderous gang meant sure death. (250) Nor could he have risked his life solely for that nonagerian granduncle, who despised them all so (214) and who was dead against arbitrary political divisions that robbed one's homeland. (215) It is more likely that he ventured out of the car in order to save May for Tridib's act surely included his concern for her, born of his love. She had been the first to move out of the car. He loved her dearly. (144, 175) He had compared himself to Tristan who loved the lady from beyond the seas. (186) Ironically he had also desired to make love to her against the backdrop of a historical ruin. (144) What better ruin then, of modern history than the riots—the ruin of nationalism—its most notable achievement? But a voluntary death, where it could achieve nothing for his love was most unbecoming of Tridib. Surely it was more than a mere capricious suicide. Besides, he must have known as May did, that the rioters wouldn't harm her for she was English. (251) He moved into the mob leaving her behind.

The larger implications of the death dawned very gradually on the narrator through the years. Initially he had been told that Tridib died in a car accident (239); later that he was killed. (238) But the more shocking aspect of the tragedy opens up when, fifteen years later, the narrator digs out old newspapers to show his doubting colleagues that serious Hindu-Muslim riots did occur in Bengal in 1964. What those papers revealed was shocking—that these riots had first begun in Dhaka and had spread to Calcutta from there. Tallying dates, the narrator now realized that Tridib had lost his life in these riots. (227)

It was the horror of this realisation—why should the likes of Tridib, who would hurt none, be killed in the riots?—that had led the narrator on to scan the papers of those days for detailed information on the nature and causes of those riots and thereby, to the true import of Tridib's death. He found that the cause had been the loss of the holy relic from the Hazratbal Shrine in Kashmir. But there the Hindus, Muslims and Sikhs had led a unified protest against the Government and the Police. Soon, the Government took steps, the relic was reinstalled and the people responded with celebration and joy. But the Pakistani Govt. declared that the theft was "an attack upon the identity of Muslims," (226) and warned of retaliation. Consequently, rioting began in East Pakistan and surprisingly, gathered force after the relic had been re-installed. (228-29) What was more shocking to the narrator was the Calcutta newspapers on the days immediately preceding the riots here had given no hint at all of the trouble in East Pakistan, and very little indeed, of the events in Kashmir. Or else, the narrator's father would never have allowed his people to go to Dhaka at that time. The narrator says that these papers, like all common men and women, had believed in the power of distance. (227) Srinagar being 1200 miles away from Calcutta, and Dhaka being in another country, were both distant, so what happened there could not probably affect life in Calcutta! This piece of news led the narrator to discover a momentous truth: national frontiers create a false sense of distance and of reality. Though Dhaka and Calcutta are at the same places nearly, and Srinagar so far away, the latter had been supposed closer, simply because it belonged with Calcutta in the same country! Experimenting now with a compass on Tridib's old atlas, he made some startling discoveries. Chiang Mai in Thailand, he realized, is closer to Calcutta than Delhi is, yet he had never heard of the place before. And further, that within a radius of 1200 miles from any city of the world as the centre, lay different cities of different countries and that the only event with the power to draw all the various citizens together, was war! So that the world was left only with "states and citizens: there were no people at all." (231-33)

While the narrator was making these discoveries on the atlas on which "the smudges left by [Tridib's] fingers were clearly visible, he had Tridib . . . watching over [him]." (231-32) So he was discovering only now with the gift of sight Tridib had given him, what the latter had already known and acted on: that riots are born of gross political manipulation of communal sympathies and nationalist passions; that political lines cannot separate people or their common land and realities. (233) Dhaka and Calcutta, the narrator now realized, were the "inverted images of one another"—what happened at one place was sure to spread out into the other. And, most interestingly, it was the 'indivisible sanity, of people like Tridib on both sides of the border, who often at the cost of their lives, tried to rescue their brethren of opposite religions, that really helped to quell the riots. (229-30)

So Tridib's had been the normal humane gesture of one whose vision had transcended the shadow lines—and the shadow realities these lines imposed upon minds that stuck by them—of national frontiers and distances. Interestingly it is Tridib—the laid-back, lazy object of grandmother's scorn who rises to an act that turn out to be tragic-heroic while Robi the man of action and grandma's pet cowers inside the car paralyzed in fear. (245-46) Equally significant is the fact that May and Tridib are not the only ones whose vision and therefore, emotions have not been constricted by nationalist fervour. The writer observes, "As always, there were innumerable cases of Muslims in East Pakistan giving shelter to Hindus, often at the cost of their own lives, and equally in India of Hindus sheltering Muslims." (229-30) These men and women demonstrated "that indivisible sanctity that binds people to each other independently relationship is the natural enemy of government, for it is in the logic of states that to exist at all they must claim the monopoly of all relationships between peoples." (230)

NOTES

1. Amitav Ghosh, *The Shadow Lines* (New Delhi: Ravi Dayal Publisher, 1989).
2. Nandita Sinha, "Perspectives in Time: The Narrator as Child in Amitav Ghosh's *The Shadow Lines*," pp. 143-48 of this book.

The Theme of Violence in *The Shadow Lines*

N. EAKAMBARAM

Amitav Ghosh's *The Shadow Lines*[1] is a complex novel interweaving memory and contemporary life, more memory than contemporary life. It converges on the traumatic life of a family in Calcutta and Dhaka in 1964 when a member of the family, Tridib was killed in a communal riot. Ghosh employs the technique of the narrator, an educated young man who travels between Calcutta and London in 1981, to tell the story which contains multiple stories of his grandmother and her sister, of his uncles—Tridib and Robi, of his cousin Ila who marries an Englishman, and of May Price, a family friend in London. Many stories that belong to the oral sphere in the extended family memory get their validation by being written in the novel—a feature of most postcolonial writing.

Ghosh depicts the urban middle class in India to whom education and professional jobs are important. Living and partly living they drift from one day to another, and so for a whole lifetime. The reward, if one is lucky, may be one's own house and a pension to lean upon. The environment of the school and/or office encourages the cultivation of the virtues of hard work, contentment, obedience, and conformity to the norms of society. Amitav Ghosh's characters inhabit this realm of life. But when misfortune strikes their lives in an unforeseen manner, they are left baffled. If it is, at least, death or disease, they may try to comprehend it. But when violence erupts like a volcano in the public sphere, they are totally disoriented. Life seems to lose its significance. The present paper examines how violence cracks the mirror of life in the fictional world of *The Shadow Lines.*

The narrative of *The Shadow Lines* is in two parts: "Going Away" (3-112) and "Coming Home." (115-252) The words "going" and "coming" are used in relation to 'home,' a place of one's birth and upbringing, a place to which a person is deeply attached, especially if one lives in another place. Though in the growth of a human being, it would be ideal to feel that all places are one's place and all people one's people, and he/she is 'a citizen of the world', most people are circumscribed by the contexts of their life. They either 'go away' or 'come home.' Ghosh's characters go as far as Delhi or London on work or travel, and come home to Calcutta or Dhaka only to learn that peace is as elusive as ever.

One disturbing feature of life in Calcutta/Dhaka and such cities is the increasing tension between the Hindu and Muslim communities and the eruption of violence which takes its toll of innocent lives and destruction of public as well as private property. As long as one learns about death and destruction in newspapers and other media, one is not touched by them. But when someone in the family is caught in the carnage, then one realizes what it is. In fact, this exactly is what happens to the characters of Amitav Ghosh.

The narrative structure of *The Shadow Lines* is fragmentary. There are sixteen sections in the first part, and fifteen in the second part, but the sections do not add up to an organic whole with a proper beginning, middle and ending. Nivedita Bagchi observes: "The 'story' or the chief narrative line evolves sporadically and is constantly interrupted and diverted by other narratives. The only fixed center is that of the chief narrative voice through whom the other narratives are filtered."[2] Ghosh's narrator shuttles not only from Calcutta to London to collect material for his Ph.D. thesis, but across the loom of time from 1981 to the 1960s onto the 1940s and earlier. Especially his mind is drawn on the troubled time of the 1960s when Tridib, his uncle, was killed in a Hindu-Muslim riot in Dhaka. At the time this tragedy took place, the narrator, a twelve-year-old boy, had been told that Tridib had died in an accident. It is onty in 1981 that he learns from Robi, another uncle, an eyewitness, how Tridib had been killed, also from May Price, an English family friend, also an eyewitness to the tragedy. The oblique manner of the revelation of Tridib's death is more effective than a direct presentation. It is a timeless moment in the tortured consciousness of the family. The narrator—whose name is not given—is the bearer of this troubled memory.

The narrator's grandmother, Tha'mma is the central character in the novel. In fact, *The Shadow Lines* is very much her story. The narrator remembers how Tridib had called her "a modern middle-class woman. . . . All she wanted was a middle-class life in which, like the middle classes the world over, she would thrive believing in the unity of nationhood and territory, of self-respect and national power: that was all she wanted—a modern middle-class life, a small thing that history had denied her in its fullness and for which she could never forgive it." She has lived a quiet life for a whole lifetime in Calcutta, but when she goes to Dhaka (her native city) on a visit, she is the unwitting witness to the most horrendous act in her life when a rioting mob kills her aged uncle and her young nephew. She is left totally disoriented as she cannot comprehend the meaning of what happens. She is the dangling woman suspended by the quirk of history.

Amitav Ghosh presents the grandmother's early life as a story told by her to the narrator. (121-26) Born in 1902 in Dhaka, she grew up as a member of "a big joint family, with everyone living and eating together." (121) But when her grandfather died, the ancestral house had to be partitioned because of the strife that broke out between her father and her uncle. While at college for her B.A. in History in Dhaka, she had known the terrorist movement amongst nationalists in Bengal: "about secret terrorist societies like Anushilan and Jugantar and all their offshoots, their clandestine networks, and the home-made bombs with which they tried to assassinate British officials and policemen; and a little about the arrests, deportations and executions with which the British had retaliated." (37)

In her own class there was a shy young man who was a

member of a terrorist organization. One day as the lecture was going on, the police entered the class and arrested the young man as they had learnt that he planned to kill an English magistrate in Khulna district. He was tried and later deported to the cellular jail in the Andaman Islands. In her youthful enthusiasm she had dreamt of terrorists like Kudhiram Bose and Bagha Jatin who had been betrayed by treacherous villagers who in turn had been bought with English money. "She'd been expecting a huge man with burning eyes and a lion's mane of a beard, and there he was, all the while, at the back of her class, sitting shyly by himself." (39) She had wanted to work for the terrorists, to run errands for them, to cook their food, to wash their clothes and to render some help. After all, the terrorists were working for freedom. When the narrator asks her whether she would have killed the English magistrate, she replies: "I would have been frightened. . . . But I would have prayed for strength, and God willing, yes, I would have killed him. It was for our freedom: I would have done anything to be free." (39) But her romantic notion of terrorism and freedom went like a bubble with her marriage. Her short married life, mostly lived in Burma, was punctuated by the birth of a son in 1925, and the unfortunate death of her husband in 1935 when she was just thirty-two.

A new phase of life began in 1936 when she took up the job of a school teacher in Calcutta. Amitav Ghosh omits this part of the grandmother's life except dropping hints from which the reader may construct the story. Starting life in Calcutta in a one-room tenement in Bhowanipore, she would dream of "the old house, her parents, Jethamoshai [her uncle], her childhood" (125) in Dhaka, but she could never go there. The big political events, the partition in 1947 and Dhaka becoming the capital of East Pakistan, divided her from her native city. But these public events did not have a direct impact on her so much as the demands of her personal life. As a school teacher she educated her son on her own, declining the help of her rich sister. The son's employment in a private company, his marriage, the birth of a grandson in 1952, her own retirement in 1962 as the headmistress of the school she had joined in 1936 are abbreviated and revealed in an oblique manner. The focus of the novel is on the grandmother from her retirement in 1962 to her death in 1965.

One feature that may be noted is the kind of house in which the grandmother lives: from the large house in Dhaka to a succession of houses in Burma with her husband onto the one-room tenement in Calcutta after her husband's death, then to a cramped little flat in Gole Park (119) where she spent most of her life. She had grown up with the school where she was a teacher and became the headmistress in the last six years of her service. But the school disappeared from her life with her retirement, and around the same time her son was promoted as the General Manager of his firm. The family moved to a large new house on Southern Avenue, opposite the Lake—with "rooms upstairs, rooms downstairs, verandas, a garden as well as a roof big enough to play cricket on." (119) She was given the best room in the house, but she dreamt of her old house in Dhaka where she was born and had grown up to adulthood.

The grandmother's younger sister, Mayadebi, is the fortunate girl in the family. Born in 1910, she grew up into a beauty and married Datta Chaudhuri, the son of the wealthy judge, who became a diplomat in the Indian Foreign Service. She lived mostly abroad, moving from one country to another, wherever her husband had his posting. Mayadebi had three sons. The eldest was Jatin, born in 1929, who had a job as an economist with the U.N., working most of the time in Africa or SouthEast Asia. He lived with his wife and his daughter, Ila who was of the age of the narrator. Tridib was the second son, born in 1931, who lived in the 1960s in the family's large ancestral house in Ballygunge Place in Calcutta with his aging grandmother. He was supposed to be working for his Ph.D. in Archaeology. The youngest son was Robi, born after a long break, almost the age of the narrator. By 1981 Robi is in the Indian Administrative Service and he stops in London to be with the narrator and Ila for a few days. On leave from his job, he is on his way to Harvard where he has a fellowship to study administration and public affairs for six months.

London figures in a prominent way in the life of Mayadebi's family. She and her husband with their eight-year-old son, Tridib, had stayed with Mrs. Price, a family friend in London in 1939 for a whole year when the war had started. Tridib had told the narrator about their life at 44, Lymington Road and other places. People in London had started living with the terror of German air raids and the Prices suffered when Mrs Price's brother, Alan Tresawsen, and his three friends were killed in an attack. They were young intellectuals whose life had been snuffed out all of a sudden. Though they were in the photograph that Tridib had shown, "nobody can ever know what it was like to be young and intelligent in the summer of 1939 in London or Berlin." (68) After more than forty years the narrator explores these places as "I wanted to know England not as I saw her, but in her finest hour every place chooses its own and to me it did not seem an accident that England had chosen hers in a war." (57)

But England comes through in a different light in the life of Ila, the narrator's cousin. After roving round many places with her parents, she had come to London to school. There was so much racism that one day she was beaten up while returning from school and she had never gone to school again. Later she did B.A. in History at the University College in London, took up a job in an office and married Nick Price whom she had known over the years. Of course, the narrator is in love with his beautiful cousin. On one occasion the narrator's grandmother is angry that Ila was living in London. She had said:

> Ila has no right to live there. . . . She doesn't belong there. It took those people a long time to build that country; hundreds of years, years and years of war and bloodshed. Everyone who lives there has earned his right to be there with blood: with their brother's blood and their father's blood and their son's blood. They know they are a nation because they've drawn their borders with blood. . . . That's what it takes to make a country.

> Once that happens people forget that they were born this or that, Muslim or Hindu, Bengali or Punjabi: they become a family born of the same pool of blood. That is what you have to achieve for India, don't you see? (77-78)

The narrator disagrees with his grandmother when she says that Ila lives in London for the money and the comforts of British life. He had known Ila to live a simple life and spend her spare time going on demonstrations and acting in radical plays for Indian immigrants in east London. (79) It is a mystery why Ila who can live like a princess in Calcutta should live in London like a martyr. Probably it is the romance of freedom in an alien land. Also she seems to be the kind of person who is not attached to any particular place.

The heart of *The Shadow Lines* is the death of Tridib and it is only towards the end of the novel the narrator approaches this experience. It is a struggle with silence as he has no words to communicate what happened: "it lies outside the reach of my intelligence, beyond words . . . it is simply a gap, a hole, an emptiness in which there are no words." (218) A little later he writes: "I can only describe at second hand the manner of Tridib's death: I do not have the words to give it meaning. I do not have the words, and I do not have the strength to listen." (228) The narrator loved and admired Tridib as a hero. So he finds it difficult to accept the fact of Tridib's death. "So complete is this silence," the narrator declares, "that it actually took me fifteen years to discover that there was a connection between my nightmare bus ride back from school, and the events that befell Tridib and the others in Dhaka." (218) The narrator's struggle with the presentation of Tridib's death makes it all the more agonizing.

The trouble started when the sacred relic known as the Mu-i-Mubarak—believed to be a hair of the Prophet Mohammed himself—disappeared from its place on 27 December 1963 in the Hazratbal mosque near Srinagar, two hundred and sixty three years after it had been installed. "Over the next few days life in the valley seemed to close in upon itself in a spontaneous show of collective grief. There were innumerable black flag demonstrations, every shop and building flew a black flag, and every person on the streets wore a black arm-band." (225) But surprisingly there was not a single incident of Hindu-Muslim animosity in the valley. Probably it was the gifted leadership of Maulana Masoodi who "drew the various communities of Kashmir together in a collective display of mourning." (226) While India was deeply agitated, Pakistan fanned communal passion, and spoke of 'genocide.' Fortunately the Mu-i-Mubarak was 'recovered' on 4 January 1964 by the officials of the Central Bureau of Intelligence, and Kashmir heaved a sigh of relief.

The narrator is concerned with the impact of this event on life in Calcutta and Dhaka. Novy Kapadia rightly points out: "Amitav Ghosh's greatest triumph is that the depiction of communal strife in Calcutta and erstwhile East Pakistan, and its continuation in contemporary India, is very controlled and taut. There are no moralizing or irrelevant digressions. Lucidity and compactness is achieved primarily by his unusual narrative device."[3]

The narrator remembers how on a certain morning in early January 1964 the school bus, which would normally be over-crowded, came with only a dozen boys. No sooner he got in than the other boys told him that 'they' had poisoned the water in the Tala Tank, which catered to the entire city of Calcutta. Everyone knew who 'they' were. At school, the classes were cancelled half-way through. On their way home the boys saw that the streets "were eerily empty now except for squads of patrolling policemen." (202) At a particular point an unruly mob had thrown stones on their bus and chased it from its normal route. The boys began to sob as they could not go home. "It would not be enough to say we were afraid: we were stupefied with fear." (204)

This fear grips the thousand million people who inhabit the Indian sub-continent and sets them apart from the rest of the world. The narrator comments upon the quality of this fear in the following manner: "It is a fear that comes of the knowledge that normalcy is utterly contingent, that the spaces that surround one, the streets that one inhabits, can become, suddenly and without warning, as hostile as a desert in a flash flood. . . . it is the special quality of loneliness that grows out of the fear of the war between oneself and one's image in the mirror." (204) This is a very evocative account of the fear that has rocked the people of our sub-continent since the partition and that threatens to engulf us any moment.

It was at the time the narrator suffered the worst of fears in Calcutta, that his grandmother had gone on a visit to her sister, Mayadebi, who was in Dhaka. Her husband had his posting in East Pakistan. When the idea was mooted that she should visit Dhaka, she had wondered whether the border between India and East Pakistan was marked by trenches or something. What could be the dividing line between the two countries? Then her son explains: "This is the modern world. The border isn't on the frontier: It's right inside the airport. You'll see. You'll cross it when you have to fill in all those disembarkation cards and things." (151-52) She was worried because "she had not been able to understand how her place of birth had come to be so messily at odds with her nationality." (152) When she flew into Dhaka on 3 January 1964, accompanied by Tridib and May Price, who had come on a visit to India, and met her sister, the grandmother's question was: "Where's Dhaka? I can't see Dhaka" (193) for the dream image of her native city had vanished long ago.

One important reason for the grandmother to go to Dhaka was her desire to see her old house and bring her uncle, Jethamoshai, to India. No sooner she had spent a few days in her sister's house than the grandmother accompanied by Mayadebi, Tridib, May Price, and Robi set out in the Mercedes car with the driver and a security guard of the High Commission. The car had to stop at a particular point in the by-lanes of Dhaka, and they had to walk to the old house. They discovered to their dismay an automobile workshop in what was a garden in their house. Their house was crumbling and a large number of families were living there. Their uncle Jethamoshai, now called Ukilbabu, was decrepit and bedridden, looked after by Khalil, a cycle-rickshaw driver, and his family.

The old man failed to recognize them, and spoke ill of his relatives when they were mentioned. As for going to India, he had not believed in that. In fact, he had told his India-bound sons: "but suppose when you get there they decide to draw another line somewhere? What will you do then? Where will you move to? No one will have you anywhere. As for me, I was born here, and I'll die here." (215) The old man would have gone on with his talk, but the car driver intervenes to say that they must leave immediately as "there's going to be trouble outside." (216) So the grandmother and Mayadebi and others depart, arranging with Khalil that he should bring their uncle to their house in his cycle-rickshaw telling him that he is taking him out. It is then that "trouble" starts. In a book-review, Girish Karnad makes the following observation on this episode: "The grandmother's visit to the ancestral home . . . is surely one of the most memorable scenes in Indian fiction. Past and future meet across religious, political and cultural barriers in a confusion of emotions, ideals, intentions and acts, leading to a shattering climax."[4]

The "climax" occurs as the grandmother and her sister are returning in their Mercedes from their ancestral home and their uncle is following them in the rickshaw (Robi's narrative 243-47, May Price's recollection 250-51). When they come to the bazaar area, they find that the shops are closed and the street is deserted, but for stray people. It was as if they were waiting for the car. In no time a lot of men surround the car, break the windscreen and the driver suffers a cut across his face. The car lurches and comes to a halt with its front wheel in a gutter. Then the security guard jumps out and fires a shot from his revolver and the crowd begins to withdraw from the car. At the same time the eerie silence is broken by a creak, and the attention of the crowd turns to the sound of a rickshaw—Khalil's rickshaw—with their uncle in it, and the people surround the rickshaw. Though the sisters could have driven away, May Price and Tridib leave the car to save the old man and they get lost in the whirlgig of the crowd. The mischief takes less than a moment and the crowd begins to melt away. The dead bodies of Khalil, the old man and Tridib lie on the road. The horror of the act is branded with fire on the memory of May Price and Robi who see the whole thing.

Amitav Ghosh dramatizes the violence that is at the heart of *The Shadow Lines*. Characters in the novel—Robi, May and the narrator (Ghosh's alter-ego)—tremble "like a leaf" to recollect the scene of Tridib's death, "fifteen years later, thousands of miles away, at the other end of another continent." (247) As in Greek tragedies, the violence comes through in a terrible manner because it is conveyed through choric characters. Robi, May and the narrator perform such a role of mediation. True, the violent bear it away. But for what? People kill for freedom. But do they achieve it? It seems to be a mirage, as the shadow lines that divide one people from another keep ever-changing.

NOTES

1. Amitav Ghosh, *The Shadow Lines* (Delhi : Ravi Dayal Publishers, 1988), p. 78.
2. Nivedita Bagchi, "The Process of Validation in Relation to Materiality and Historical Reconstruction in Amitav Ghosh's *The Shadow Lines*," *Modern Fiction Studies*, 39.1 (Winter 1993), p. 188
3. Novy Kapadia, "Imagination and Politics in Amitav Ghosh's *The Shadow Lines*," *The New Indian Novel in English: A Study of the 1980s*, ed. Viney Kirpal (New Delhi: Allied, 1990), p. 208.
4. Girish Karnad, "Worlds within Worlds: Book Review of *The Shadow Lines*," *Indian Express Magazine*, December 18, 1988, p. 5.

The Shadow Lines: A Quest for 'Indivisible Sanity'

MURARI PRASAD

> The novel is not required—even assuming the task is within the realm of possibility—to describe the specific historical forms of a society; that is not where the truth lies. Nor of course is it a matter of saying that the author's ideas are necessarily correct. But literature is always an attempt to reveal to us "an unknown side of human existence," as Kundera says somewhere, and thus although it has no privileged access to truth, it never stops searching for it.[1]

Amitav Ghosh's *The Shadow Lines* is one of the most readable and least frivolous of the recent Indian novels in English. An effective fiction, it emanates from a particular historical moment which intersects the narrator and the nation at a crucial point of their evolution and growth. While capturing the high points of the historical moment in credible and efficient narrative action, the novel eventuates into a search for the vibrant concerns essential for the survival of central strength and sanity in society. The novel is rich in signifying transactions that do not depend for their effect on "solid slabs of continuous experience" but on the potentiality of materiality marshalled by the author to anchor his perception of reality. It quickens our conscience and triggers our response to the mingled frenzy of violence, idealism, passion and intrigue that has amputated the narrator's intimate history and geography. By skilfully manipulating the narrator's developing sociological consciousness and his interaction with multicultural representatives in a fictional construct, Ghosh makes his novel a supple medium of sophisticated comment on current realities. Although the situations are bound by their historical and geographical co-ordinates, they enlarge the spatial and temporal axes and offer a melange of insights into a kind of 'reality' that can sustain inter-personal bond across cultural boundaries and contain the threats flowing from the absurdities of borders and frontiers.

The novel tells the story of the three generations of the narrator's family spread over Dhaka, Calcutta and London and lines up characters from different nationalities, religions and cultures in a close-knit, palpable fictive world. Written against the backdrop of the civil strife in post-partition East Bengal and riot-hit Calcutta, the events revolving around itinerant Mayadebi's family, their friendship and sojourn with their English friends, the Prices, Tha'mma, the narrator's great mother, ties with Dhaka and the later wrench from her roots, spontaneous communal combustion in 1964 in Dhaka claiming the lives of Jethamoshai, Khalil and Tridib pose the challenge of intercultural understanding and friendship in contemporary society divided by arbitrary demarcations of national boundaries. The narrator's mnemonic fund is enriched by his uncle and mentor, Tridib, who lets him in on the creative powers of memory and imagination. On one hand is the narrator's family consisting of his grandmother, Mayadebi's elder sister, and his parents; on the other are Mayadebi, her husband, a diplomat, and their three sons, Jatin, an economist with the UN, Tridib and Robi. Jatin's daughter, Ila, is always away with her parents. While the narrator's family is settled in Calcutta where his grandmother is a schoolmistress, Mayadebi's family except Tridib keeps on going around the world. Tridib, who lives in his ancestral house in Ballygunge place, is seen at a loose end at Gole Park among his *adda* acquaintances. Stay in close vicinity brings the narrator and his uncle Tridib together, although much to the dislike of Tha'mma, who is stern middle-class matriarch.

Tridib saw May Price as a little baby when he went to England with his parents in 1939. The friendship between the families began when Mrs. Price's father, Lionel Tresawsen, and Tridib's grandfather, Mr. Justice Chandrashekhara Datta-Chaudhury, met in Calcutta at seances. By the time Tridib meets May in India in 1962, their friendship through correspondence since 1959 has ripened into love. The narrator who is Ila's age and is drawn to her apparently liberated charms loses his chance to Nick Price, May's younger brother. It is May-Tridib relationship which is central to the thematic concerns of the novel. The narrator's close interaction with May who accompanied Tha'mma, Mayadebi and Tridib to bring his grandmother's uncle, Jethamoshai, from Dhaka to Calcutta and was witness to the killing of Tridib, is the most moving part of the novel. The narrator recalls his meeting with May at crucial point in the chronology of the novel: "I met May Price for the first time two years after that incident, when she came to Calcutta on a visit. The next time I met her was seventeen years later, when I went to London myself."[2] (19) The stretch of history during these seventeen years between 1962 and 1979 is the effective background of the novel against which the author evokes postcolonial situations, cultural dislocations and anxieties, and interprets the issues of fractured nationalities in close and telling encounters.

The historical baggage shouldered by the novel includes the freedom movement in Bengal, the Second World War, the partition of India and the miasma of communal hatred breaking out into riots in East Pakistan (now Bangla Desh) following the Hazratbal incident in Srinagar in 1964. The novel is not a recapitulation of these historical upheavals; it catches alive the trauma of emotional rupture and choked human relations as also the damaging potential of the siege within people sundered by politics. The materiality of Ghosh's novel constituted by the web of material relations at a certain time in a certain location binds the narratives and authenticates the nexus between the historical moment and the fictive world. The reconstruction of the past through houses, photographs, maps, road names, newspapers, advertisements and other concretizations allows the reader to examine the text with diverse co-texts and validate the author's perception of the time and milieu covered by the novel. A close look at the principal episodes with reference to their historicity and materiality is significantly revealing in that the author's insight into the issues troubling the consciousness of characters can be identified and gleaned. "In *The Shadow Lines*," writes Nivedita Bagchi, "the very materiality of objects plays a vital role in validating the narrative. Tridib, we are told, is an archaeologist, and the chief narrator is a history research fellow. The importance of material objects to the archaeological-historian for validation of oral narratives, for dating and establishing chronology in the reconstruction of history, cannot be overstated."[3]

The looping, non-linear progression of the narratives underpinned by the narrator and the historical sweep entail active and alert audience participation. In the opening lines, the narrator refers to his grandmother's sister's visit to England and establishes the narrative framework: "In 1993, thirteen years before I was born, my father's aunt, Mayadebi, went to England with her husband and her son, Tridib." (9) We gather that Mayadebi was born in 1910 and Tridib in 1931. The novel also telescopes the political ferment in Bengal and the upbringing of Tha'mma, who was born in 1902, and Mayadebi in the revolutionary decades of the present century. As soon as we infer the details of Mayadebi's visit to England, the narrative shifts to 1960 when Tridib first shared his experience of London with the narrator:

> Over the years, although I cannot remember when it happened any more than I can remember when I first learnt to tell the time or tie my shoelaces, I have come to believe that I was eight too when Tridib first talked to me about that journey. I remember trying very hard to imagine him back to my age, to reduce his height to mine, and to think away the spectacles that were so much a part of him that I really believed he had been born with them. It wasn't easy, for to me he looked old, and I could not remember him looking anything other than old—though, in fact, at that time he could not have been much older than twenty-nine. In the end, since I had

> nothing to go on, I had decided that he had looked like me. (9)

Thus the narrative spills back and forth but all the episodes are held in simultaneous focus nonetheless to illuminate the major burden of the novel.

Chronologically, the story begins with a passage of time in colonial India when the narrator was not born. The year 1939 is historically significant for the outbreak of the second world war and phenomenal changes caused by that agonizing epochal event. Mayadebi's visit to London around this time, her warm and consequential contact with the Price family and Tridib-May component of the story is recounted by Tridib to the narrator twenty-one years later when the latter is an eight-year-old inquisitive child. Although May was a little baby when Tridib saw her in London—and they have not met since then—a romantic relationship develops through correspondence between them, transcending the shadow lines of nationality and cultural boundary. Amitav Ghosh explores the mysterious pull between Tridib and May and the abiding intimacy between the two families, when the countries were pitted against each other. This search for invisible links ranging across the realities of nationality, cultural segregation and racial discrimination is the central theme of *The Shadow Lines.* The author questions the validity of geographical boundaries and celebrates the union of aliens pulled together by self-propelling empathy and attachment. Tresawsen and Mayadebi, Tridib and May, Jethamoshai and Khalil rise above the prevailing passion of war, hatred and communal bad blood and vindicate the political logic of partition and border demarcation to define national and cultural particularities. Ghosh's maturer view of reality was missed glaringly by Bruce King in his review of *In an Antique Land* in *World Literature Today.* The reviewer notes: "Amitav Ghosh's novels *The Circle of Reason* and *The Shadow Lines* are somewhat difficult to place on the current literary map; they have an unusual perspective and cover unexpected territory. *In an Antique Land* fills in some of the picture of how Ghosh sees the world and, besides the interest of the book itself as social anthropology and what it tells us about Ghosh, might be a starting place for future discussion of his fiction."[4] Without questioning the merit of *In an Antique Land*, the present writer differs with Bruce King's comments on *The Shadow Lines* in that the latter, as a seminal piece of fiction, does bring out the rare and remarkable talent of Ghosh who passionately searches for strategies for survival in a violent, hate-filled world of narrow divisions and finds in love the enabling and productive action to tide over separatist propensities of communities and nationality groups. The novel addresses the challenge of geographical fluidity and cultural dislocations with a new consciousness and firm grasp of socio-cultural and historical material. The experience of aliens and immigrants in postcolonial setting furnish us with the clue to the novel's larger project of cultural assimilation, friendship across borders and adjustment with the altered face of the world. The theme is first sounded when in a conversation with the narrator in London in 1978 May Price shares her growing intimacy with Tridib:

> Smiling at the memory, she told me how his card had reached her just when she was trying to get over an adolescent crush on a schoolboy trombonist, who had had no time for her at all and had not been overly delicate about making that clear. It was nice to feel that someone wanted to befriend her. She had written back, and after that they had written to each other regularly—short, chatty letters, usually. Soon, pen-friendship, they had exchanged photographs. (23)

The narrator recalls that Tridib's made-up story of his English relatives through marriage recounted to his *adda* acquaintances at Gold Park around 1960 sprang from his passionate longing for May:

> Where have you been all this while Tridib-da! somebody said. It must be three or four months. . . .
>
> I've been away, I heard him say, and nodded secretly

> to myself.
>
> Away! Where!
>
> I've been to London, he said. To visit my relatives.
>
> His face was grave, his voice steady.
>
> What relatives!
>
> I have English relatives through marriage, he said. A family called Price. I thought I'd go and visit them.
>
> Ignoring their grunts, he told them that he had been to stay with old Mrs. Price, who was a widow. Her husband had died recently. She lived in north London, he said, on a street called Lymington Road; the number of their house was 44 and the tube station was West Hampstead. Mrs. Price had a daughter, who was called May. (17)

Tridib realizes May concretely and warmly in his imagination with all the attendant excitement stored in his senses. He can visualize her shape and appearance precisely even without meeting her. Their love has instrinsic reality; it crosses all borderlines and shadow-lines. The narrator also owes his broadened horizons to Tridib's influence. He has become an imaginative traveller of distant locations beyond the limits of his mind and experience at a fairly young age. He is verily enamoured of the Tridib who had pushed him to "imagine the roofs of Colombo" for himself and "had said that we could not see without inventing what we saw, so at least we could try to do it properly." (37) The narrator's psyche absorbs cross-cultural interactions and sheds particularity of his origin and narrow nationalism fostered and instilled in him by his grandmother. Unlike Ila's pragmatic cosmopolitanism, either lukewarm or lacking in vibrant reciprocity, the narrator learns the lesson of love and sacrifice untrammelled by exclusionary nationalism and spatial limits, first under the spiritual tutelage of Tridib, and later, in the warm embrace of May towards the close of the novel. He contrasts the cross-cultural perspectives of Tridib and Ila at several places in the novel. For instance:

> I tried to tell her, but neither then nor later, though we

> talked about it often, did I ever succeed in explaining to her that I could not forget because Tridib had given me worlds to travel in and he had given me eyes to see them with; she, who had been travelling around the world since she was a child, could never understand what those hours in Tridib's room had meant to me, a boy who had never been more than a few hundred miles from Calcutta. I used to listen to her talking sometimes with her father and grandfather about the cafes in the Plaza Mayor in Madrid, or the crispness of the air in Cuzco, and I could see that those names, which were to me a set of magical talismans because Tridib had pointed them out to me on his tattered old Bartholomew's Atlas, had for her a familiarity no less dull than the lake had for me and my friends; the same tired intimacy that made us stop on our way back from the park in the evening and unbutton our shorts and aim our piss through the rusty wrought-iron railings. (26)

Yet the narrator is hooked on to Ila's exotic appeal. It is her striking foreignness, her western ways and easy informality that attract him. Her liberated gestures and overtly off-beat demeanour arouse Tha'mma's contemptuous dislike for her. While the narrator develops a mesmeric fascination for Ila in the flush of adolescence, his grandmother hates her vulgar transgressions. Ila's preference for Nick Price and her later disappointment expose her wobbly transplantation in the western culture. Her dislocation stems from her penchant for illusions devoid of any real understanding of the cultural interface. The adult narrator sees through Ila's hidden anxieties and discomfiture. Her last words in the novel are aimed at consoling the narrator and her cousin that everything is all right between her and Nick. Commenting on Ila's role in the novel, Suvir Kaul notes that she is central to the narrator's coming-of-age and functions "as a narrative scapegoat, a figure who acts as a lightning-rod for a great many sexual and cultural anxieties, and the telling of whose unhappy and even sordid itinerary, especially her relationship with Nick, takes on all the cautionary tones of a modern fable."[5] Nick-Ila pairing is a counterpoint to Tridib-May kinship in the thematic framework of the novel. When the narrator looks at Ila's seductive foreignness with unstinted eye in his mature stage, he notices her snooty ways and cultural contradictions. Significantly, the novel ends with May and the narrator lying in close embrace after the former has recounted Tridib's tragic killing in Dhaka. May interprets Tridib's act as sacrifice and defines the manner of his giving up his life while rushing to Jethamoshai for his unsuccessful rescue from the frenzied rioters. Tridib appreciates May's ideals of humanitarianism and acts like her soul-mate. Jean Sudrann makes a perceptive comment on the thematic concerns of Amitav Ghosh: "As in his first novel, *The Circle of Reason,* where Ghosh pitted rationality against emotion as warring forces within and among people, so here the conflict has been resumed in epistemological terms. Knowledge can set us free, but only if it is bred of heart as well as head. May's love—of the narrator, of Tridib, of the cycle-rickshaw man, of the hate-filled lawyer—which prompts her to reveal her innermost thoughts to the narrator, releases him from the silence which is outside his intelligence into the perhaps equally unspeakable mystery of love."[6] The novel insists on the imperatives that assure empathy and unimpeded flow of friendship, and mock the conception of militant nationalism, exclusive national pride and identity. The outbreak of communal strife in Dhaka following the disappearance of the prophet's hair in Srinagar exposes the fragile demarcation of political frontiers. The author's postcolonial angst for the disrupted subcontinental commonality and snapped cultural bonds is evident in the instant communal reaction to the Hazratbal incident in Calcutta and Dhaka. Tha'mma's ideals of nationalism nurtured since the Swadeshi movement do not stand the test of time. Hers is a misplaced sense of pride reminiscent of the 'tardy late-bourgeois world.' Drawing national borders with blood is bound to be undone by the inherent logic of and propensity to separateness and divinations. Her senile old uncle has a grasp of ambiguous and tenuous geographical boundaries: "Once you start moving you never stop. That's what I told my sons when they took the trains. I said: I don't believe in this India-Shindia. It's all very well, you're going away now, but suppose when you get there they decide to draw another line somewhere! What will you do then! Where will you move to! No one will ever have you anywhere. As for me, I was born here, and I'll die here." (216)

The message of the novel underlines the need of friendly ambience for co-existence and humanitarian ties across cultures independent of political managers. The 'indivisible sanity' of people beyond borders has the potential to ensure warm and wholesome international amity and exorcise divisive streaks and madness. Mayadebi and Tresawsen realize the palpable evidence of this desire among people both in England and Germany even as the second world war is looming ahead:

> Well, she said, laughing, the couple of months she had spent in London had been so exciting—the atmosphere had changed so dramatically, even within the last few weeks. People were becoming friendlier; in the shops, on the streets, she couldn't help noticing. Everyone was so much nicer now; often when she and Tridib were out walking people would pat him on the head and stop to have a little chat with her; the shopkeepers would ask her how her husband was, and when he was to have his operation. But it wasn't just her—everyone was being friendly with everyone; why just that morning his sister, Elisabeth, had said that old Mrs. Dunbar who lived down the road had actually been civil for the first time in living memory. . . .
>
> Yes, he said, that's true—there's a kind of exhilaration in the air.
>
> Yes, that's the right word, said Mayadebi: exhilaration. I've been lucky, I've been lucky to watch England coming alive. I wouldn't have seen that if I hadn't been here now.
>
> Tresawsen laughed. People don't believe me, he said, but it's the same over there—in Germany—though of course in a much more grotesque way. It was odd com-

> ing back here—like stepping through a looking glass. (70-71)

The narrator with his expanded horizons and imaginative understanding of the world caught up in the vortex of violence and murderous rampage stresses on the urgency of preserving the memories of saner and humane transactions for cultural self-determination and inter-personal communication. The media and public memory must keep alive the 'indivisible sanity' of communities to prevent recurrence of insane frenzy. Ghosh has edged up his novel to confront the memory of traumatic events and shake up our indifference to the gathering potential of tragedy. All in all, the novel is "an eloquent critique of colonial hangover and cultural dislocation in postcolonial situation as also the psychological make-up of the contemporary man who thrives on violence."[7] Amitav Ghosh projects these genuine Indian vibrations with remarkable competence.

NOTES

1. Tzvetan Todorov, "A Dialogic Criticism," *Literature and Its Theorists*, trans. Catherine Porter (London: Routeledge and Kegan Paul, 1988), p. 164.
2. Amitav Ghosh, *The Shadow Lines* (London: Black Swan, 1988), p. 19.
3. Nivedita Bagchi, "The Process of Validation in Relation to Materiality and Historical Reconstruction in Amitav Ghosh's *The Shadow Lines*," *Modern Fiction Studies*, 39 (Winter 1993), pp. 187-201.
4. Bruce King, "*In an Antique Land*," *World Literature Today*, 68:1-2, 1994, p. 430.
5. Suvir Kaul, "Separation Anxiety: Growing Up Inter/National in Amitav Ghosh's *The Shadow Lines*," *The Oxford Literary Review*, 16 (1994), pp. 125-45.
6. Jean Sudrann, "Goings and Comings," *Yale Review*, 79 (1990), pp. 414-38.
7. G.R. Taneja, "*The Shadow Lines*," pp. 302-4 of this book.

The Quest for Meaning: A Study of *The Shadow Lines*

S.P. SWAIN

Basically a memory novel, Amitav Ghosh's *The Shadow Lines*[1] presents a dexterous blending of private lives and public events into a desultory mosaic of history. The narrator's story unfurls itself through fragmentary streams of consciousness where the private turmoil of the individual is reflected in the public chaos and crises. It is through the stories narrated by Tridib that the narrator, a young boy, validates his experiences: "Tridib had given me worlds to travel in and he had given me eyes to see them with." (20)

The question that Amitav Ghosh raises or seems to ask his readers is that whether or not one can draw a demarcating line between imagination and reality and the implied response that he offers is "No." There indeed cannot be a dividing line between imagination and reality. Ghosh seems to suggest that there can only be a "shadow line" between imagination and reality, since reality is too vast and complex a concept to be circumscribed within historical chronology or geographical contours. A place is more than its geographical and historical features. It carries a deep imaginative meaning. The narrator disapproves of Ila's down-to-earth perception of reality. He says: "I could not persuade her that a place does not merely exist, that it has to be invented in one's imagination; that her practical bustling London was no less invented than mine, neither more nor less true, only very far apart." (21)

The interpretation of reality in mundane terms, as does Ila, is a falsification of it, since such a perception of reality is shorn of its true meaning. It lacks imaginative perception of feeling. It is gross. But Ila is obsessed with such feelings and hence the narrator's failure to persuade and convince her to a meaningful imaginative interpretation of reality. Amitav Ghosh seems to say that it is imagination alone which can portray a lucid and an enduring picture of reality. Hence he gives more emphasis to the creative role of imagination in delineating the uncoiling of memories through the stream-of-consciousness of Tridib and other characters in the novel like the grandmother. Exploration of meaning occurs at two planes—the private and the public. In the first section of the novel—"Going Away," the novelist focusses on London on the eve of, and during the war. London is vividly portrayed through the narrator's deft dispensation of his historical imagination. The significance of war is explored both at the personal and the human level. At the personal level there is a feeling of pity and sympathy, of fellow-feeling brought about by the shadow of an impending death and at the national (public) level, there is a feeling of masked and counterfeit exhilaration across national borders, and both in England and in Germany. Sharmila Guha Majumdar opines that this sense of exhilaration is "the defence mechanism that people developed to combat the sense of doom."[2] The personally experienced reality of Tridib colours the imagination of the story-teller. It is through Tridib and the grandmother that the narrator views reality and lends meaning to his meaningless infantile fancy. The title "The Shadow Lines" becomes an ambivalent symbol. It suggests the dichotomy of one's mind, the shadow lines that pervade the minds of the people. Grandmother's son says: "This is the modern world. The border isn't on the frontier; it's right inside the airport. You'll see. You'll cross it when you have to fill in all those disembarkation cards and things." (151-52)

In the absence of any clear-cut division, the meaning of nationalism as described in the novel becomes quite blurred and vague. The narrator, unable to vividly comprehend "these physical equivalents of the division,"[3] says: "They had drawn their borders, believing in that pattern, in the enchantment of lines, hoping perhaps that once they had etched their borders upon the map, the two bits of land would sail away from each other like the shifting tectonic plates of the pre-historic Gondwanaland." (233) Amitav Ghosh aims to drive home the meaning of nationalism, in the minds of the readers, through the characters in the novel. The narrator's grandmother thinks nationalism a holy and sacred word which has become the focus of political thinking in the nineteenth and twentieth century. It suggests everything that is anti-British. Sharmila Guha Majumdar observes: "In her desire to win political freedom she dreamt of killing English officials. She even considered war as a necessary evil which inspired the idea of nationalism and thus strengthened the foundation of a nation." (146)

Nationalism in the late twentieth century degenerated into political animosity between the Indians and the Englishmen. Such was the narrowmindedness of the grandmother that she viewed nationalism as a belligerent and recalcitrant attitude held by the Indians towards the Englishmen. She failed to have a proper grasp of nationalism in her mind. Not only the grandmother but also Irishmen like Mike thought that "for a person to be righfully Indian, it was necessary to kill Englishmen." Such is the individual enmity between the Indian and the Englishman, that they fail to form a meaningful interpretation of nationalism. In the section "Coming Home" Ghosh explores the meaning of political freedom. Indian nationalism, a manifestation of political freedom fails to guarantee the territorial integrity of the coutry. The historic event of Partition gave a jolt to the Indians' sense of nationalism. Majumdar holds that "Nationalism in the Indian context changed its meaning to exclude people on the other side of the border but could not include everybody on this side of paradise." (146) But I feel that the characters fail to form a cogent picture of nationalism because of the lack of an inner harmony, or rather the lack of a mutual sense of love and regard for each other. After all what is nationalism and political freedom without the element of love and regard for oneself as well as others? But the grandmother, with her perspicacity and clarity of vision gives her own views of nationalism. She thinks that the sentiments of nationalism can only develop through war and bloodshed. Her feelings of nationalism are related to the ideals of self-esteem and national power. The grandmother tells the narrator: "It took those people a long time to build that country . . . years and years of war and bloodshed. Everyone who lives there has earned his right to be there with blood. . . . War is their religion. That's what it takes to make a country." (77-78)

In a bid for political freedom, people have frenziedly and madly given themselves to terrorism and communal violence. "Even characters like the grandmother and Ila who do not indulge in violence are on the fringe of it."[4] Her willingness to run errands for the Bengal terrorists and kill the English magistrate at Khulna during her youth bears testimony to her love of violence and war. If in the grandmother the quest for political freedom manifests in her belligerent and violent motives, in Ila it manifests in her personal freedom, her breaking away from her family for a cosmopolitan way of life in London. It is this quest for freedom—personal and political—that imparts a realistic touch to the novel. With a dialogic narrative approach Ghosh reveals the motive behind everyone indulging in violence and mutual hatred. Robi, the IAS officer, philosophises to Ila and the narrator: "You know, if you look at the pictures on the front pages of the newspapers at home now, all those pictures of dead people—in Assam, the North-East, Punjab, Sri Lanka, Tripura—people shot by terrorists and separatists and the army and police, you'll find somewhere behind it all, that single word: everyone doing it to be free." (246)

Amitav Ghosh does not elaborate the meaning of concepts and ideologies. On the other hand, he insinuates the readers into the world of history through the mind of characters, their painful and nostalgic recallings and recollections and it is these psychic intrusions that destroy the narrative sequence of the story. The novel, therefore becomes a series of random reflections, for it reflects "reality itself in the process of its unfolding . . . tendencies of a new world still in the making."[5] Personal histories, family histories and the history of the nation are weaved into a thin and transparent gossamer of imagination. They are restructured in a quest for meaning, a quest for knowledge since what the characters reminisce has the touch of inaccuracy. Hence Tridib is not sure as to the accuracy of his memory: "he didn't know whether it had really happened or he had imagined it" (29) to make it sensible and meaningful. It is through imagination that the "I" narrator experiences much of his life in the process of knowing through a search for meaning:

> I shook my head violently. . . . You're lying. I shouted at her. That can't be a staircase because it's flat, and staircases go up, they aren't flat. And that can't be upstairs because upstairs has to be above and that isn't above; that's right beside the drawing room. I dropped to my knees and began to scrabble around in the dust, rubbing out the lines, shouting: You're lying, you're mad, this can't be a house. (70)

This is nothing but the travesty of a quest by the half-knowing young narrator who makes a fancifully naive approach to validate materiality. But the narrator, despite his imaginative skill fails to comprehend the real when his childhood hero, Tridib, falls a prey to the "seamless silence," (270) that meaningless violence in Dhaka. It was May Price who finally recounted the incident that gobbled Tridib. K. Damodar Rao observes: "The silence that preceded and followed the revelation was a moving statement on the actualisation of internal violence. The search and the revelation together cause a harrowing experience for the narrator." (65) In fact, the search for meaning amidst communal frenzy and political chaos is motivated by the awareness of a need, that is the need to know the cause and nature of silence that permeates the life of the inquisitive young narrator:

> Every word I write about those events of 1964 is the product of a struggle with silence. It is a struggle I am destined to lose—have already lost—for even after all these years I do not know where within me, in which

> corner of my world, this silence lies. . . . It is simply a gap, a hole, an emptiness in which there are no words. (218)

The silent quest of the narrator for meaning in life, for filling up the inner void in him with words forms the focus of the novel and it is this search for words, the need to articulate silence that "throws the notions of secularism, nationalism and freedom into disarray."[6] But could the narrator fill the gap, the silence in him with words and voice? All voices seem to be stifled in that traumatic psychic state where uncertainty and horrific apprehensions make our otherwise peaceful existence on this earth meaningless. Look at Ghosh's graphic account of the communal situation in the subcontinent where all forms of quest for meaning are rendered futile: "It is like the fear of the victims of an earthquake, of people who have lost faith in the stillness of the earth. . . . It is a fear that comes of the knowledge that normalcy is utterly contingent, that the spaces that surround one, the streets that one inhabits, can become, suddenly and without warning, as hostile as a desert in a flash flood." (204)

Such a psychological situation alienates man from man and even sets apart the subcontinent from the rest of the world. It is this that has "the special quality of loneliness that grows out of the fear of the war between oneself and one's image in the mirror." (204) Such meaningless absurdity of our shaky existence where, in the words of Matthew Arnold, "ignorant armies clash by night," where incertitude rules our life, man's quest for meaning and value turn into a cry in wilderness.

The novel urges the reader's involvement in actively constructing for himself an interpretive framework that runs parallel to the characters' traumatic and anguished recounting of the past. Especially the grand-mother's remembrances of her painful and haunting past have been vividly and dramatically presented. They give validity to her existence, meaning to her chaotic and tense life. The grandmother, the narrator, Tridib, Ila and many other non-Indian characters present a multiplicity of voices characterised by variegated discourse and language to recount their experiences. This is nothing but a striving after meaning and reason for the stifled thoughts of the past tormenting their psyche. Replete with interpretive potential, an appealing aspect of the novel is its multivocal dimension, and a structure fragmented and episodic, successfully leading to a conclusion that the historical events of the past, political rivalry, religious and communal strife and even personal trauma and nostalgia are beyond objectification. Through multivocal narrative, Ghosh lends meanings to social and political chaos reflected in the individual's search of a meaningful existence personified in memory as a relived experience.

The meaning of political freedom in the modern world is for Ghosh a complicated and an intricate one. It is without a clear solution. In a land where culture and communities thrive on mutual hatred and antagonism, the quest for meaning is liable to end in failure. The 'journey motif' which runs through the fabric of the story like the grandmother's journey to Dhaka in the second part of the novel and the narrator's journey backwards in time is symbolic of the quest for meaning in life. It is the quest for wholeness, an attempt to impose a pattern on our otherwise chaotic experience. It is a shadow line. The novel which depicts violence and crude barbarity through the recounting of riot memories seems to convey the message that man's running after self-esteem, his search for an authentic selfhood through freedom to act the way he likes, is a mirage. It would only come to a point of no return. Hence the futility of the quest for the validation of one's existence. Hence it is difficult to say why Tridib gave up his life, why he threw himself to his own death. Louis James maintains that he was "drawn by the 'shadow-line' of imaginative sympathy."[7] But the question that crops up in our mind is why he did it. It is a mystery. Ghosh does not give any clear answer to this and so Tridib's death, though a real sacrifice, becomes a mystery, an absurdity for the common man who fails to find any meaning in it. The quest for meaning thus continues without finality.

NOTES

1. (New Delhi: Ravi Dayal Publisher, 1988).
2. "Amitav Ghosh's *The Shadow Lines* and *In an Antique Land*: Some Thematic Considerations," pp. 120-31 in this book.
3. K. Damodar Rao, "Silence as Possible Mode of Response in Amitav Ghosh's *The Shadow Lines*," pp. 265-73 in this book.
4. Novy Kapadia, "Imagination and Politics in Amitav Ghosh's *The Shadow Lines*," in Viney Kirpal, ed., *The New Indian Novel in English* (New Delhi: Allied, 1990), p. 205.
5. Mikhail Bakhtin, "Epic and Novel," *The Dialogic Imagination*, ed. Michael Holquist, trans. Caryl Emerson and Michael Holquist (Austin: Univ. of Texas Press, 1981), p. 7.
6. Rao, p. 65.
7. "Shadow Lines: Cross-Cultural Perspectives in the Fiction of Amitav Ghosh," pp. 112-19 in this book.

Silence as Possible Mode of Response in *The Shadow Lines*

K. DAMODAR RAO

Amitav Ghosh's second novel, *The Shadow Lines*,[1] creates a rich tapestry of eloquence and silence. It offers a vintage formula of sketches, memories, and glimpses in an intricate pattern of past and present gushing through the prismatic view of the personal and the historical. With its axis on the Indian subcontinent's specified context, the novel's breath-taking compass coils together geographical distances and deliberately attempts to break many myths while taking the country's history, culture and political situation in its stride. Amitav Ghosh's first novel, *The Circle of Reason,* is about eloquence, search for metaphor, and the narrative capabilities of the narrator and his characters. The story-teller-audience interaction is marked by understanding, expectancy and involvement. While the zest for narration is evident in *The Shadow Lines,* it allows just enough space, and in it lies its eloquence, to see the limitations of the normally accepted notions of love, history, violence, freedom, communication and justice. The text, as such, is important for things eloquent as much for things left unsaid. The metaphors, in themselves all-pervading and eloquent, with all their contours of language and creation, are oriented towards capturing the possibilities and nuances of silence. Since the text is studded with myriad possibilities and multiple points of view, an attempt is made in this paper to view silence as employed in the text by means of subversion as a possible mode of response.

The novel puts to test some of the personal experiences, relations, memories and historical processes in which the realization of the futility of metaphor on the one hand and an awareness of the 'illusion of knowledge created by deceptive weight of remembered detail' (67) are evidenced at many levels. This process of testing is achieved by constant juxtaposition of silence with powers of communication, and of experiential realities with those notions supposed to have been theorized, defined and categorized. The pathetic situation of finding oneself beyond or below the categorized parameters throws into relief some seemingly undefined, vague and unreal conditions. This incongruous element is approached by the novelist from different angles by applying different frames of reference covering different areas of human experience. If irony is one mode of reference, silence is the other mode of reference as well as response, a strategy to probe deep into the validity or otherwise of words and notions. The questions dealt with are both experience and eloquence.

The division of the novel into two parts—'Going Away' and 'Coming Home'—is in itself a conscious attempt on the part of the novelist to dismantle some of the time-tested notions of experience and eloquence. These words, all by themselves, cannot encompass the subtleties of coming and going which overlap any number of times. In an on-going process of continuity, strict compartmentalization of the notions of coming and going might become arbitrary as the text testifies to the intricacies of these in both the parts. And when national boundaries are constantly drawn and re-drawn, the meaning could take an ambiguous turn while the processes of coming and going get marginalized.

The grandmother of the narrator, born and brought up in Dhaka and now living in Calcutta, recalls her childhood days and mentions to her son that in those days before partition there were no forms to be filled up and says: "I could come home to Dhaka whenever I wanted." (152) At this the narrator who was a child then jumps up at the ungrammatical expression of his grandmother-headmistress and wonders why she could not make out the difference between coming and going: "Tha'mma, Tha'mma! I cried. How could you have 'come' home to Dhaka? You don't know the difference between coming and going!" (152) The question involved here is twofold: one of capturing in words the actual processes of coming and going and the other relates to national boundaries, notions of patriotism and the like. Words and meanings have got to be defined and re-defined in accordance with the changing physical boundaries and political affiliations. Even for the grandmother, a mental division must entail a physical division. Now it is her turn to pose a question, not a childish one by any means. She thinks that there were 'trenches perhaps, or soldiers, or guns pointing at each other, or even just barren strips of land' that would give an indication of the thing happened, the division of physical borders as it happened in the minds of the people of the subcontinent. But, to her dismay, much like her grandson's, she learns that the mental equivalent of the division was not physically visible on the frontiers, and the natural question would be: 'What was it all then—partition and all the killing and everything—if there isn't something in between.' (151) Her son's remark brings to the fore the dichotomy, the shadow lines, that existed in the minds of the people: "This is the modern world. The border isn't on the frontier; it's right inside the airport. You'll see. You'll cross it when you have to fill in all those disembarkation cards and things." (151-52) The myth of nationalism gets broken in the absence of these physical equivalents of the division. The narrator himself is worried about the problem when he grows up and broods on this: "They had drawn their borders, believing in that pattern, in the enchantment of lines, hoping perhaps that once they had etched their borders upon the map, the two bits of land would sail away from each other like the shifting tectonic plates of the prehistoric Gondwanaland." (233)

The conspicuousness of words and logic is presented, in the first instance, in the case of the narrator's love for Ila. He thinks aloud on the futility of metaphors in this context of a love, unreciprocated:

> Perhaps those miles and yards are my own living metaphors, my attempt to claim a share of justice. For I had already thrown everything else I had on the scales; not

> insubstantial things after all, for I was a human being too, with my own worth and weight, not ugly, not without substance, educated, and with other qualities too, like patience and good humour—what more could a human being have, in fairness—I had thrown in all of that, everything I had, and by not so much as a tremor had the scales acknowledged their weight. (96)

One may, in fact, go on heaping the metaphors and still not find the state itself and there is also the danger of finding its opposite. Hence, the virtue of the other extreme, silence. For Ila, the current, cut off from the past and future, alone was the real. It was as though she was completely overwhelmed by the present which was like "an airlock in a canal, shut away from the tidewaters of the past and the future by steel floodgates." (30) The narrator has not travelled extensively around the world as Ila did since her childhood. Yet he could invent these places in his imagination on the basis of the described places and narrated events first by Tridib, by Ila's parents and then by Ila herself. But when he goes to London years later—to collect data from the India Office Library on the textile trade between India and England in the 19th century—and mentions 'Cairo' to Ila, what all she could remember was 'Ladies' in the airport which she says was on the other side of the departure lounge. Probably, the 'tired intimacy' (20) made her forget the aspects which precisely held a magic aura for the narrator. As Tridib would say of her, "the inventions she lived in moved with her, so that although she had lived in many places, she had never travelled at all." (21)

The worlds they had essentially belonged to were understood by Ila in the first place. The narrator could not help loving her and it was in the very personality of Ila not to spare a loving space for the likes of him. Even as the narrator feels that his invented England was no less real and concrete than the actual base of Ila and leads her and Nick Price, based on memory of description, to the old building in which Nick Price's maternal grandfather, Mike Tresawsen, and others of a socialist outfit carried on their activities on the mid-thirties, Ila's slight comes as a shocker:

> You wouldn't understand the exhilaration of events like that—nothing really important ever happens where you are . . . well of course there are famines and riots and disasters. . . . But those are local things after all—not like revolutions or anti-fascist wars, nothing that sets a political example to the world, nothing that's really remembered. (104)

The thoughts that cross the mind of the narrator at this would provide a fitting commentary on the 'mystery of difference' (32) between the two, on the futility of metaphors and of a life that fits in with such an ability of communication only: "She seemed immeasurably distant then, in her serene confidence in the centrality and eloquence of her experience, in her quiet pity for the pettiness of lives like mine, lived out in the silence of voiceless events in a backward world." (104)

Ila's love for Nick Price, by the same token, defies logic. Even as a child she hides the essentially mean and the timid in Nick Price whom she was to marry later on, and presents a cosy picture of an incident supposed to have taken place at school in London in which Nick Price does the rescuing act while in reality he runs away from the scene of action for fear of being seen with a non-native. She persists with her illusion and does not hesitate to marry him in later years despite his proven qualities of inconsistency and waywardness. The narrator whose love was unreciprocated ('You were always the brother I never had'—Ila) soon establishes his superiority but the agony, the silence, that made him do away with metaphors remains much the same.

The shadow lines, queer turns, absence of logic, sheer absurdity, and defiance of well-defined systems of thought and ordering might often prove to be the hallmarks of the notions of governance, excellence, freedom and justice as in the case of a purely personal experience of love. Tridib was the narrator's childhood hero. Apart from the fact of Tridib being at the centre of things, the narrator also accepted his influence as part of his own being. Tribid, he feels, has given him "worlds to travel in and . . . eyes to see them with." (20) One thing of substance he had learnt from Tridib was to use his imagination with precision. He knew that what Tridib could see in his imagination "was infinitely more detailed and more precise" (29) than he could ever possibly hope for. All the same he could not forget his advice that if he didn't try it himself he would never be free of other people's imagination and invention.

Despite the art of imagination the narrator has assiduously cultivated, he fails to grasp the actual when his childhood hero and mentor becomes a victim of meaningless violence in Dhaka. It was only much later that he finds himself, despite the promise he had made to his father that he would not be interested in knowing the cause of Tridib's death, on the look out for the bits and pieces that would connect him to the cause of Tridib's death. It was May Price who at the end actually recounts the incident of communal frenzy that engulfed Tridib. The silence that preceded and followed the revelation was a moving statement on the actualization of internal violence. The search and the revelation together cause a harrowing experience for the narrator. The stoic understatement of the entire narration is informed by this awareness, an awareness of the need and result of silence: "Every word I write about those events of 1964 is the product of a struggle with silence. It is a struggle I am destined to lose—have already lost—for even after all these years. I do not know where within me, in which corner of my world, this silence lies . . . it is simply a gap, a hole, an emptiness in which there are no words". (218)

The silent search of the narrator which forms the core of the novel throws the notions of secularism, nationalism and freedom into disarray. In effect, it implies a search, a probe that has been orientated towards the prime cause for the creation of illusions, thc shadow lines. Political domain which has thrown many such illusions is sharply contrasted with a sensitive individual's attitude that rises above narrow considerations and shallow confines of the political exigencies. Hence, the basic problem one is confronted with in this sphere is not merely that of eloquence, but that of communication which comes to the fore any number of times. So complete is this silence—"of an absolute, impenetrable banality" (218)—in the life and mission of the narrator that it took nearly fifteen years to discover that there was a connection between the theft of the Prophet's hair from the Hazratbal shrine in 1964, the nightmarish bus ride back from his school and the events that befell Tridib and others in Dhaka.

The communal riots follow their own 'grotesque logic' (229) fed by rumours, devoid of the basic human streak, as evidenced in the life of the subcontinent at frequent intervals since independence. The carnage let loose on such occasions is beyond description. The loss of life, the manner in which people get killed and the animal instincts that come to the fore in an atmosphere of frenzy and violence convert human life into a huge pretension or an accidental freak. Before the riots erupt there would not be 'any hint or augury' that would suggest the impending carnage. The situation would be 'replete with the fullness of normalcy.' (227)

And then all the mayhem would follow as if by design, in a pattern. Unable to measure the 'stirrings of silence' Tridib had fallen a prey to that 'seamless silence.' (227) The grandmother of the narrator and May were witnesses to the ghastly scene of Tridib's murder at the hands of a fanatical mob. What could be reactions of the intimate ones of the victims or the actual witnesses to such gory deaths? The grandmother of the narrator attempts to wreak psychological revenge at the time of the war with Pakistan in 1971 by offering blood in a frantic hurry, as if in a fit of madness. As for May, she thinks that she was, to some extent, responsible for the thing happened, as it was she who wanted to rescue the old man and Khalil, the rickshaw puller, who were following their car. She applied the same previous logic of stopping the car and requesting Tridib to relieve the dog, that fell under their car, of its pain. But to her dismay, as she herself revealed it to the narrator in the last pages of the novel in a vivid manner as if she could not forget the tragic event, as if she has been living with the painful experience ever since, she becomes a witness to the murder of three persons: "When I got there, I saw three bodies. They were all dead. They'd cut Khalil's stomach open. The old man's head had been hacked off. And they'd cut Tridib's throat, from ear to ear." (251) She feels she could have gone right into that mob—'they wouldn't have touched me, an English memsahib'—and saved them all. But an understanding of the strange dynamics of the communal tension peculiar to the subcontinent makes her conclude that Tridib had given himself up. She considers it 'a sacrifice.' (252)

The day Tridib and others were murdered in Khulna on the outskirts of Dhaka, the narrator himself, as a school-going boy, was undergoing a traumatic experience as the riots erupted in Calcutta also. The narrator could remember it vividly, more so because only the previous day the cricket match with England had started in Madras and the wicket-keeper-batsman, Budhi Kunderan, scored a century on debut. The school was closed abruptly and he could remember, on their way back home in the school-bus, how 'the streets had turned themselves inside out,' and how 'the city had turned' against them all, children. Tublu, one of his school-mates, wept all the way—'for all of us' (204)—and all the others gathered around him. At any other time they would have laughed, but that day they remained silent. The 'texture' of the fear, although indescribable, could still make a lasting and powerful impact on the mind of the narrator, and in later years he tries to reconstruct his mental state which must be regarded as, perhaps, the most eloquent statement on the communal situation in the subcontinent:

> It is like the fear of the victims of an earthquake, of people who have lost faith in the stillness of the earth. And yet it is not the same. It is without analogy, for it is not comparable to the fear of nature, which is the most universal of human fears, nor to the fear of the violence of the state, which is the commonest of modern fears. It is a fear that comes of the knowledge that normalcy is utterly contingent, that the spaces that surround

> one, the streets that one inhabits, can become, suddenly and without warning, as hostile as a desert in a flash flood. (204)

This psychological state is peculiar to our cultural and political context. This is a peculiarity that sets us apart from the rest of the world: "It is this that sets apart the thousand million people who inhabit the subcontinent from the rest of the world—not language, not food, not music—it is the special quality of loneliness that grows out of the fear of the war between oneself and one's image in the mirror." (204)

What could be the attitudes of the governments involved in this peculiar geographical and political context? In fact, the theatre of war, 'where generals meet, is the stage on which states disport themselves,' where violence is considered justified by the state. They have no use for 'memories of riots' (230) that bring feelings of oneness among sections of society independent of the state intervention that might be detrimental to the interests and welfare of the state mechanism. Hence, the governments follow a fairly predictable line. Initially they start with 'rhetorical exchanges' such as symmetrical accusations for remaining passive in the face of a 'frenzy of looting, killing and burning.' And when the riots get subsided on their own, congratulatory notes are exchanged 'over their respective successes in quelling disturbances.' The measure of governments's success or failure depends on the number of deaths occurred. When only a few people get killed, governments have no use for them. The irony that killed Tridib and others was conveniently forgotten and the murderous frenzy itself disappeared from the collective imagination "into the crater of a volcano of silence." (233) Conversely, the impact on the consciousness of the concerned individual could be a shattering one. The best course would be to take recourse to silence, as the novel eloquently does.

NOTE

1. Amitav Ghosh, *The Shadow Lines* (New Delhi: Ravi Dayal Publisher, 1988).

Historicizing Memory in *The Shadow Lines*

PALLAVI GUPTA

Let sea-discoverers to new worlds have gone,
Let maps to others, worlds on worlds have shown,
Let us possess one world, each has one, and is one.

John Donne, "The Good-Morrow"

"I could not persuade her that a place does not merely exist, it has to be invented in one's imagination; that her practical, bustling London was no less invented than mine, neither more nor less true, only very far apart."[1] It would appear from the above statement that although places "exist" for some people and are "imagined" by others, both are inventions, and this act of inventing entails not only the creation of worlds but also the history of those worlds. These histories may or may not square with those available in records and books but this does in no way challenge the veracity/authenticity of these histories. And intimately connected with the attempts at history-writing is the exercise of the memory: in a way each mnemonic effort is an attempt at historicization and each recollecting individual is an amateur historian. As the narrator in *The Shadow Lines* states, "people like my grandmother who have no home but in memory, learn to be very skilled in the art of recollection," (194) as is Tridib, as is Ila. Hayden White opines that "it is possible to tell several different stories about the past and there is no way, finally, to check them against the fact of the matter."[2] This idea is further strengthened by the American historian Carl Becker, who in his preface to *The Eve of the Revolution* confessed to having frequently resorted to the literary device of telling a story. For him, "the point of greatest relevance [is] the truth and effectiveness of the illusion aimed at—the extent to which it enables the reader to enter into such states of mind and feeling. The truth of such history [or whatever the critic wishes to call it] cannot of course be determined by a mere verification of references."[3] Fred Weinstein observes a shift in the novelistic concerns vis-à-vis history and claims: "Unlike earlier generations of novelists who did not like history or historians, for whom history was a nightmare from which they were trying to awake and who would have escaped from history into a world of art, not only are there novelists currently who have come to appreciate the uses of history, but a number of them want to claim history for their own." (11) The list is endless starting from Chinua Achebe and Ngugi wa Thiong'o and ending with Carlos Fuentes, Allan Sealy, Maxine Hong Kingston et al.

Moreover, characters in *The Shadow Lines* appear to have an intimate relation with history: Tridib pursues a Ph.D. in Archaeology, Tha'mma has lived through the Partition, and the narrator's visit to London is prompted by the need to "collect material from the India Office Library, where all the old colonial records were kept, for a Ph.D. thesis on the textile trade between India and England in the nineteenth century." (13) The opening of the novel itself smacks of historiographisation, as does the background of wars against which the narrator plots his own history and that of others. One might question the use of the term "history" for a rendition which might well be called an autobiography or a biography. However one might argue that "there are records of events, well preserved in public and private archives; but how these events affected ordinary people and ordinary families may never be known without the autobiographies of ordinary people."[4] Moreover, autobiographical/novelistic discussions are intended to bring readers closer to the real world of people, to the turmoil, divisions, and conflicts that they experience in their everyday lives. This point is well illustrated in *The Shadow Lines* with regard to the riots of 1964 and the political condition in India at that time. Referring to the newspaper in the archives, the narrator tells us the complete facts regarding the sacred relic, the rumours of poisoned water, and the reactions of the governments of India and East Pakistan. These are the ostensible fragments from which mainstream history is constructed. What he does tell us later is his own bewildered experience as a child during the riots, his estrangement from his best friend Montu, who is a Muslim, and the death of Tridib which form the "real world" of ordinary people who live history. Though not available in records of history, these events are not falsifications. Moreover, the history which we are referring to is the history of imagination which, although "it occurs at a certain time, and in a certain context of other acts of thought, emotion, sensations and so forth," it has the characteristic of being able to "sustain itself through a change of context and revive in a different one."[5] As is evident from the novel where the thoughts—regarding the past—are Tridib's while the narrator goes on a mnemonic journey visiting the places and the people that figured in Tridib's past.

In this regard, the narrator becomes the historian while Tridib appears as his authority; in other words—as the "common-sense theory" in history goes—"the believer is the historian and the person believed is called the authority."[6] However, it is true enough that the individual's thought process cannot be replicated by the historian; nevertheless, what matters is "the act of thought itself, in its survival and revival at different times and in different persons: once in the historian's own life, once in the life of the person whose history he is narrating,"[7] e.g., Tridib's comments on Ila's imperviousness to places which matches the narrator's own feelings, (20-21) May's comment on Nick—"he's not at all like us" (53)—and the narrator's eventual realization of the truth of the statement, Tha'mma's comment regarding the narrator's obsession with Ila and the narrator's eventual discovery of it. (89-90) Collingwood also stresses the pre-requisite for the writing of history, which is that "the object [of the historian] must be of such a kind that it can revive itself in the historian's mind; the historian's mind must be such as to offer a home for that revival."

(298) The proximity which the narrator shares with Tridib—evident in his merging of personality with Tridib's—makes him, undoubtedly, the best person to play historian to a past which exists only in memory and has no visible traces left in the present to go by. The only resources, the "relics of the past," which the narrator-historian possesses to graft his history are memories, photographs, and Tridib's stories which are difficult to dismiss because they are factually correct yet set in a medium of fiction. A point driven in through a book advertisement in the November 1984 edition of the *New York Times Book Review*: "Non-fiction gives you the facts. Fiction gives you the truth."

This is to say that if Tridib is the novelist and the narrator the historian, it posits the question whether the narrator-historian's history is more credible than Tridib's history. In Collingwood's appraisal, "As works of imagination, the historian's work and the novelists do not differ. Where they do differ is that the historian's picture is meant to be true. The novelist has a single task, i.e., to construct a coherent picture, one that makes sense. The historian has to do both." (306) The tentativeness of Collingwood's statement with regard to historical truth—"meant to be true"—is confirmed by White who argues that "literary artists give us truer, because they are more honest, representations of the human experience of historical events than do historians themselves." In White's opinion, historical truth, which is capable of being described, should be the responsibility of the novelists because of their superior intuitive access to the intentions and motives of people.[8] This brings us to the question of objectivity in historical narration and as the narrator repeatedly reveals, his narrative is unwittingly/unconsciously coloured by the manner in which he relates to his object. However, the question to ask here would be whether a historical study must fulfil the condition of objectivity to be considered 'history.' Christopher Blake in his article "Can History be Objective?" argues that asking this question is like asking, "Can novels be well written?" (334) And James B. Conant wisely adds, "history is not a deductive science and there are no rules for detecting fact."[9] So while the narrator can go over his archives to locate the "bombed-out Solent Road," (57) he does not expect to find it as Tridib had seen it. Although he cannot recreate the event—factually—in the present, he has already seen it in the imagination bestowed on him by Tridib, which is truer, for him, than facts are or the testimonials of Ila, Nick and Robi. Memory thus appears to function as a more reliable source for history than the present. It is to be noted, however, that the whole-hearted trust, which the narrator places in Tridib's narrative, is not shared by any other character. They seem to register only the fictive aspect of his stories and consequently dismiss the facts, which are connected with them. This is why the "story" regarding Tridib's life—"don't you know he's married and has three children and lives with his widowed mother in a slum near Santoshpur," (10)—seems more credible to people than his "history" of belonging to a family which "was rich and powerful, his father was a diplomat, the son of a wealthy judge, and his brother was a brilliant economist who had a job with the U.N. and lived abroad." (10) Moreover, novelists reconstruct events, often as accurately and carefully as any historian, "putting real people in imaginary situations, and imaginary situations in documentary narratives, augmenting the significance of historical events by plausible, internally consistent, but more obviously unverifiable depictions of the subjective intentions of people."[10]

Another way of looking at the relationship of Tridib-novelist and the narrator-historian is by positing that Tridib weaves a fictional thread into facts available to him e.g., his concocted story of having gone to London to visit the Prices. It is in this "document" that the narrator-historian has to separate the facts from the fiction. It is interesting to see how Amitav Ghosh never lets us rest in the certainty of knowing the facts from the fiction; having stressed the validity of the mnemonic activity, Tridib's visit to London and May's physical description are presented as facts which have been arbitrarily unified in the novelist's imagination, which renders them valid and credible. We know from the narrator-historian's record that Tridib had gone to London as a child, and as May tells him later, she had sent a photograph to Tridib, and the narrator conjectures, "I like to think that Tridib received May's photograph the day he came to Gole Park and told us that made-up story." (17)

What is perplexing, however, is the narrator-historian's stance vis-à-vis his authority-object, i.e., Tridib. While on the one hand he unquestioningly trusts Tridib's memory—"because Tridib told me" (56)—there are instances—as illustrated above—when he can be sceptical about him. And so can we, as readers, as the smooth structure of his mnemonic recollections often shows fissures, as in the beginning of the novel when Tridib remarks, "If you believe anything people tell you, you deserve to be told anything at all." (12) On the one hand, Ghosh implies the unreliability of Tridib's narrative while at the same time proving the authenticity of the facts, on the other hand, he also makes us aware of the narrator's reliability. Though his matter is furnished by Tridib, his narration is more credible, because it is "necessitated by the evidence, it is a legitimate historical construction of a kind without which there can be no history at all."[11] For example, a couple of days after the narrator arrives in London; he comes across a sign with the name "Victor Gollancz" painted on it. This obscure sign contains the history of Alan Tresawsen—which had been told to him by Tridib. The narrator recounts, "I tried to recall for her [Ila] how Tridib had told us that Alan Tresawsen, Mrs. Price's brother, had worked there before the war, in the Left Book Club [which] had been a part of Victor Gollancz's publishing house." (31) To Ila it appears "like any musty office now," whereas for the narrator the memory in the past juxtaposes itself on the present and makes the past "concurrent with the present." (31) This however, is not the case with Solent Road although the event is kept alive in the narrator's mind as it was in Tridib's. The historical past is seen in Collingwood's *The Idea of History* as "a living past, kept alive by the act of historical thinking itself," (226) and hence Tridib's time never "stinks" because it is never wasted, it never dies but is kept alive in the narrator's thought process.

There are, however, other characters in the novel whose historical memory functions as the obverse of recorded factual history as codified in history books. Tha'mma, who is technically a refugee from Bangladesh—though she vehemently denies it—is a living testimonial of the Partition in 1947. The narrator himself is an eyewitness of the riots in Calcutta in 1964, though when he tries to prove it to his colleagues using the traditional medium of recording history—the newspapers—he initially meets with disappointment. While material on the war with Pakistan floods the newspapers, there is no visible record of the narrator's mnemonic history: "I nodded silently unnerved by the possibility that I had lived for all those years with a memory of an imagined event." (222) Eventually, he does find it along with discovering that its mirror image had occurred on the other side of the border, in Khulna, East Pakistan. He also discovers that the main historical events such as the trouble in East Pakistan, and the restoration of the sacred relic in Kashmir find no mention in the local newspaper and he wryly comments, "It was after all, a Calcutta paper, run by people who believed in the power of distance no less than I did." (227)

Meenakshi Mukherji observes, in this regard, that "the public chronicles of nations are interrogated in this novel by highlighting on the one hand the reality of the fiction people create around their lives, and on the other hand by recording the verifiable graphic details of individual memories that do not necessarily tally with the received version of history."[12] And it is owing to the latter that Tridib's "unreliability" as a source of history becomes acceptable. But there are also discontinuities, fissures, gaps in the history which can only be filled up by silence because the narrator knows nothing about them. His authority—Tridib—has been selective about stories, he has maintained his interiority in secret, e.g., the narrator has no idea of Tridib's romantic entanglement with May. The unreliability attributed to Tridib appears in another form, which is, the inability of the historical discourse to speak/enunciate in totality because something will, inevitably, elude its grasp From the apparently continuous model of memory translated into history, we are thrown into an arena of silences, of discontinuities. This is highlighted in the last section of the novel where the narrator confesses his inability to describe/record the circumstances of Tridib's demise because he has not received it first-hand from Tridib: "I can only describe at second hand the manner of Tridib's death." (228)

Weinstein in his work *History and Theory after the Fall* makes a distinction between historians and novelists by pointing out that "historians and social theorists, as a means of establishing a sense of order in the world, have constantly searched for underlying unities." (95-96) However, critics and novelists point out the "heterogeneity and discontinuity" (5) which is implicit in the history that people have lived. As the narrator confesses, in the section titled "Coming Home," with regard to his task as a historian:

> Every word I write about those events of 1964 is the product of a struggle with silence. It is a struggle I am destined to lose—have already lost—forever after all these years, I do not know where within me, in which corner of my world, this silence lies. I know nothing of this silence except that it lies outside the reach of my intelligence, beyond words—that is why this silence must win, must inevitably defeat me, because it is simply a gap, a hole, an emptiness in which there are no words. (218)

This feeling of vacuum is the resultant of the lack of memory and imagination owing to the absence of Tridib. It is at this point that the implication of Tridib as the narrator's "authority"—stated earlier in the article—hits us with full force. The narrator is caught in an expanse of absolute silence because he does not have Tridib as his guide and has no clue as to what has happened to him.

It takes him fifteen years to realize that the construction of history as time-bound, separate, and nation-specific is ridden with contradictions. Through his imaginative legacy he projects an image of history which cuts across the "shadow lines";

which has to do with a sense of history as experienced, not with recorded facts or absolutist historical pronouncements:

> They had drawn their borders, believing in that pattern, in the enchantment of lines. The simple fact [was] that there had never been a moment in the four-thousand-year-old history of that map, when the places we know as Dhaka and Calcutta were more closely bound to each other after they had drawn their lines. (253)

NOTES

1. Amitav Ghosh, *The Shadow Lines* (Delhi: OUP, 1995), p. 21.
2. Qtd. Fred Weinstein, *History and Theory after the Fall: An Essay on Interpretation* (Chicago: Chicago UP, 1990), p. 1.
3. Carl Becker, *The Eve of the Revolution: A Chronicle of the Breach with England* (New Haven: Conn. 1921), pp. vii-viii.
4. R.G. Collingwood, *The Idea of History* (1946; Oxford: OUP, 1994), p. 288.
5. S.N. Mukherjee, *Citizen Historian: Explorations in Historiograhy. Sydney Studies in Society and Culture* (Delhi: Manohar, 1996), p. 139.
6. *Ibid.*, p. 282.
7. *Ibid.*, p. 298.
8. Hayden White, Rev. of *The Paradox of History* by Nicola Chiaromonte, *NYTBR*, 22 Sept. 1985, 7.
9. Qtd. Christopher Blake, "Can History be Objective," *The Philosophy of History*, ed. Patrick Gardiner (London: OUP, 1974), p. 334.
10. Weinstein, p. 12.
11. Collingwood, p. 283.
12. Meenakshi Mukherjee, "Maps and Mirrors: Coordinates of Meaning in *The Shadow Lines*," *The Shadow Lines* (Delhi: OUP, 1995), p. 255.

Imagination and Reality in *The Shadow Lines*

URBASHI BARAT

> The novel is no more the work of imagination than it is a reflection of reality: its essence, its necessary quality, lies in the expression of the connection between the real and the imaginary.[1]

Amitav Ghosh's *Shadow Lines* resists classification. It is 'basically a memory novel'[2] that weaves together past and present, childhood and adulthood, India and Bangladesh and Britain, Hindu and Muslim, story and happening, through the 'coil within coil of memories [that] unfurl within it'[3]; it establishes its socio-historical situation through its careful observation of concrete social reality and as such can be regarded both as a social document and a political novel[4]; it is also in many ways a bildungsroman, tracing the growth and development of the narrator from childhood to maturity. It is part of the Indian experiment with the non-fiction novel whose first significant landmark was Salman Rushdie's *Midnight's Children;* it is as postmodernist a work of fiction as Farrukh Dhondy's *Bombay Duck.*

Several more labels can be affixed to *The Shadow Lines*, each as valid as the others; after all, as Henry James noted in *The Art of the Novel*, 'the Novel remains still, under the right persuasion, the most independent, most elastic, most prodigious of literary forms.'[5] But one of the most rewarding ways of reading the novel is, I believe, to see it as belonging to that long tradition of fiction that includes *Don Quixote* and *Tristram Shandy* on the one hand and *Travels with My Aunt* and *Haroun and the Sea of Stories* on the other: fiction, that is, that examines its symbiotic relationship with fact and explores the role of the imagination in creating and evoking reality, which, 'in the artist's sense,' in the words of A.A. Mendilow, 'is always something created: it does not exist *a priori.*'[6]

This theme is established in *The Shadow Lines* through the use of the geographical metaphor and the journey motif implicit in its title—derived, significantly, from Conrad—and in the titles of its two parts, 'Going Away' and 'Coming Home.' This metaphor pervades the book and enables it to extend and to expand spatially and temporally (a journey, after all, takes place sequentially and in time). This is of course a traditional method for the novel that sets out to discover the relationship between imagination and reality; indeed, even Edward Said uses it when he observes of the novel, 'stories are at the heart of what explorers and novelists say about strange regions of the world.'[7] It is through its imagination, perception and rendering of human experience in everyday life, through what Proust calls the 'gross dimensions of social phenomena,' that the novel is able to 'evoke the essentially non-finite quality of existence.'[8] Ghosh's approach has in fact a close affinity with Graham Greene's in *Travels with My Aunt* and *The Captain and the Enemy*, which are likewise concerned with this relationship and which are similarly based on the metaphor of the journey.

Appropriately, *The Shadow Lines* begins with a statement about a journey, one that Mayadebi, the narrator's great-aunt, her husband and Tridib, her son, undertook in 1939, from India to England: a journey which will be undertaken again and again, and by other characters in the novel, too, both physically and in the imagination, sometimes, however, from England to India as well. Tridib's father is a diplomat, living abroad or in Delhi and only occasionally visiting Calcutta; but Tridib himself prefers to stay on in their family house in an upper-middle-class neighbourhood of Calcutta with his elderly grandmother. Why he has rejected his parents's peripatetic lifestyle is not known, but the narrator's grandmother (and Tridib's aunt) puts it down to incompatibility with his father. The fiercely bourgeois old lady disapproves not of her nephew's estrangement from his father but of what she considers his flippancy in letting so trivial a matter stand in the way of his material prospects. In her eyes Tridib is an untrustworthy and dangerous nonconformist, though outwardly he may seem the quintessential middle-class Bengali, living staidly in Calcutta and looking after his grandmother, and engaged in research for his doctoral degree. The apparently everyday quality of his life, paradoxically, only emphasizes his uniqueness, and he is a source of perennial fascination for the boy who as a young adult is the narrator of the 'story' of the novel.

Tridib, too, is a story-teller, 'happiest in neutral, impersonal places—coffee houses, bars, street-corner addas—the sort of place where people come, talk and go away without expecting to know each other any further,'[9] for it is detachment and objectivity that allow the imagination to soar. He spends much of his time in gossip with young ne'er-do-wells at street corners and tea-stalls, much to the distaste of the grandmother, who has a Gradgrind-like belief about time: 'For her time was like a toothbrush: it went mouldy if it wasn't used,' and stank. Tridib, however, 'never seemed to use his time, but his time didn't stink.' (4) For he is caught up with the non-essential, the non-material, the imaginary and the imaginative: the world of story, the world of the creative imagination. He himself, like his tales, constantly skirts the border between truth and falsehood, reality and the imagination, so that it is difficult to say whether it is fact or fiction that prevails with him. Sometimes his imagination creates a story that is truer than reality; once he speaks gravely of visiting his English relatives by marriage in London, describing them in graphic and truthful detail—the only caveat being that they are not his relatives at all, nor has he been to London to meet them. The boy blurts out what he believes is the reality, and Tridib's exciting story falls apart, so that the truth of his account of the Price family is dismissed: the irony being, of course, that they do literally become his relatives by marriage in course of time.

Tridib's niece Ila sometimes comes to Calcutta, and the boy tries to remind her of their shared experiences of her uncle's stories. She is surprised by the vividness of his memories, for she cannot understand how, sitting in a little room in Calcutta, 'Tridib had given me worlds to travel in and . . . eyes to see them with.' (20) Ila has travelled all over the world with her parents, but too great an exposure to reality has erased the magic from her eyes, so that all those places on the map which are to him 'a set of magical talismans' are for her merely familiar, commonplace, dull, significant only by virtue of the position of Ladies toilets in the airport lounges, which become for her the signs of stability, 'the only fixed points in the shifting landscapes of her childhood.' (20) She is therefore irritated by the narrator's enthusiasm for the London Underground: 'To her the Underground was merely a means of shifting venue,' and he comments: "I could not persuade her that a place does not merely exist, that it has to be invented in one's imagination; that her practical, bustling London was no less invented than mine, neither more nor less true, only very far apart. It was not her fault that she could not understand, for as Tridib often said of her, the inventions she lived in moved with her, so that although she had lived in many places, she had never travelled at all." (21)

Ila believes that her emphasis on reality has had a salutary effect on the narrator: 'at least you learnt that those cities you saw on maps were real places, not like those fairylands Tridib made up for you.' But Tridib, the archaeologist who makes the past come alive for the present, has never believed in fairytales: what he had taught the boy was 'to use my imagination with precision.' (24) For instance, when Ila's mother described an encounter with a snake in Colombo, the boy tries to earn his mentor's approval by asking what kind of snake it was. Tridib, however, is disappointed. The snake has little to do with real life, and what kind it is is merely factual information; what is interesting, rather, is to imagine life under a sloping roof, so unlike the flat ones of Calcutta. This is what reality is, something that must be seen and known through the imagination, which works out of 'real desire,' 'a longing for everything that was not in oneself, a torment of the flesh, that carried one beyond the limits of one's mind to other times and other places, and even, if one was lucky, to a place where there was no border between oneself and one's image in the mirror.' (29) The mirror-image, repeated later in the novel too, is especially significant, for it is the traditional symbol of art. Art is expected to represent or reflect reality, and the novel is a mirror walking along a highway, in Stendhal's picturesque phrase; but how far a mirror-image is 'real' and how far a distortion of 'reality' is to be questioned. As Michel Zeraffa observes, 'the "real" is what fate must reveal, sooner or later, for us to know. Fiction, on the other hand, consists in what can never be brought to our knowledge except through "splendidly wandering" thoughts and desires' (57)—through, that is, the imagination, which is thus no less 'real' than so-called 'reality.'

Indeed, even the apparently unimaginative Ila cannot do without imagination. As a child her only souvenirs of the faraway places she has lived in are the Yearbooks of her schools—'the places themselves went past her in an illusory whirl of movement' (23)—with photographs of her fellow-students, about whom she weaves many stories. So the most beautiful and talented among them are her special friends, and yet she herself is never photographed with them; and when she finds that her cousin has discovered a photograph of a boy she has claimed to be her boyfriend with his arms around other girls, while Ila herself stands a little apart from everybody else, the page with the incriminating photograph is torn from the book. The boy realizes then that the exotic and unapproachable Ila is like him after all, creating her own reality, her own space, out of her imagination.

Similarly, when Ila teaches her cousin to play Houses with her in the dark basement (note the significance of this setting) of the family house in the village, she talks about Nick Price, with whom she has evidently played this game before and whom she describes as coming to her rescue when she is attacked by a group of racist children in London. It is only later that the adult narrator learns what the reality was like: that Nick was ashamed of her and had certainly not gone to her aid at all. Ila is obviously in love with Nick, and she inveigles him into marrying her, with her father's money as bait; but she soon discovers that Nick does not care for her and is openly unfaithful. The only way in which she can cope with the situation is by pretending to herself and to her cousin that the reality is actually imaginary and that the imaginary world of well-being she creates is the reality.

Everyone in the novel, in fact, hovers over the shadow lines between imagination and reality; everyone has his or her stories and memories that are based partly on imagination, partly on reality, and when they are retold they are relived as well. They interlink and participate in each other, so that in the end the boundary between fact and fiction, imagination and reality, disappears, and everything becomes part of an imaginatively perceived experience of real life. The shadow lines between people and between the countries they inhabit and call their own, too, merge and become one. When, therefore, Ila shouts out that she has chosen to leave India and live in London because she wants to be free of her past, of her people and of the inhibitions they impose on her, the narrator shouts back at her, 'You can never be free of me. . . . If I were to die tomorrow you would not be free of me. You cannot be free of me because *I am within you* . . . [sic] just as you are within me.' (89)

Imagination is not just a part of reality, it can and does create its own reality. Rumour can start a riot; so that the story of the loss of the Prophet's hair in faraway Srinagar can kill Indian Hindus in Dhaka and make vast crowds of people believe that their water supply has been poisoned and break up a friendship in Calcutta. For it is imagination that links a people together, not the fact of geographical contiguity. The Bengali feels closer to what is happening on the Indian subcontinent than to events in Chiang Mai in Thailand or Chendu in China, which are closer to Calcutta than Delhi or Srinagar; while places in Europe as far away from each other as Khulna and Srinagar in South Asia remain uninvolved with each other, for there is no imaginative connection between them. Indeed, the physical fact of geographical boundaries between nations is of no real importance: the border drawn between the two Bengals has in fact pulled them even closer together, 'So close that I, in Calcutta, had only to look into the mirror to be in Dhaka; a moment when each city was the inverted image of the other, locked into an irreversible symmetry by the line that was to set us free—our looking-glass border.' (233)

Facts can in fact distort reality much more than imagination can. Thus the intensely felt horrors and the betrayals of the riots in Bengal following the theft of the Prophet's hair hardly find a mention in the newspapers outside Bengal, and when the narrator recalls the event his friends suggest that he might have imagined it all. He is naturally 'unnerved by the possibility that [he] had lived for all those years with a memory of an imagined event,' (222) until he remembers that the riot had coincided with a Test Match in Madras. Searching through the papers of that day he finally discovers a brief mention about them—except that the report is about Khulna, not about Calcutta or Dhaka. The riots in these two cities of Bengal have 'dropped out of memory into the crater of a volcano of silence' (230) because neither the newspaper nor the reader was at the time or later imaginatively involved with what had happened then. To bring them back to light now requires the narrator to make the 'strangest journey' of all: 'a voyage into a land outside space, an expanse without distances; a land of looking-glass events.' (224) Zeraffa's comments about what he calls the 'documentary novel'—the nonfiction novel, as it is most commonly known—are of relevance here: "This idea of reality is suited to a mass society whose eyes and ears are daily assailed with innumerable aspects of the world so that the imagination is clogged, instead of being inspired. The idea of society and social structures is beginning to disappear under an increasing flood of social facts, always being revised, which are represented as instances." (147) Reality is as subjective as the imagination; facts are not, and so cannot be as true as imaginatively comprehended experience.

Perhaps the character who most clearly illustrates this is the narrator's grandmother, posited from the beginning of the novel as Tridib's opposite. She may disapprove of Tridib's unconventionality, but Tridib can sympathize imaginatively with her, and sums her up as "a modern middle-class woman—

though not wholly, for she would not permit herself the self-deceptions that make up the fantasy world of that kind of person. All she wanted was a middle-class life in which, like the middle classes the world over, she would thrive believing in the unity of nationhood and territory, of self-respect and national power: that was all she wanted—a modern middle-class life, a small thing that history had denied her in its fullness and for which she could never forgive it." (78) For her nationality is not something nebulous and ambiguous but a reality built over 'hundreds of years, years and years of war and bloodshed. . . . They know they're nation because they've drawn their borders with blood. . . That's what it takes to make a country. Once that happens people forget they were born this or that, Muslim or Hindu, Bengali or Punjabi: they become a family born of the same pool of blood.' (77-78) As a young girl in the turbulent years of the freedom struggle she had seen for herself what shedding blood for the sake of the country had meant, and she had been inspired enough by the freedom-fighters to join the terrorist movement, even to kill, for her cause, and she retains this fierceness till the end. That is why she believes Ila is wrong to make England her country; if she does so, it is 'because she's greedy; she's gone there for money.' (79) The grandmother knows that Ila's claim to be free outside India is false; freedom cannot be bought 'for the price of an air ticket,' for it is much more than being 'left alone to do what [one] pleases.' (89) Ila's horizons are shrunken because she does not use her imagination to find out the real meaning of freedom. The narrator knows, however, that freedom lies in being bound and in living with 'the clamour of voices within [him]' that his imagination gives rise to: the freedom to imagine and to feel.

The grandmother is so angry about her grandson's defence of Ila that she believes he shares the young woman's view of freedom and that, accordingly, he must visit prostitutes in Delhi, where he is studying; she even writes to the dean of his college complaining about his character and demanding his expulsion. The narrator easily denies the charges; but the fact remains that her imagination has not run too far away from reality. (93) As she sinks into dementia following her retirement, she lives more and more in her imaginary world and rejects the 'real' one.

The grandmother's memories of the Dhaka of her childhood are so sharp, vivid and concrete that her grandson can easily visualize it for himself, in another kind of imaginative reconstruction of reality. When she gets an opportunity to go there again as an old woman, she is at first a little reluctant, for reality often destroys memories and dreams. But she convinces herself that she has a mission ahead, to rescue her old uncle living alone in their old family house, although he and her father had long been estranged. She is full of excitement when her plans are finalized, but not because, as the boy thinks, of the prospect of her first flight, but because, she hoped to see the border between India and East Pakistan from the plane. She cannot believe that there are no lines or marks to separate the two countries; obviously, then, partition has failed, if things are as they used to be before with no definite boundaries; it has merely made her, and thousands like her, aliens in their own home.

Dhaka itself no longer seems the same Dhaka, but it is only when she and Mayadebi see their old house that reality overtakes memory and imagination. The house is changed beyond recognition, but the uncle has not: he clings to the only reality he knows, the old family feud, and refuses to go with them: "Once you start moving you never stop. . . . It's all very well, you're going away now, but suppose when you get there they decide to draw another line somewhere? What will you do then? Where will you move to? No one will have you anywhere." (215) And when he does agree to move, it is the end for him. The stay-at-home can survive, because his imagination keeps him alive; reality can kill.

The old uncle's end is the end also for Tridib, who had accompanied the two elderly ladies to their ancestral home to rescue their recalcitrant relative. On their way back, the riots break out and their car is attacked by a frenzied mob. They would have got away had it not been for May, the girl he is in love with, the kind considerate girl whose honesty is assailed so scornfully as barren by her brother Nick and who is distressed by what the Victoria Memorial symbolizes, the harsh reality of power games. On the Indian streets she had once killed a dying dog, run over by Tridib's car, with her pen-knife; now in Dhaka she re-enacts what she had done then with Tridib as her victim. For she sees coming behind them the old uncle in a rickshaw pulled by his trusted Khalil; and when 'the mob [goes] after them instead,' (250) May jumps out of the car, against everybody's advice, to help them, and Tridib runs after her to help her, as he had always done. She herself is untouched, for she is 'an English memsahib,' (251) but the old man, the rickshaw-puller and Tridib are slaughtered. May realizes now that her earlier kindness had been insensitive, and that it was because of her that Tridib died. Clearly, then, kindness is not enough if it is not accompanied by understanding, which is the gift of imagination. For years May has blamed herself for his death. But now she has seen the reality behind Tridib's death: 'He gave himself up; it was a sacrifice. I know I can't understand it, I know I mustn't try, for any real sacrifice is a mystery.' (251-52) Ultimately, then, it is imagination which triumphs, for it gives her and the narrator and the reader a 'glimpse' of 'a final redemptive mystery' that must remain distanced from reality.

NOTES

1. Michel Zeraffa, *Fictions: The Novel and Social Reality* (Harmondsworth: Penguin, 1976), p. 20.
2. Novy Kapadia, "Imagination and Politics in Amitav Ghosh's *Shadow Lines,*" *The New Indian Novel in English: A Study of the 1980s*, ed. Viney Kirpal (New Delhi: Allied, 1990), p. 201.
3. A.K. Ramanujan, pre-publication comment on the back of the jacket of the novel.
4. A political novel is one 'in which political ideas play a dominant role or in which the political milieu is the dominant setting,' according to Irving Howe's definition in *The Idea of the*

Political Novel (NY: Fawcett, 1967), p. 19.

5. Qtd. Damian Grant, *Realism* (London: Methuen, 1985), p. 1.
6. *Ibid.*, p. 16.
7. *Culture and Imperialism* (NY: Knopf, 1993), p. xii.
8. Zeraffa, p. 20.
9. *The Shadow Lines* (Delhi: Ravi Dayal, 1988), p. 9.

Perspectives in Time: The Narrator as Child in *The Shadow Lines*

NANDITA SINHA

On reading *The Shadow Lines* one is struck by the extraordinary density of its narrative texture. The story emerges in layers and each layer is a fusion of private lives and public events, all linked into a thematic unity. This paper proposes to show how Ghosh uses first-person narrative from a dual viewpoint—that of the child and the adult "I, thus giving us a sense of inhabiting both past and present simultaneously. The narrator as child comes into close contact with the protagonists of the story and thus serves to weave together its multiple facets—through his grandmother with her East Bengal background and memories of her girlhood days in Dhaka in a sprawling house with its idiosyncratic occupants, the narrative takes us to the odyssey of her search for an old uncle left behind in what was by then East Pakistan and its tragic consequences; through his relationships with his uncle Tridib and cousin Ila and their connections with the Price family in London, the narrative takes us back in time to war-torn London and doubles back again to a time when he is a student in London himself. And once again, through Tridib, whom the child hero-worships, we have an authentic vista of Calcutta life—the streetside addas, the strollers round the Lake, the squalid tenements—as well as a lovingly drawn portrait of childhood in a middle-class Bengali family. The child observes and assesses his world—a world in which "children were sent to school to learn how to cling to their gentility by proving themselves in the examination hall"; where the women possess a "peculiar manipulative worldliness which comes from dealing with large families," where there is a subtle balance of power between the mother and grandmother. His intuitive insights give a grounding to what is one of the novel's most appealing features—its remarkable air of authenticity.

The personal drama in each case is played out against a canvas of sweeping historical events—the freedom movement and the rise of insurgency in Bengal, England's war against Hitler's Germany, the Chinese aggression and the Indo-Pak war, the desecration of the Hazratbal shrine in Srinagar in 1963, and the communal riots in Khulna and Calcutta in 1964—each of which directly or indirectly impinges on the child's experience.

The Shadow Lines is a novel about time, about growing up, not so much in years as in understanding. It is not what happened, but the meaning of what happened that is the central concern and the meaning emerges when the past and the present are considered together. Ghosh discards linear narrative in favour of multiple perspectives and here the narrator as child plays a significant role. People and events encountered in childhood are once again brought into focus when the adult narrator views them from a perspective of cumulative knowledge. The narrative voice, now that of the child's, now the adult's criss-crosses the novel. The juxtaposition of an incident as it appeared to the child while he was experiencing it with a later view of it from an unexpected angle is one of the recurrent devices of the narrative and introduces an effect that is almost cinematic. The movement back and forth in time is not merely a structural device, it serves to image a central theme—that the line dividing past and present is only a shadow, that the past lives in the present and that the present is shaped by the past or, as the novel puts it, "the past is concurrent with the present."

The inseparable tie between past and present manifests itself in the two love relationships that develop in the novel—Ila's infatuation with and later marriage to Nick Price and Tridib's love for May. Each is a bid for freedom from the past, but the irony lies in the fact that such freedom is an illusion. Ila desires freedom from a petty middle-class orthodoxy, but she discovers that the free world she had tried to build for herself was not free from the squalor of betrayal. Tridib wants to meet May as "the completest of strangers, far from their friends and relatives—in a place without a past, without history, free, really free, two people coming together with the utter freedom of strangers." But both are caught up inexorably in the backlash of history.

The child's involvement in these relationships takes him to the threshold of awareness, but his understanding remains partial till adulthood, when fresh perspectives heighten his sensitivity to the deeper meaning of his earlier experience. In the beginning it is his fascination for his cousin Ila that forms the core of his existence. To the boy, brought up in the humdrum routine of a "small, puritanical world" Ila appears as an exotic butterfly, with her easy intimacy with places which are magic names in the boy's atlas. But his love for her makes him vulnerable and with the clarity born out of despair he sees himself defenceless in her power and faced with the adult truth—"that need is not transitive, that one may need without oneself being needed." At age nine jealousy enters his world in the form of Nick Price, whom he has never seen, but who appears bigger and better and more desirable, because he was so in Ila's eyes. But the boy is puzzled at the way she bursts into tears while recounting the story of Nick's heroic rescue of a girl in distress. Much later, he learns from May what really happened—that the story was only make-believe, the truth was Nick Price's rejection of Ila because he was ashamed to be seen by his friends walking home with an Indian, an act of betrayal that reveals its full implications when the adult narrator is confronted with the reality of Nick's later betrayal of Ila, now his wife. This incident surfaces into the memory of the adult narrator many years afterwards when Ila takes him down to Mrs. Price's cellar in London and weeps as she tells of Nick's unfaithfulness. It is a telescoping of time and the two images appear to coalesce. But now he sees things differently. He sees Nick Price as vulnerable and fallible as he himself once was, "facing in future of helpless dependence coupled with despairing acts of rebellion." "I wanted to get up then and hold him, chest to chest, his shoulders to mine. But of course I didn't—he did not know of the part he had played in my life, standing beside me in the mirrors of my boyhood." (189)

The relationship between May and Tridib, too, unfolds from the child's point of view; he instinctively knows that there is something between them which he could never understand or share. "I was jealous, achingly jealous, as only a child can be, because it had always been my unique privilege to understand Tridib and that day, at the Victoria Memorial, I knew that I had lost that privilege, somehow May had stolen it from me." Understanding comes seventeen years later, when bits of information fall into place to create a pattern of meaning. He becomes aware of the true nature of their unique bond. The values that May cherishes and which motivate her to put a helpless dog, hurt in an accident out of its misery at personal risk are the same values that inspire Tridib's act of selfless heroism. Cutting across the superficial barriers of nationality, gender and similar divisions is human nature's "indivisible sanity."

The image of the journey is central to the novel—its two parts being entitled "Going Away" and "Coming Home" Tridib goes away from India to England with his family and the child relives the experience vicariously through Tridib's imaginatively vivid descriptions, so that when he himself grows up and goes to London, it is an effortless transition, a "coming" rather than a "going." It is Tridib who expands the frontiers of his boyhood world, giving him "worlds to travel in" and "eyes to see them with." It is Tridib who explains to him how one could be carried beyond the limits of one's mind to other times and other places "and even if one was lucky, to a place where there was no border between oneself and one's image in the mirror." Thus the boy learns to value the imaginative as revealing a world as concrete and real and infinitely more exciting than the world experienced through the senses. His journeys into the past with Tridib leave him with a vivid recollection of war-torn London and later, though he does not see the "uprooted trees or splintered windows or buckled flagstones "that have been lost in a forty year old past" he realizes that he has been shown something more valuable—England in her finest hour. As the adult voice puts it, "despite the clear testimony of my eyes it seemed to me still that Tridib had shown me something truer about Solent Road a long time ago in Calcutta." (57) In contrast, the narrow limits of Ila's imagination baffles the boy and makes him aware of the mystery of difference between people, a difference that is not based on distance in time and space, but on attitudes of the mind, as for instance between himself and Ila "who lived in a present which was like an airlock in a canal, shut away from the tide-waters of the past and the future by steel floodgates, so that though she had lived in many places, she had never really travelled at all."

In the second part, the grandmother's journey to Dhaka becomes a symbolic search for a point of fixity. The prospect of a return to a home where she has inexplicably become a foreigner bewilders her. The child innocently misinterprets her confusion as anxiety at the prospect of travelling in a plane and his naive response strikes a note of touching humour: "I could see, then, that she was going to land up in a hopeless mess. I was sure, for example, that she would roll her window down in midair unless I warned her not to." Many years later, he comes to understand the true source of her mental conflict—her inability to understand how her place of birth had come to be so messily at odds with her nationality. The irony of this situation permeates the account (told to the now adult narrator) of her encounter with her old uncle who does not recognize her. In her bid to resurrect the past that memory has so indelibly imprinted in her mind, she fails to take into account the realities of the present, so that it is she who is the alien, the Muslims Khalil and Saifuddin who have befriended the old man are his family in the truest sense of the word. Her total allegiance to her past (symbolized by her changing into a red-bordered saree at the moment of departure) limits her vision, so that in the end, she remains isolated in the Mercedes, while the mob butchers the old man in his rickshaw as well as Tridib who sacrifices his life in trying to save him.

The meaning of political violence is one of the major themes of this novel. Violence is seen as destructive, but also as redemptive, for it can bring out heroism in unexpected ways. Ghosh draws a parallel between the heroism of ordinary Englishmen like Alan Tresawsen, Dan and Mike in facing the knowledge that "their world and in all probability, they themselves, would not survive the war" and Tridib's act of foolhardy courage, reinforcing thereby his belief that people are not so different after all, that geographical lines of division cannot change human values.

The child's experience touches both these situations at second- hand—through an old photograph in Tridib's room taken in London in 1939, and through his parent's reluctance to speak of Tridib's death to him as other than an accident. The child accepts their explanations unquestioningly: "for me, 'dead' was just a word, associated vaguely with films and comic books. That was all. I had no means of attaching that word to a real presence, like Tridib's. I felt nothing—no shock, no grief. I did not understand that I would never see him again, my mind was not large enough to accommodate so complete an absence." The boy is more concerned with his own immediate experience of violence when an ordianry school day turned into a nightmare with rioting mobs on rampage in the streets giving his school bus chase. He understands the terrifying power of rumour and its frightening ability to demarcate a division between "we" and "they." He also experiences a gut-wrenching fear, which is translated into a perception about the nature of this sort of fear by the adult narrative voice: "It is a fear that comes of the knowledge that normalcy is utterly contingent, that the spaces that surround one, the streets that one inhabits, can become, suddenly and without warning, as hostile as a desert in a flash flood. It is this that sets apart the thousand million who inhabit the subcontinent from the rest of the world—and language, not food, not music—it is the special quality of loneliness that grows out of the fear of the war between oneself and one's image in the mirror." (204)

The boy's experience is juxtaposed with the adult experience when the narrator, now in London as a student, hears two separate accounts of the violence that led to Tridib's death from Robi and May, both of whom had been present there. For Robi, the memory is a nightmare from which there is no deliverance, for his experience as an administrator has by now shown him how human nature remains unchanged, that the concept of freedom has become a catchword to condone killing, and that political freedom is an illusion, so that to draw thousands of little lines through the whole subcontinent and give every little place a new name would not change anything at all. For May, who is guiltridden at the thought that in some way she is responsible for Tridib's death, it is a luminous mystery that defies understanding a sacrifice and a martyrdom, an idealist's heroic stand against the tide of madness and bloodshed.

All these perceptions radiate from the focal incident of communal violence in Calcutta which the narrator experienced as a child, and which he later realizes is the obverse side of the same violence in Dhaka that took Tridib's life. These separate insights coalesce into a final awareness which forms the core of the novelist's vision. What matters is people and especially, as far as the subcontinent is concerned the indivisible links between them. The relationship could be positive as Ghosh records in his documentary account of the disappearance of the Mu-i-Mubarak from the Hazratbal shrine in Srinagar—that there was not one single recorded incident of animosity between Kashmiri Muslims, Hindus and Sikhs. It could as easily flare up at a moment's notice into the "pathological inversion" of communal riots in places as far apart as Khulna in East Pakistan and Calcutta. This indivisible tie governs the paradox that while the people of Khulna did not care about the fate of the mosques in Vietnam or South China which were much nearer in terms of geographical distance than Srinagar, in the other direction (i.e. Calcutta) it took no more than a week to rouse a frenzy of looting, burning and killing. Thus the irony of our political processes, which seek to give people separate identities by drawing boundary lines, is highlighted. As the novel puts it in a major setting forth of theme: "They had drawn their borders, believing in that pattern in the enchantment of lines, hoping perhaps that once they had etched their borders upon the map, the two bits of land would sail away from each other like the shifting tectonic plates of the prehistoric Gondwanaland. What had they felt, I wondered, when they discovered that they had created, not a separation, but a yet-undiscovered irony—the irony that killed Tridib: the simple fact that there had never been a moment in the four-thousand-year-old history of that map, when the places we know as Dhaka and Calcutta were more closely bound to each other than after they had drawn their lines—so closely that I, in Calcutta, had only to look into the mirror to be in Dhaka; a moment when each city was the inverted image of the other, locked into an irreversible symmetry by the line that was to set us free—our looking-glass border." (238)

The novel can therefore be described as the narrator's journey backwards in time in quest of a fuller meaning in life. It is an attempt to impose a pattern on experience. By putting the child in the centre of the narrative and surrounding the events of the past with later interpretations, Ghosh leads the reader through the same deepening of perception that the narrator experiences.

The Shadow Lines: A Note

G.R. TANEJA

The new Indian English fiction of the eighties is free from the self-consciousness, shallow idealism and sentimentalism that characterized the work of the older generation of novelists such as Raja Rao, R.K. Narayan or Mulk Raj Anand who started writing in the thirties. The fiction of the eighties takes a maturer view of Indian reality. There is freshness and vitality and the writers betray remarkable confidence in tackling new themes, and experiment with new techniques and approaches to handle those themes. Amitav Ghosh, whose first novel, *The Circle of Reason* appeared in 1986, has strengthened the new English novel in more than one way.

The Shadow Lines takes us into the mnemonic fund of a young narrator who as a wide-eyed adolescent hero-worshipped Tridib, an uncle, who fed him on his memories of his one visit to London during the war; and his grandmother, who shared with him her nostalgic memories of East Bengal where she was born and spent her childhood. And then there is Ila (his cousin, for whom he nurtures a secret passion), who travels all over the world with her diplomat glob-trotting parents and occasionally comes home to tell a wonderstruck boy accounts of her peregrinations abroad. Their memories "form a part of my secret map of the world, a map of which only I know the keys and coordinates, but which was not for than reason any more imaginary than the code of a safe to banker."

From the three whose memories form his own consciousness, he learns to see in different ways. Ila sees much but experiences little. With her superficial response to life, she only remembers how one airport differed from the other by its less or more conveniently located ladies'. Tridib teaches him to see with precision because he teaches the boy to see with imagination ("we could not see without inventing what we saw"). He evokes for the young boy "the worlds to travel in and . . . eyes to see them with." The grandmother establishes to him the oneness of the memory for according to her neither space nor time can divide it.

The Shadow Lines spans three generations of the narrator's family spread over in East Bengal and Calcutta: the English family-friends, the Prices, whose histories include the two Wars and contemporary London. And the web of life in *The Shadow Lines*, which encompasses many countries, many religions, is a collage of memories, the narrator's own, and others, dusty photographs, yellowing newspaper clippings, but strengthened above all by imagination. While nations, religions, war, violence and partition divide people, memory does not. Imagination creates a world that cannot be divided, any more than nations break and float away when geographical boundaries are arbitrarily recreated. Life in *The Shadow Lines* loses its chronological logic. Past invades the present and enriches and transforms it and in the process strengthens the narrator's ability to encounter and even reshape his own future when it invades his present at a later date. (In that sense one of the major concerns of the novel is about growth and experience and maturity.) The very structure of the novel—coil within coil opening up vistas of new worlds, new experiences—reflects this giddying whirl of life, memory and imagination. His remarkably brilliant handling of his linguistic medium is one of his major achievements. He writes fluently, and his narratives move with grace, ease and understatement.

Ghosh's evocation of the city of his birth and adolescent years, Calcutta, depicted in remarkably vivid details, is comparable only with Anita Desai's re-creation of Bombay in *Baumgartner's Bombay* (1988). His experience as a social anthropologist at the Universities of Delhi and Oxford shows in his handling of the characters and the context in which they exist. He reveals a sense of history and a firm grasp of socio-cultural and historical material that underlies his narrative. He confesses to one of his earliest memories of Calcutta as that of a mob surrounding his house, a memory that he decided to "exhume" and confront after he witnessed the 1984 riots (the most traumatic event in contemporary Indian history) which spread through the country after Indira Gandhi's assassination. *The Shadow Lines* takes in the war-devastated London, civil-strife in post-Partition East Bengal, and the riot-hit Calcutta and embodies a major critique of the psychological make-up of the contemporary man that thrives on violence.